CLAWS
OF THE
PANDA

WITHDRAWN
FROM
COLLECTION

D0951838

WITHDRAWN
FROM
COLLECTION

CLAWS
OF THE
PANDA

Beijing's Campaign of Influence
and Intimidation in Canada

JONATHAN
MANTHORPE

Cormorant Books

Copyright © 2019 Jonathan Manthorpe
This edition copyright © 2019 Cormorant Books Inc.
Second printing 2019.

No part of this publication may be reproduced, stored in a retrieval system or transmitted,
in any form or by any means, without the prior written consent of the publisher or a licence from
The Canadian Copyright Licensing Agency (Access Copyright). For an Access Copyright licence,
visit www.accesscopyright.ca or call toll free 1.800.893.5777.

  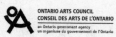

The publisher gratefully acknowledges the support of the Canada Council for the Arts
and the Ontario Arts Council for its publishing program. We acknowledge
the financial support of the Government of Canada through the Canada Book Fund (CBF)
for our publishing activities, and the Government of Ontario through
Ontario Creates, an agency of the Ontario Ministry of Culture,
and the Ontario Book Publishing Tax Credit Program.

LIBRARY AND ARCHIVES CANADA CATALOGUING IN PUBLICATION

Manthorpe, Jonathan, author
Claws of the panda / Jonathan Manthorpe.

Includes bibliographical references and index.
Issued in print and electronic formats.
ISBN 978-1-77086-539-6 (softcover). — ISBN 978-1-77086-540-2 (html)

1. Canada—Foreign relations—China. 2. China—Foreign relations—
Canada. 3. Espionage—Canada. 4. Espionage—China.
I. Title.

FC251.C5M36 2019   327.71051   C2018-906260-6
                                                          C2018-906261-4

Cover photo and design: angeljohnguerra.com
Interior text design: Tannice Goddard, tannicegdesigns.ca
Printer: Friesens

Printed and bound in Canada.

CORMORANT BOOKS INC.
260 SPADINA AVENUE, SUITE 502, TORONTO, ON, M5T 2E4
www.cormorantbooks.com

In memory of Tom Manthorpe,
who lived some of the happiest years
of his short life in Hong Kong.

CONTENTS

CLAWS
OF THE
PANDA

INTRODUCTION
RETURN OF THE MIDDLE KINGDOM

China does not see itself as a rising, but as a returning power ...
It does not view the prospect of a strong China exercising influence
in economic, cultural, political, and military affairs as an unusual
challenge to world order — but rather a return to a normal state of
affairs.

— HENRY KISSINGER, *ON CHINA*

MUCH OF THIS book is about how the Chinese Communist Party (CCP) is riding roughshod over Canadian values and interfering in Canadian internal affairs to a degree that sometimes amounts to a challenge to Canadians' sovereignty within their own country. But this is not a book arguing that Canada should distance itself from the current regime in Beijing. As China under the leadership of President Xi Jinping and the Chinese Communist Party sees itself re-emerging as the world's natural, irreplaceable superpower after two centuries of "humiliation" at the hands of Western nations, engagement with China cannot and should not be avoided. But what the often sad and difficult story of Canada's 150 years of involvement with China tells us is that we need to find a less self-delusional, more courageous, and more intelligent way of dealing with the new version of the Middle Kingdom. If Canada does not reassess and rework its approach to Beijing, this country may be steamrollered by the new juggernaut of history.

The tectonic plates of international power are shifting, thankfully peacefully — so far. But as I write in mid-2018, even two years ago the world and its prospects looked very different. There were few visible hints of the cascade into political dysfunction and isolationism that overtook the United States in November 2016. And it still looked as though Xi would follow the collegial style of leadership adopted in China following the depredations of Mao Zedong and the bone-jarring shock of the 1989 Tiananmen Square uprising and massacre. But at the nineteenth Communist Party Congress in October 2017, Xi set the stage for his own continuation in power beyond the two five-year terms that had become the norm. His personal power is now unmatched by any of his predecessors since Mao, and perhaps even further back than that. Meanwhile, Canada's chances of continuing the last seventy years of economic and security dependency on the United States look less and less secure. Donald Trump is a symptom of the isolationism that for many Americans has always accompanied their belief in the exceptionality of American society. More important, perhaps, is that Trump is the face of one side of the widening political and social divide within the United States that is making it nearly impossible for political and administrative life to function. That destructive friction between conflicting views of the world shows no sign of being resolved any time soon. It is already contributing to the withering of the American imperium, and it is accentuating the contrast with the rise of other nations, especially China.

In the rapidly approaching future, Canada is not going to be able to rely on Washington as an ally in regional security or a trustworthy partner in investment and commerce. More than that, the end of the Pax Americana means that the champion of the international liberal values that have characterized global discourse and institutions since the Second World War and that are at the heart of Canadian nationhood is withdrawing from the field. When China began opening up in the 1980s, Western nations assumed that as the CCP became a stakeholder on the global stage, it would adopt the values of the established international liberal-democratic order. That is not what has happened. China has not emerged as a benign and benevolent beast. Far from it. It has all the hallmarks of a fascist regime, if one accepts the definition of fascism as being a country with a centralized autocratic government headed by a dictatorial leader, severe economic and social regimentation, and forcible suppression of opposition. And yet the word *fascist*, while handy and accurate, is not quite appropriate. It is too Eurocentric in its associations. Xi's China is most like that other post-communist dictatorship, Russia, which is sometimes described as being driven by "Mafia capitalism." But that also falls somewhere outside the truth. Whatever the Chinese Communist Party does, it does with Chinese characteristics. The management and style of the economy, the internal administration, the attitudes toward neighbouring and foreign states — these all owe more to Chinese traditions than to the country's experience of the outside world since the end of isolationism in the 1970s. The Communist Party in Beijing oversees a modernized version of a classic Chinese imperial dynasty.

It is clear that the CCP's dynastic ambitions include running a one-party state and resisting political reform with all the tools at its command. The CCP's political legitimacy comes from massive internal repression tempered by efforts to provide a standard of living that discourages dissent. This has worked well since the era of revised Marxist economics began in the 1980s. Hundreds of millions of Chinese have seen their standard of living improve beyond what they could have imagined. But with that improvement has come the expectation that their quality of life will continue to improve. This carries a threat for the CCP: if the party fails to continue to feed the desires it has created, it will lose the Mandate of Heaven, the historic concept of divine political legitimacy conferred on Chinese rulers only so long as they are successful.

Flowing naturally from China's economic success is a heightened sense of patriotism and nationalism. State-controlled media incessantly pushes the theme of China riding a wave of national revival, to the point of stoking xenophobia, which is fed by appeals to ancient animosities toward neighbours such as Japan. The CCP misses no opportunity to fabricate warnings that, behind a facade of democratic pacifism, Japan remains a militaristic country.

Beijing also nurtures more recent suspicions that the United States and other Western countries are bent on containing China's rise and reimposing the semi-colonialism of the last half of the nineteenth and early twentieth centuries. Ending what the CCP calls the "century of humiliation" is fostered in part by reviving a sense of superiority over neighbouring countries. These were vassal states in imperial times, and the CCP suggests they will be vassals again. Indeed, some — such as Cambodia and Laos — already are. This trumpeting of refreshed Chinese imperialism includes pursuing territorial claims over

Taiwan and in the South China and East China seas. The CCP's construction of island military bases in the South China Sea has turned one of the world's most important routes for international trade into what amounts to a Chinese lake. Much of the CCP's colonialism is surreptitious. In the last two decades, about one million people from China's southwestern Yunnan province have moved over the border into northern Myanmar. They are taking advantage of the business opportunities in the city of Mandalay and the attractions of the casino towns that have sprung up in the lawless regions under the control of Myanmar's ethnic minority warlords.

For two decades or so, CCP state-owned companies and banks have been using the gargantuan profits from the export of manufactured consumer goods to acquire control of natural resources worldwide. Beijing has also been astute in offering cheap loans to governments others considered too risky. Too late, the recipients find that when they are unable to repay the loans, the CCP's agents are ruthless in demanding assets instead. That's how the CCP got control of the strategic Sri Lankan port of Hambantota and sixty square kilometres of land around it. Something similar happened when Greece fell on hard times and could no longer get loans from its European Union partners. Beijing stepped in to help, but the upshot is that a Chinese state-owned company owns half of Athens' port of Piraeus.

The acquisition of Greek and other European ports is part of Xi Jinping's most lavish imperial enterprise. His multi-trillion-dollar "One Belt, One Road" scheme envisages a vast rail, road, air, and sea network that directly links China to two-thirds of the world's population in Europe, the Middle East, Africa, Central Asia, South and Southeast Asia. All roads will lead to Beijing and will be a route for the CCP's projection of power and influence throughout this modern version of the old Silk Road.

President Xi has made it clear that he has no regard for the values of democracy and human rights that have been at the heart of the international liberal order since the end of the Second World War. He is an evangelist among developing countries for China's model of economic advances achieved by a secure one-party state managing a close-knit family of oligarchs and state-owned enterprises. It is a model that the leaders of many developing countries find attractive, especially when contrasted with the apparent disorder and internal disruption of North Atlantic liberal-democratic culture. Xi is equally skeptical about international institutions such as the United Nations, World Bank, the International Monetary Fund, and all the agencies that have flowed from them. Those institutions do not represent the values of the world that Xi wants to create. He will either bend them to his will or supplant them with new bodies more to his liking.

The current CCP regime will not last forever. Dynasties never do, and the historical record in China is that they all die violently. This will likely happen to the CCP, but it's not a good bet that it will happen anytime soon. Thus, Canada and all other countries having to engage with China while maintaining their own liberal-democratic institutions face some harsh realities. If Canada wishes to preserve its values and its standards of living based on trade in a world dominated by China, if it wishes to expand its influence as a global middle power, present and future governments in Ottawa need to prepare the ground. They need to cement political, economic, social, and security ties within NATO and the G7, along with other like-minded countries. Canadian politicians need to assume a much tougher and more self-assured attitude toward Beijing than is now the case.

That change of attitude is not going to be easy to accomplish, for reasons that this book aims to set out. Canada's fascination with China surfaced in the 1880s, when this country began to send Christian missionaries across the Pacific. Then, as now, China appeared to be a vast market just waiting to gobble up what Canada had to sell. However, the belief that Chinese would rush to become Christians was just as much of an illusion as the conviction today that Chinese yearn to buy Canadian manufactured goods if they have the chance. Canadian missionaries, mostly from the Presbyterian, Methodist, and Catholic churches, were spurred by not only the zeal of Christian evangelism but also the notion of the Gospel as a charter for social change. That belief, that Canada could change China by the self-evident appeal of Canadian values, remains deeply embedded even today. Events in China show this view to be delusional. A recent example was in November 2017, when Chinese officials rejected proposals by Prime Minister Justin Trudeau that a bilateral free trade agreement include his progressive agenda for commercial relations. This would have committed the CCP to following Canadian standards on such things as labour laws, gender equality, and environmental standards. The CCP will never allow a foreign country to dictate its civic and human rights policies. Canada is never going to change China, neither by example nor by compelling arguments.

Far more pertinent is the question: Is China changing Canada? Since before it came to power in 1949, the Chinese Communist Party has been establishing links through which it can influence Canadian political, commercial, media, and academic discourse to its own advantage. The construction of that network has grown and spread dramatically since diplomatic relations were established in 1970. The CCP now has the capacity to ensure its interests are voiced, and can often dominate, when matters of concern to Beijing are raised in Canada's Parliament, its provincial legislatures and municipal council halls, its media, and its lecture theatres. There is no question that the CCP's capacity to influence Canadian public discussion has grown with immigration from Hong Kong and China in the last forty to fifty years. But it is crucially important to understand that the vast majority of the approximately 1.56 million immigrants from greater China, who make up about 4 percent of Canada's population, are here to escape the depredations of the CCP. And it is because the CCP knows that among those 1.56 million people are many political dissidents working to change the politics of China that the party is intent on maintaining an espionage network in Canada that keeps watch on these people and intimidates them when necessary.

The major victims of the Chinese Communist Party's determination to influence public discourse in Canada are Canadians of Chinese heritage or those from territories occupied or claimed by the CCP. But they are not the only victims. Canada as a whole is suffering from the imposition of the values of the CCP on this country's citizens and institutions. Corruption in all its forms now permeates many walks of life. Most of this is Canada's own fault. Canada has become a haven for laundered fortunes of CCP princelings and red aristocrats (a privileged class whose status springs from family ties to the leadership of the CCP). This is because Canadian governments at all levels have not put checkpoints in place to ensure that money coming into the country was acquired honestly and is in Canada to serve a law-abiding purpose. Inevitably, because of China's restrictions on the export of money, corruption, including the corruption of business partners in Canada, must be involved in the illegal movement of money into this country. Once corruption has taken hold in one aspect of public life, it swiftly moves to others. There are signs that the culture of corruption that travels with the CCP has infected many areas of Canadian life, including academic credentials and the many regulatory and licensing requirements overseen by the municipal, provincial, and federal governments.

Canada is not alone in having these experiences flow from contact with the CCP. Similar things are happening in the United States, Europe, and especially New Zealand and Australia. Indeed, the Australian experience of infiltration by the CCP is almost exactly the same as that of Canada. The difference is that Australian politicians, academics, media, and the public have been a good deal louder and more pointed in their objections to the CCP's campaigns.

Why Canada hesitates to recognize these incursions is a troubling question. Is it because the CCP's agents of influence have been so effective that any discussion is deflected? There is some truth in that. The way the government of Conservative Prime Minister Stephen Harper was turned away from its original skeptical attitudes toward contacts with China carries evidence of the potent pro-Beijing lobby deep-seated in Canadian political, business, and academic establishments. But the effectiveness of CCP intrusion into Canadian public life should not be overstated, certainly not to the point of seeing every public figure who speaks up for reasonable relations with China as Beijing's Manchurian Candidate.

Canadian politicians constantly show skepticism about the extent of CCP intrusion, even when compelling evidence is put before them. One reason for this appears to be a historic lack of respect for Canada's security and intelligence services. These agencies do indeed have a troubled history; as will be described later, the difficult birth pains of the Canadian Security Intelligence Service (CSIS) in the 1980s and 1990s involved the much-maligned report about CCP infiltration code-named Operation Sidewinder. However, the relationship between Parliament and the secret service agencies seems to have stabilized in recent years. Mutual respect has grown. Credit for this must go to several former heads of CSIS and the Communications Security Establishment who have doggedly and with appropriate circumspection in their public pronouncements continued to warn about CCP predation in Canada. At CSIS, the confidence in being able to speak out about this issue is evident in the Academic Outreach conference it held in March 2018. The conference was a closed one, conducted under the Chatham House Rule, under which what was said can be reported but not attributed to a specific person. The 163-page report of the conference published by CSIS two months later at the end of May 2018 is called *Rethinking Security: China and the Age of Strategic Rivalry*. It is the most pointed and comprehensive description made public by CSIS to date of the threat posed by the CCP to Canada and other countries. The report's summary lists the elements of CCP interference in Canadian life and their dangers.

It warns that it is irrelevant whether a Chinese company doing business with a Canadian partner is a state-owned enterprise or not. All Chinese companies "have close and increasingly explicit ties to the CCP." Unless trade agreements are carefully vetted for their security implications, the CCP "will use its commercial position to gain access to businesses, technologies and infrastructure that can be exploited for intelligence objectives, or to potentially compromise a partner's security," the report states. "China is prepared to use threats and enticements to bring business and political elites on its side, and motivate them to defend the Chinese perspective on disputes such as the status of Taiwan and the South China Sea."

The report says the CCP works actively to influence the Chinese diaspora (the Chinese community that has dispersed around the world) and Chinese students and business people living in other countries, "often curtailing their freedom of expression to promote a narrative favourable to its views." It goes on to say, "academics and reporters who question [CCP] activities are harassed by Chinese diplomats and Chinese-controlled media."

Fear of being labelled racist has resulted in restrained public discussion on the activities of the CCP's agents in Canada. This country has an indefensible history of racist laws and regulations aimed at Chinese and other Asian would-be immigrants. Remorse over that record has bred a defensive attitude among public figures when talking about any component community of Canada's multicultural society, thus handing a weapon to the CCP's agents of influence. It is noticeable that whenever questions are raised in public about relations with China, there is an immediate retort that these questions are racially motivated.

But it is wrong, and ultimately dangerous, to view the CCP's infiltration of Canada as racial. It is not. It is the story of a particular regime working for its own ends at a particular stage in its history. A threat both to Canada in general and to Canadians of Chinese heritage in particular is that the CCP sees the Chinese diaspora as an asset to be used and abused. A few Chinese Canadians are undoubtedly vulnerable to appeals of Chinese nationalism. But the vast majority of those who have immigrated to Canada want nothing more than to live prosperous lives as Canadians, and a large number have escaped the clutches of the corrupt and power-addicted men who live in the villas around the lakes in the Zhongnanhai leaders' compound next to the Forbidden City opposite Beijing's Tiananmen Square.

This book is not a doomsday saga — far from it. As the story develops, what becomes apparent is that while the CCP has been successful in infiltrating and influencing some aspects of Canadian life, it has failed in others. What emerges from this war in the shadows is that the CCP is most sure-footed when operating within familiar Chinese cultures or among people from traditional vassal states. In contrast, the party and its operatives are often off balance when dealing with established democratic societies, including Canada, Australia, the United States, and the countries of Western Europe. They are most comfortable operating in Western democracies when they find people who can be charmed or suborned. And it is never hard to find people whom the old Soviet communists used to call "useful idiots." Canada has offered up to the CCP a steady stream of useful idiots, including political party and government leaders, rank-and-file politicians, naive and hubristic academics, greedy and gullible business people, and even some parochial and inexperienced journalists. Many of these people justify their cupidity by telling themselves that more contact with the CCP will expose the party to the virtues of Canadian values. Once party members have seen the benefits of the freedoms and rights associated with liberal democracy, they will be eager to launch China on the road to reform.

It is important not to react blindly to the CCP and its agents. They have had significant successes, especially in stealing intellectual property and industrial and military technology, as well as in creating a largely benign image among Western political, business, and academic elites. Yet Canada and the other Western democracies under attack by the CCP have so far shown that their institutions and democratic cultures are able to resist the onslaught. The CCP has not been able to take the commanding heights of Canadian and the other Western societies in the way it has in non-democratic or authoritarian countries in Asia and Africa.

But the saga is not over, and as the power of the CCP grows, as it seems destined to do, the pressure on countries like Canada to adopt the views and values of the Beijing regime will increase. The signs of what the future most likely holds are already evident. The influence of the United States, which since the First World War has championed North Atlantic and Enlightenment values, is beginning to wane under the weight of the country's internal political and social discord. And there is little reason to expect that the only possible replacement as the superpower promoter of liberal values, the European Union, has either the will or the capacity to fill that role in the foreseeable future. Thus, the space on the international stage being vacated by Washington is inexorably being filled by Beijing. With this comes the replacement or remodelling of the architecture of international life and institutions to fit the CCP. Its values do not include freedom of expression, respect for political dissent, and — most importantly — acceptance of the supremacy of the rule of law.

The phrase "the rule of law" is of profound importance when dealing with the CCP. It means that the sovereign power in a country — whether a constitutional monarch, president, or parliamentary government — is answerable to the laws of the land, as is every citizen. Acceptance of this concept by England's King John in June 1215, when he signed the Magna Carta, set Western society on the long road to democracy. But the CCP does not accept the concept of rule of law, nor does it accept the concept of an independent judiciary. The CCP maintains that the interests of the party outweigh all other considerations. In cases involving issues the CCP finds threatening, such as the prosecution of people it considers dissidents or challenges to the party's omnipotence, party committees meet secretly to determine the sentence and write the script for the judicial process to be acted out later in court. As the CCP's China becomes an ever more influential arbiter of international discourse, the refusal to accept the rule of law presents a profound threat to all countries with which it trades and in which its influence is growing. Canada is not, nor will it be, an exception to this; the agents of the CCP are already acting here with what can only be described as contempt for Canadian values.

ONE

FIGHTING THE FIVE POISONOUS GROUPS

Enemy forces abroad do not want to see China rise and many of them see our country as a potential threat and rival, so they use a thousand ploys and a hundred strategies to frustrate and repress us. The United Front ... is a big magic weapon which can rid us of 10,000 problems in order to seize victory.

— MANUAL OF THE CHINESE COMMUNIST PARTY'S
UNITED FRONT WORK DEPARTMENT

CANADA HAS BECOME a battleground on which the Chinese Communist Party seeks to terrorize, humiliate, and neuter its opponents. It is a war being conducted in plain sight, but largely unremarked, as the CCP's diplomats, spies, security officers, and local agents of influence go about the daily business of trying to nullify the efforts of those it believes are set on over-turning China's one-party state. It is a war of intimidation and harassment of Canadians and others from the Five Poisonous Groups — advocates of independence for Tibet, Xinjiang, and Taiwan, promoters of democracy in China, and adherents of Falun Gong (also known as Falun Dafa), a group that advocates a Buddhist approach to spiritual and physical health. The attacks range from abusive midnight phone calls to character assassinations in social media, intimidation of Chinese students attending Canadian colleges and universities, holding hostage in China the family members of Canadian dissidents, and hacking the communications networks of dissident groups. In extreme cases, dissidents have been either physically attacked or detained and tortured — though the violent physical attacks have been in China or Hong Kong, not in Canada. In all cases, however, the aim is to smother the voices of dissent in Canada, either by intimidating Canadians into silence or by so discrediting them that what they say or do no longer has public or political impact.

The breadth and intensity of the CCP's campaign to exert pressure on immigrants in Canada from China and its possessions, such as Tibet and Xinjiang, has grown in recent years as Canada has become an increasingly popular destination. Canada is not alone, however, as a target for the CCP's spies, secret police, influence peddlers, and propagandists. Australia and New Zealand are the subjects of very similar campaigns and for similar reasons. So are other countries with substantial populations of people of Chinese ethnic heritage or emigrants from Tibet and Xinjiang. These include the United States, many of the countries of Southeast Asia, and the European Union.

Despite the best efforts of the CCP and its friends in various sectors of the Canadian establishment to obscure or downplay the campaigns here against dissidents, an increasing number of incidents in this war in the shadows have become public. Early in 2017, a group of Canadian human rights non-governmental organizations produced a report detailing "harassment and intimidation of individuals in Canada working on China-related activism." The thirty-page confidential report was prepared largely by the Canadian Coalition on Human Rights in China using mostly information already in the public domain. Members of the coalition include Amnesty International Canada, the Canada Tibet Committee, the Canadian Labour Congress, the Falun Dafa Association of Canada, the Federation for a Democratic China, the Movement for Democracy in China, the Canadian Committee to Protect Journalists, Students for a Free Tibet Canada, the Toronto Association for Democracy in China, the Uyghur Canadian Society, and the Vancouver Society in Support of Democratic Movement in China.

The report was delivered to the Greater China Division of Global Affairs Canada, the current name for Canada's department of foreign affairs, in April 2017. Members of the China coalition had a follow-up meeting with some of the Global Affairs officials and Royal Canadian Mounted Police officers who had been present at the first gathering. The RCMP and officials asked the coalition for permission to share a redacted version of their report with "like-minded governments." This was granted, and the report has become part of the material being shared among Canada, the United States, Australia, the United Kingdom, and New Zealand, who make up the Fives Eyes intelligence-gathering alliance founded during the Second World War.

Amnesty International Canada, which has over half a century of experience investigating and assessing the veracity of human rights abuses, led the inquiry. As it always does, Amnesty took a conservative and cautious approach when writing the report. "In many cases highlighted in this report, Chinese authorities cannot be directly implicated," it reads. "Yet, despite the anecdotal and inclusive nature of many experiences, Amnesty International Canada considers that the scale and consistency of many reports of rights violations to be consistent with a coordinated, Chinese state-sponsored campaign to target certain political, ethnic, and spiritual groups considered to be opposed to Chinese government interests."

The report says the Chinese government has a long record of trying to exert political and cultural influence abroad in order to promote the objectives of the CCP. "In Canada, these goals of projecting soft power abroad have led Chinese authorities to allegedly exert influence on elected officials, foreign media, and education to promote political positions consistent with Chinese government policies," the report claims. "The combination of efforts aiming to promote pro-government policies and an apparent campaign to target dissident groups has led to a significant chilling effect on human rights activism in Canada and interfered with many Canadian citizens and residents of Canada's rights and freedom of conscience, expression, and association."

The list of methods used by CCP agents to victimize Canadians and Canadian residents is long. It includes cyberattacks, harassing phone calls, the distribution of hate propaganda, following and monitoring of individuals by CCP agents, harassment at anti-CCP demonstrations, detention and bullying of Canadians visiting China, intimidation of relatives in China, and using political connections in Canada to interfere with the rights to freedom of expression and assembly.

Canada has become a hunting ground for the CCP's agents because the country has attracted so many immigrants from greater China intent on escaping the CCP. The flow started after the Second World War and the civil war in China (1945–1949) that followed when those associated with Chiang Kai-shek's defeated Kuomintang regime sought sanctuary abroad. During the 1960s and 1970s, the streams of refugee immigrants came to Canada from China and its possessions Tibet and Xinjiang. Chinese émigrés fled persecution, the chaos and famine of the Great Leap Forward, the inhuman brutality of the Cultural Revolution, uncertainties about the future of Hong Kong after the 1997 return of sovereignty to Beijing, and the crackdown against reform movements during and after the 1989 Tiananmen Square demonstrations.

Tibetans fleeing the CCP's cultural genocide in their homeland began arriving in Canada in the 1970s after a personal plea by the Dalai Lama to the Canadian government to provide them refuge. Close to five thousand Tibetan Canadians make up one of the largest ethnic Tibetan groups outside Asia.

The CCP has intensified its campaign to control and erode the religion and culture of the Turkic Uyghurs in Xinjiang since the 2001 Al-Qaeda attacks on New York and Washington gave them licence to persecute Muslims. As in Tibet, the CCP is flooding Xinjiang with ethnic Chinese settlers. About four hundred Uyghurs have settled in Canada, and among them are several who are active in the exiles' movement for autonomy and democracy in their homeland.

Taiwanese Canadians are collateral damage in the CCP's drive for control of its diaspora. There are now about one hundred thousand Canadians of Taiwanese ancestry. In the 1950s and 1960s, people began to flee the small island nation, which is slightly larger than Vancouver Island and is 180 kilometres off the coast of China. Their flight to Canada, the United States, Australia, and Europe was spurred by the occupation of the island by Chiang Kai-shek and his two million Kuomintang followers after their defeat by the CCP in China's civil war. Chiang responded to Taiwanese outrage at the invasion by imposing martial law and launching what was known as the "White Terror." Immigration to Canada from Taiwan grew through the 1970s and has continued after the lifting of martial law and transition to democracy in the 1980s. But the CCP claims to own the island nation of twenty-three million people; it does all it can to undermine Taiwan's democratic institutions and continues to hold out the threat of invasion if the islanders do not accept Beijing's sovereignty. The CCP considers Taiwanese Canadians an important target because many of them support international recognition of the island's independence and are active opponents of the Beijing regime.

The beginnings of negotiations between London and Beijing in 1983 over the return of Hong Kong to Chinese rule in 1997 after 156 years as a British colony set off an exodus of emigrants from the territory to Canada. During the following decade, at least five hundred thousand Hongkongers moved to Canada, many of them bringing with them the antipathy toward the CCP that had prompted them to flee. About three hundred thousand of those people, armed with the protection of Canadian citizenship, continued to spend at least part of their working lives in Hong Kong, where many also renewed their political activism as supporters of democratic reform. Thus, political reform in Hong Kong and China became a domestic Canadian issue. With that came the determination of the CCP to watch with increasingly intrusive interest the activities of China's Canadian émigrés.

The April 2017 report by Amnesty International Canada and the Canadian Coalition on Human Rights in China sets out details of attacks over several years on people from the Five Poisonous Groups. Cyberattacks are the most common, usually involving emails purporting to come from friends or contacts, but with attachments containing malicious software. The malware may contain annoying computer viruses or, more commonly, spyware that gives the CCP agency a window into the dissidents' communications networks. This enables the CCP's spies to not only follow plans and discussions within the dissident groups but also know the whereabouts of individual members. It was this type of malware that was discovered in an ongoing forensic study of CCP agency cyberattacks undertaken by Citizen Lab, an interdisciplinary agency based at the Munk School of Global Affairs at the University of Toronto.

In 2013, Citizen Lab examined a suspicious email with an attachment that had been received by a Tibetan Canadian organization. The email purported to be from a prominent member of the Tibetan Canadian community and contained three attached documents, which, if opened, would have infected computers with the malware Citizen Lab named Surtr, after the fire giant in Norse mythology. "A computer compromised by Surtr would be susceptible to having all of its keystrokes logged, its file directories and contents listed, as well as allowing the operator to remotely execute commands," they reported.

Pursuing its interest in attacks on human rights groups, in 2014, Citizen Lab published a report, "Communities @ Risk," after studying suspicious emails and attachments from ten civil society organizations that volunteered to take part in the research project.

A Tibetan Canadian group involved in this study gave a lead into which Chinese intelligence agency was behind some of the attacks. The hacker was identified as an operator known to Western agencies as APT1, which had targeted many government agencies and Fortune 500 companies. APT1 was identified by the United States Federal Bureau of Investigation and the Department of Justice as Unit 61398. This is the cover name for a cyberespionage operation in the second bureau of the third department of the Chinese People's Liberation Army (PLA). In May 2014, the U.S. Department of Justice filed charges of economic espionage against five officers in Unit 61398, or APT1, involving six American nuclear power, metals, and solar products industries.

Amnesty International found that other groups in Canada working on issues in China have been the target of cyberattacks, in particular Falun Gong, the movement with tens of millions of followers that combines spiritual discipline with a health regime of tai chi exercises. The group was founded in 1992 by Li Hongzhi with the aim of combining traditional tai chi exercises and Buddhist concepts of self-cultivation to achieve both physical and spiritual health. Falun Gong became very popular very quickly. Within a few years, thousands of parks in cities all over China saw scores of Falun Gong practitioners gathering to exercise in unison. The CCP began to be concerned by the popularity of Li Hongzhi's movement; authorities began to persecute the group, especially in northeast China, where it was most popular. The gathering conflict came to a crisis point on April 25, 1999. CCP leaders awoke that Sunday morning, in their Zhong-nanhai walled compound next to the Forbidden City, to be told by guards that about fifteen thousand followers of Falun Gong were demonstrating outside in protest against the persecutions. Premier Zhu Rongji invited representatives into the leaders' compound to discuss their grievances.

Had the issue stayed with Zhu, the outcome might have been different. However, Zhu was never in the mainstream of the CCP leadership, mostly by his own choosing, and his reputation was stained by having returned the day before from an unsuccessful visit to the United States and Canada, trying to win approval for China to join the World Trade Organization. Harder-nosed members of the CCP leadership looked at the Falun Gong situation and were alarmed by two things. First, most of the demonstrators were middle-aged former middle-rank members of the CCP. They were the party stalwarts trusted by the centre to carry out orders across China, the people whose adherence to the humanitarian ideology of the CCP was essential to the survival of the one-party state. But they had lost faith in what might be called the spiritual element of communism as China rushed into unabashed crony capitalism, led by the CCP and the red aristocracy. Seeking another spirituality in which to believe, they had turned to Falun Gong. Some Chinese people have adopted Christianity, but most obvious in China is a resurgence of traditional Buddhism.

The second cause for alarm for the CCP leaders was the date. The country was approaching the tenth anniversary of the 1989 nationwide protests in favour of reform and the eradication of corruption, which ended in the June 4 massacre in Beijing's Tiananmen Square and similar crackdowns in other cities across China. In anticipation of the anniversary, security in

Beijing was meant to be absolutely watertight. And yet this army of fifteen thousand people had managed to travel to Beijing from all over the country and to gather outside the leaders' compound without state security officials having any advance warning. This was a nightmare scenario for the CCP. Its conclusion after Tiananmen in 1989 was that it must never again allow a nationwide movement to emerge that could challenge and topple the CCP's rule. Yet here one was on their doorstep. The CCP moved with speed and utmost brutality against Falun Gong. In July 1999, the group was outlawed and declared an "evil cult." The party then rushed to see how deeply embedded adherence to Falun Gong and similar groups had become in Chinese society. It found to its alarm that a disturbingly high proportion of people, not only in society at large but also in the government, the CCP, and the armed forces, found comfort and solace in tai chi exercises and meditation. Falun Gong members were purged, and many thousands have been imprisoned and killed. The CCP continues to regard the group as one of the main threats to its rule, in part because the Falun Gong leader, Li Hongzhi, now lives in the United States.

Following this crackdown, the CCP launched a propaganda war to justify its labelling of Falun Gong as an evil cult. The party claimed that the group is a menace to society, brainwashing people with superstitious ideas that are damaging to a person's mental health. State-owned media told stories of practitioners committing suicide or mutilating themselves and going on crime sprees under the influence of Li's ideas. But the CCP was never able to produce convincing evidence to support its allegations against the group. Western human rights organizations that managed to examine the so-called evidence on which the party's allegations were based found either that the people identified in the stories did not exist or that the people who had committed the crimes described in the allegations were not Falun Gong followers. New York based Human Rights Watch dismissed the CCP's claims against the group as "bogus."

Yet the CCP's counterattack against Falun Gong has had considerable success in creating ambivalence and suspicion about the group in Western countries, including Canada. In part, this is because the West is predisposed to question the motives and authenticity of spiritual movements coming from Asia. The West has also had unhappy experiences with homegrown cults of one sort or another, which have sometimes created serious social problems. And Falun Gong did not help itself. Soon after being banned, it launched an unremitting public relations campaign aimed at Western media. But the campaign was so relentless, the volume of material fired at journalists and politicians so large, and some of the claims so apparently outlandish that it smacked of hysteria and was counterproductive. Instead of fostering credibility among Western journalists, the campaign bred irritation and skepticism about the group's claims. When evidence began to emerge of gross abuses by CCP authorities against detained Falun Gong members, including the harvesting of body parts for lucrative transplant operations, Western media and politicians hesitated to treat the allegations with the seriousness they demanded.

Falun Gong is high on the list of the CCP's targets in Canada. Grace Wollensack, a representative of the Falun Dafa Association of Canada, told Amnesty International's assessors that cyberattacks on the group were first noticed in 2010. She said that people impersonating Falun Gong practitioners sent emails to federal government ministers and members of Parliament in an apparent attempt to discredit the group. Messages reviewed by Amnesty appeared to be aimed at reinforcing the characterization of Falun Gong as the fanatical cult claimed by the CCP. Emails were sent to former Conservative MPs Jason Kenny and Stephen Woodworth. Insults were levelled at both men in the messages for not attending a Falun Gong celebration, and they were warned that a forth-coming meeting was their last chance to be "saved." Amnesty was also shown copies of an email chain sent in April 2016, containing a picture of Conservative MP David Anderson, the opposition critic on international human rights and religious freedom, and saying he "supports Falun Gong." The Amnesty report does not give details of the picture, but it seems it was abusive because Anderson's office forwarded the email to the Royal Canadian Mounted Police.

Threatening telephone calls are a favourite harassment technique used by the CCP's spy agencies and their affiliates. In the study, Amnesty International looked into many reports of harassing telephone calls, including some containing death threats, brought to them by the civil society organizations. In most cases the caller didn't speak but instead played a pre-recorded hateful or abusive message. Ottawa resident Lucy Zhou, a Falun Gong practitioner, got pre-recorded calls in the middle of the night denouncing the movement. Other phone calls blasted her with propaganda songs lauding the CCP and its leaders. Zhou also got calls from a man speaking impeccable Chinese who appeared to know details of her recent travels. These quickly became sexual harassment calls, she said in an interview with *The Globe and Mail* in June 2005.

Zhou's case emerged a few months after the February 2005 defection and appeal for asylum in Australia of Hao Fengjun. Hao said he was a part of the 610 Office, a special unit of the Chinese Public Security Bureau responsible for a vast network of informants watching Falun Gong in Australia, New Zealand, Canada, the United States, and other countries. He claimed that documents he saw as part of his work showed that the CCP operated a counter-Falun Gong intelligence network in Canada that included more than one thousand spies — more, he thought, than in the United States, Australia, or New Zealand. He said that the 610 Office recruited Canadians of Chinese origin to collect information on Falun Gong members, dispatched professional agents from China, and enlisted business people and students visiting Canada. Hao said Vancouver and Toronto were the centres of activity for the 610 Office and its civilian informants, who were often instructed to use recorded messages to harass and intimidate Falun Gong practitioners.

When the issue was raised in the House of Commons on June 16, 2005, Liberal Prime Minister Paul Martin responded to a question from Conservative opposition leader Stephen Harper by saying the government took very seriously Hao's allegation that one thousand CCP spies were operating in Canada. Martin said he had raised the issue with Chinese leaders when he was in Beijing the previous January. "I dealt extensively with Canada's interests," Martin told the House. "I dealt extensively with

Canada's sovereignty and the need to respect state sovereignty between countries." Martin went on to say that Canada had "a vigorous counter-intelligence program to safeguard Canada's security. It is also very clear, and Canadians can rest assured that we maintain a very strong law enforcement and security system that will enable Canadians to be assured of their own protection and their own security."

Even without Hao's allegations, there was already plenty of evidence for Canadian authorities and the members of the public to know that Chinese government officials were mounting a persistent campaign against people in Canada considered a threat to the CCP regime, especially followers of Falun Gong.

Falun Gong is the target of the most clear-cut case of Chinese diplomatic officials distributing hate propaganda in Canada. The case stems from the out-break of severe acute respiratory syndrome (SARS) in the southern China province of Guangdong in mid-November 2002. Local health officials quickly understood how contagious the disease was, and they were aware of the dangers of a possible epidemic. Reports about SARS went up the chain of command to Beijing, and in late January 2003, a team arrived in Guangdong from the Ministry of Health. On January 27, a report was completed by the officials, but it was classified Top Secret, which meant that no one — not doctors, health officials, nor journalists — could talk publicly about the disease without risking prosecution for leaking state secrets.

The reason for the information blackout was that the authorities feared a major epidemic would threaten China's economic growth and public confidence in the competence of the CCP. So it was not until February 11, 2003, three months after the outbreak of the disease and two weeks after the examination by officials from the Ministry of Health, that Guangdong provincial health officials were authorized to give a news conference in which they set out what was known about the disease, the extent of the epidemic, and what could be done by the public to both avoid infection and treat themselves once infected. Officials minimized the extent of the problem and the risks of the disease spreading. A further news blackout occurred during the period of the meeting of the National People's Congress in March. It was politically unacceptable to risk embarrassment for China's ersatz parliament. Beijing did not send information about the outbreak to the World Health Organization until early April. At about the same time, the Chinese Center for Disease Control and Prevention issued a bulletin to hospitals nationwide on how to prevent SARS from spreading. But it was not until mid-April, five months after the epidemic had been first identified, that the ministry in Beijing issued an order requiring SARS to be closely monitored and new cases to be reported daily to the ministry.

Meanwhile in Canada, on March 5, 2003, SARS claimed its first victim, Kwan Sui-chu, a seventy-eight-year-old woman from Hong Kong. Before the outbreak was over, 438 Canadians caught the disease and 44 died. Widespread criticism of Beijing's politically driven silence in the first days after the disease was identified began appearing in April. On April 16, when the death toll in Canada had reached nineteen and the WHO had warned against travelling to Toronto, the *Toronto Star* published a letter by Joel Chipkar, a Falun Gong practitioner. Chipkar was a Toronto businessman who had often written to the newspapers and to the Chinese consulate in Toronto appealing for an end to the persecution of the Falun Gong in China. In his letter to the *Star*, Chipkar expressed concern at Beijing's cover-up of the outbreak and laid responsibility for the deaths resulting from it at the door of the CCP. On May 1, a rebuttal appeared in the same newspaper from Pan Xinchun, the deputy consul general for China in Toronto. Pan vehemently denied the Beijing government had covered up the SARS outbreak and dismissed Chipkar's allegations as the ranting of a member of a "sinister cult."

Chipkar filed a lawsuit against Pan in August 2003, saying the deputy consul's letter was evidence of Chinese diplomats spreading hatred and inciting Canadians against Falun Gong. In February the following year, the Ontario Superior Court heard the case. Pan was not present during the trial and did not send a representative to defend his position. The court held that even though, as deputy consul general, Pan was an employee of the Chinese diplomatic service, his immunity from Canadian law was more limited than that of a full diplomat at the embassy in Ottawa. More than that, Pan's immunity only applied when he was engaged in consular work. In the court's view, Pan's letter to the *Star* did not qualify as a consular function.

The court found Pan guilty of libelling Chipkar and ordered him to pay $1,000 in damages and $10,000 toward Chipkar's legal costs. Chipkar had asked the court for only the token amount in damages, saying he was more interested in the symbolism of the guilty verdict. After the verdict, the Beijing government issued a statement: "Mr. Pan was protecting the interests of the PRC [People's Republic of China] in Canada, and acting on the instructions of the PRC to respond to an attack ... Mr. Pan was acting in the exercise of consular functions and is thus immune from Canadian courts' jurisdiction."

One could be forgiven for believing that taking a robust approach to what constitutes protecting the interests of the People's Republic of China, even to the point of distributing hate material and interfering in domestic Canadian affairs, is part of the job description of Chinese diplomats in Canada. On March 5, 2007, Zhang Jiyan, the wife of an accountant at the Chinese embassy in Ottawa, defected and asked Canada for political asylum. Her account of activities in the embassy covers several of the activities that the Amnesty International report identifies as harassment and intimidation.

Zhang became a Falun Gong follower in 1995 while she was attached to the Chinese embassy in Paris, when the system of Buddhism-infused tai chi was still legal in China. Although Falun Gong had been outlawed in China by the time Zhang and her husband were posted to Ottawa in 2003, she saw practitioners demonstrating on Parliament Hill and decided to join them. After she had been distributing material for the group for a while, she realized she was being monitored by embassy staff. She stopped her public displays of support. She told reporters after her defection that she also became aware of the extent of anti-Falun Gong activities within the embassy. "At the embassy, I personally witnessed materials to incite hatred against Falun Gong," she said in her press conference, published in several Canadian newspapers. "The embassy has a special unit dedicated to collecting information [on practitioners]. The Chinese ambassador mentioned at meetings attended by all embassy personnel that he went to deliver materials defaming Falun Gong to the MPs, the Canadian government officials, and the former Governor General."

Zhang said the embassy's aims to influence Canadian society went much further than the desire to discredit Falun Gong. "The embassy has been in control of the Chinese communities to reach the goal of generating impact and influence on the mainstream [Canadian] society," she was quoted as saying in the *Vancouver Sun*. She pointed to a failed attempt by Chinese diplomats in Canada to prevent a New York-based broadcaster, New Tang Dynasty TV (NTDTV), from getting a television broadcasting licence in Canada. The network has links to Falun Gong, is operated by Chinese expatriates, and usually takes an editorial line critical of the CCP. Zhang said the embassy "mobilized the pro-communist Chinese groups and the Mainland Chinese students to write letters to the CRTC [Canadian Radio-Television and Telecommunications Commission] to stop NTDTV from entering Canada." When that failed, embassy staff lobbied the Canadian cable company, Rogers, to try to prevent NTD from being given a local broadcast channel, she said.

Another case of hate peddling cited in the Amnesty report is far less clear-cut. Amnesty's assessors heard from a well-known and highly regarded Chinese Canadian writer and journalist, Zang Xi Hong, whose pen name is Sheng Xue. Sheng grew up in Beijing and moved to Canada soon after the Tiananmen Square massacre in 1989. As Sheng Xue, she is a correspondent for Radio Free Asia and the North American correspondent for the German public broadcaster Deutsche Welle. Sheng is a member of PEN Canada, a branch of the international organization that defends persecuted writers. In 2007, she was writer in residence at Carleton University in Ottawa. In 2009, she had the same post at McMaster University in Hamilton, and in 2010 she was the writer in exile of Edmonton. She is a member of a dozen or so organizations promoting democracy and reform in China and supporting human rights in Tibet, Xinjiang, Hong Kong, and Taiwan.

Sheng told the Amnesty interviewers that for several years she had been the target of defamatory websites and also of personal attacks by a man named Zhang Xing Yang. From November 2015 until April 2016, Zhang paraded every day on Parliament Hill in Ottawa, carrying large signs denouncing Sheng as being a "China Spy." She reported Zhang to the police, and he responded by launching a civil suit against her demanding $10 million in damages. Zhang's statement of claim filed in the Superior Court of Ontario contains many bizarre allegations, including that Sheng was responsible for kidnapping him in the United States and that she arranged the killing of his wife's cousin in a car crash in China. The brunt of Zhang's claim appears to be that his family's commercial property in Zhengzhou, capital of Henan province, was stolen in 2006 by local officials — an all-too-frequent and believable occurrence. But Zhang then claims that the profits from this theft were used, among other things, to finance the CCP's spy agencies abroad, of which he claims Sheng is a member. Sheng holds that Zhang is doing this on behalf of the CCP in order to discredit her work and position with the many dissident groups with which she is involved. That's a common modus operandi for the CCP's spy agencies. It is also common for people with fixations and a penchant for conspiracy theories to focus their grievances on public figures. What the Sheng/Zhang story illustrates is the smoke-and-mirrors world of suspicions and insecurities within Chinese Canadian communities bred by the activities of the CCP espionage and intimidation campaigns.

From the evidence assembled by Amnesty International Canada, it seems that the CCP's diplomats and agents use surveillance and monitoring of their targets as much for intimidation as for information gathering. There are purposeful efforts to let victims know they are being watched and their activities monitored.

Several of the accounts about the monitoring of individuals gathered in the Amnesty report come from Canadian universities and colleges. In most cases, Amnesty does not name those who gave accounts of their experiences in order to offer them some protection from further attentions. In one case, a Canadian professor told the Amnesty investigators "he had been subjected to a long campaign of harassment and intimidation by Chinese officials attempting to monitor his activities in Canada." This wording suggests the professor is of Chinese ethnic origin or came from territory controlled by China. The professor told Amnesty that his administrative assistant had been contacted by "Chinese people" asking for information on him and that he had personally been approached by members of Xinhua (or New China News Agency), as well as people who he believed had infiltrated an organization of which he is a member. "He also said that colleagues had warned him that the staff of the Confucius Institute at his university have been asked for information of his activities by the Chinese consulate. Recently, his university's Chinese Faculty Association has reportedly received funding from the Chinese Consulate, and he suspects that this support may be predicated on information sharing." The professor told Amnesty that it also appeared that CCP agents had taken a more direct approach to attempting to intimidate him. His house was being watched by two people in a car who left only after being confronted by his wife.

Mehmet Tohti, the head of the Uyghur Canadian Association in 2007, had a similar experience. In an interview with *Maclean's* magazine, published on May 14, 2007, Tohti said he was frequently the target of telephone harassment from people he suspected of being CCP agents. The previous October, he had seen three Chinese men in a black SUV watching his home. Tohti told the magazine he couldn't sleep for days afterwards, even after complaining to CSIS and the Department of Foreign Affairs. In desperation, he moved to a condominium with twenty-four-hour security, but told the magazine, "I no longer feel secure in Canada."

That appears to have been just the reaction the CCP agents hoped for among the 450-strong Canadian Uyghur community. Three years before, there had been an even more direct attempt to intimidate Tohti. The phone rang late one evening at his home. The call was from Tohti's mother, Turmisa, who lived in Karghilik in the largely Uyghur Chinese-occupied territory of Xinjiang. He had not seen her for sixteen years, not since he had fled from China. Turmisa quickly passed the phone to a man, who immediately began berating Tohti about his political activities. The man identified himself as an official of the Overseas Chinese Affairs Office, a major agency for using people in China's diaspora as vehicles for achieving the CCP's international objectives. He instructed Tohti to stop working in Canada to draw sympathy to the Uyghur cause. In particular, he wanted Tohti to stop claiming that Beijing was engaged in a campaign of cultural genocide against the Uyghurs. He also instructed Tohti not to attend an upcoming conference in Germany of many groups of Uyghur exiles. The threat behind the official's demands was explicit. "We have your mother here, and your brother, too," he said, adding that police had brought them nearly three hundred kilometres to the regional police headquarters at Kashgar in order to make this phone call. "We can do whatever we want," the official said.

That was no empty threat. Another Uyghur leader, Huseyin Celil, is a Muslim imam who fled with his family to Canada in 2001, became a Canadian citizen, and settled in Burlington, just west of Toronto. Celil was active in Uyghur politics and took part in demonstrations outside the Chinese consulate in Toronto, where he was photographed by Chinese officials. In March 2006, Celil went to visit his wife's family in Uzbekistan, a Central Asian country close to China's Xinjiang region. He was arrested, handed over to Beijing's officials, and bundled across the border into China. Despite increasingly agitated insistence by Canadian diplomats that Celil was a Canadian citizen and must be treated as such, he was swiftly tried for terrorism and sentenced to fifteen years in prison. The incident brought a distinct chill to Canada-China relations. In response to Prime Minister Stephen Harper's demand that the Chinese government explain Celil's treatment, Chinese Ministry of Foreign Affairs spokeswoman Jiang Yu said the Chinese government considers Celil a Chinese citizen and therefore the "consular agreement between China and Canada does not apply in this case." Jiang also said that Celil is "a member of the East Turkestan Islamic Movement. He's a criminal."

Celil's Canadian lawyer, Chris MacLeod, believed the swift removal of Celil from Uzbekistan to China could not have been arranged without espionage efforts in Canada. "I've maintained all along that the reason Huseyin came on the radar of the Chinese authorities was because of activities here," he told *Maclean's*. "Obviously, they monitored him and they knew he was travelling. They certainly didn't want other Uyghurs speaking publicly about the cause. I guess this is their way of sending a message."

The CCP's campaign of subjugation in Xinjiang has intensified. In August 2018 a United Nations human rights panel issued a report saying it had received many credible accounts indicating that as many as two million Uyghurs were being held in camps. Gay McDougall, a member of the UN Committee on the Elimination of Racial Discrimination, said "We are deeply concerned at the numerous and credible reports that we have received that in the name of combating religious extremism and maintaining social stability (China) has changed the Uyghur autonomous region into something that resembles a massive internment camp that is shrouded in secrecy." China rejected the charges and accused the United Nations of relying on "unsubstantiated and irresponsible information."

Threatening family members in China or holding them hostage is a well-established technique used by the CCP's agents to control the behaviour of dissidents abroad or to force people to return to China for retribution.

Perhaps because she is an actress and beauty queen, and is therefore photogenic and has a significant fan base, Anastasia Lin's case has received international publicity. Lin emigrated from China to Canada with her mother in 2003 when she was thirteen. Her parents were divorced, and her father continued to live in Hunan province. She majored in theatre at the University of Toronto, forged an acting career, and won the Miss World Canada pageant in the summer of 2015.

Writing about her experience in *The Washington Post* in June 2015, Lin said that despite the censorship in China, word of her victory in the Miss World Canada pageant reached her family and friends:

But things soon took a dark turn....

Shortly after my victory, my father started receiving threats from Chinese security agents complaining about my human rights advocacy. As an actress, I frequently take on roles in films and television productions that shed light on official corruption and religious persecution in China, and my Miss World Canada platform reflects these passions. No doubt fearing for his livelihood and business, my father asked me to stop advocating for human rights. He told me that if I did not stop, we would have to go our separate ways.

Many Chinese rights advocates have had similar experiences. Even after they immigrate to the West, the Communist Party uses their family members in China as leverage to silence and intimidate them.

Lin wrote that she wrestled with the choice between her relationship with her father and her human rights advocacy. "The answer is simple: If I allow myself to be intimidated, then I am complicit in continued human rights abuses. If I and others who share my concerns allow ourselves to be silenced, the Communist Party will continue abusing its people with impunity," she declared. "[S]ilence will not protect my father, and even if he can't understand or accept why I speak out, I know he is safer in the light of international attention than in the shadows sought by the authoritarians."

In November, despite the threats, Lin was set to go to Sanya, on China's Hainan Island, for the Miss World finals, but she didn't get there. Chinese authorities would not let her into the country, declaring her *persona non grata*, apparently because of her outspoken support for human rights and religious freedom in China, including condemnation of the persecution of Falun Gong.

The Amnesty report documents several cases of harassment and bullying of Canadians' relatives in China, Tibet, or Xinjiang. In most cases, the names of those interviewed have been blacked out to protect their privacy. One case referred to directly is that of Xie Weidong, a former judge of the Supreme People's Court who moved to Toronto in 2014 and became an outspoken critic of the Chinese judicial system. In an interview with *The Globe and Mail* published on January 11, 2017, Xie said he has no doubt the Chinese authorities were trying to force him to return to China for questioning. They have publicly accused him of corruption, a catch-all charge frequently used by the CCP to remove and silence its critics.

"They are using the methods which hurt me most," he is quoted as telling the newspaper. "The whole family has fallen into extreme terror. They don't dare even call each other. My son was arrested for no reason, and everyone in the family knows him. Are they going to be arrested next?"

The wife of Xie's son, Xie Cangqiong, gave a graphic account of what happened when the newlywed couple went to the underground car park of their Beijing apartment complex at the end of 2016 to drive to a party for his grandfather's one hundredth birthday. The tires on their car had been slashed, and they were immediately surrounded by a group of men dressed in black. Xie Cangqiong, who was twenty-seven, was carried off, howling in pain. "We are enforcing the law. You must cooperate with us," Xie's wife quoted one of the men as saying. The young man was taken thirteen hundred kilometres south to Hubei province, where he was held on suspicion of embezzlement. The harassment didn't stop there. Xie Weidong's sister was detained, and other relatives were barred from leaving China.

The Amnesty report cites several instances where Chinese diplomats have ridden roughshod over Canadian tenets of freedom of speech, assembly, and media in order to suppress criticisms of the CCP. In another case of interference in Canadian freedom of expression, the report cites a letter China's consul general in Vancouver, Liang Shugen, wrote in March 2011 to the city's mayor, Gregor Robertson, urging him to boycott a dance performance at the Queen Elizabeth Theatre by the Shen Yun Performing Arts group.

"As you know, the Falun Gong cult has been engaged in activities aimed at undermining the Chinese government and poisoning bilateral relations between China and Canada," Liang wrote in the letter obtained by the *Vancouver Courier* newspaper after a Freedom of Information request. "One of their tactics is staging the so-called Shen Yun Performance Arts across Canada in the name of 'promoting classical Chinese dance and music.' But in reality, the show is filled with cult messages and political attacks on the Chinese government. This year's performance will be no exception." Liang concluded by urging Robertson and Vancouver's city council not to issue a letter of congratulation to the troupe, "let alone attend their performance." Robertson's office told the newspaper the mayor did not attend the show because he was out of town on holiday.

Many, though not all, of the CCP's spies, secret police, agents of influence, and other clandestine operations have parts in the Amnesty-led report on harassment and intimidation of human rights and political reform groups in Canada. The full picture of the agencies and agents at the CCP's disposal is much larger, and all of those additional servants of the party are also working away in Canada.

TWO

THE HUNDRED STRATEGIES TO FRUSTRATE ENEMY FORCES

Use the past to serve the present, make the foreign serve China.
— XI JINPING, QUOTING MAO ZEDONG

THE MACHINERY THAT the Chinese Communist Party has fashioned to control, influence, and milk its relationships with foreign countries is a fabulous example of craftsmanship and ingenuity. The intelligence and sub-version apparatus is massive, and its component parts are interlocked and interdependent in ways that are unfamiliar, and therefore not always recognizable, to non-Chinese. Like other countries, the CCP has the usual military and civilian counter-intelligence agencies to winkle out foreign spies targeting China. Where the CCP differs, however, is the emphasis it places on using a plethora of unofficial bodies and people-to-people links to provide windows into target countries.

As with most of what the Chinese Communist Party has undertaken since its founding on July 1, 1921, in Shanghai, there is a strand of political philosophy guiding these endeavours, learned from the Soviet Union, which mentored the CCP in the business of managing a Marxist revolutionary organization. Mao Zedong edited and embellished Joseph Stalin's text-book to fit Chinese social and cultural imperatives. He produced Stalinism with Chinese characteristics.

Mao tried to destroy ancient China and create a country with a Marxist culture uncoupled from its past. But the murder of the land-owning class, the brainwashing and indoctrination of re-education, the bloodletting of the Great Leap Forward, the internecine warfare of the Cultural Revolu-tion — none of these fundamentally changed Chinese society. Those catastrophic government-created events only proved that ancient and modern China are inexorably intertwined and that some cultural attitudes are too deep to be uprooted. The importance to Chinese strategic thought of the fifth-century BC military handbook *The Art of War* by Sun Tzu has become a cliché. But its advocacy of the use of intelligence to outfox enemies, especially more powerful ones, remains central to the strategy of the CCP. Beijing's security and power projection is still driven by the notion that the intensive gathering of intelligence about opponents and careful analysis of their weaknesses will give China the upper hand before any armed conflict begins. If properly undertaken, this intelligence will force an enemy to capitulate before actual physical conflict is initiated. Writing about the influence of Sun Tzu on modern Chinese leaders in his 1994 book *Chinese Intelligence Operations*, Nicholas Eftimiades, who had a thirty-year career in various American defence, security, and intelligence agencies, said, "Today's policymakers show the same appreciation for the value of foreknowledge and the proper application of espionage activities in support of the affairs of state. The People's Republic of China's intelligence apparatus is more than just a support department for policy makers. It is inextricably linked to the foreign decision-making process and internal methods of economic development and political control."

An excellent example of Beijing's use of intelligence to allow sophisticated judgment on the likely actions and reactions of its adversaries is its takeover of the South China Sea over the last twenty years, almost without a shot being fired. During that time, the CCP has made small but persistent advances in its claims and in its military presence in the sea and on the islets and atolls whose possession are the justification for broad maritime territorial claims. The South China Sea is one of the world's most important maritime highways, and also the repository of significant seabed oil and gas reserves, as well as major stocks of fish and other seafood. Beijing carefully judged the speed and size of its approach to establishing sovereignty. None of China's advances was in itself large or threatening enough to excite major international responses, especially from the United States. None was a *casus belli*. The reality now is that, despite claims from half a dozen of the other littoral states, the South China Sea is essentially a Chinese lake, defended by ever-enlarging military outposts on seven artificial islands. It will now take a major war to dislodge Beijing's military from the sea, and there are no indications that anyone, least of all Washington, is prepared to try to evict Beijing or otherwise challenge its squatter's rights.

The Chinese Communist Party's main civilian security and intelligence agency is the Ministry of State Security. The MSS was formed in 1983 and, like some other CCP institutions, was modelled on a Soviet counterpart. The modern MSS resembles the Soviet Union's main domestic and foreign security service during the Cold War, the Komitet Gosudarstvennoy Bezopasnosti (KGB). China's MSS is responsible for counter-intelligence at home, gathering foreign intelligence, and defending the political security of the CCP.

The head of the MSS at the time of writing in mid-2018 is Chen Wenqing. Chen's position makes him a member of the two-hundred-plus-member Central Committee of the CCP. He is also on the thirty-five-member State Council, which is the public face of the government of China.

The MSS benefited greatly from the Cold War. While the United States and its allies were preoccupied with the Soviet Union and its Warsaw Pact satellites in Eastern Europe, the MSS and the CCP's other intelligence agencies were able to grow and extend their tentacles almost undisturbed. From the creation of the People's Republic of China in 1949 until the death of Mao in 1976, the interest in China by Western intelligence agencies was spasmodic at best. Mao's sending hundreds of thousands of "volunteers" to fight with North Korea in the Korean War of 1950–52 excited attention. So did the prospect in the 1950s that Mao might attempt to complete his conquest of claimed Chinese territory by invading Taiwan. In the 1960s, China was involved in the war in Vietnam and in the spread of communism throughout Southeast Asia. This reached a boiling point when the Beijing-backed Khmer Rouge seized power in Cambodia in 1975. Four years later, however, it was not Washington but Vietnam that invaded Cambodia and put an end to the Khmer Rouge bloodbath.

With Mao's death and the accession of Deng Xiaoping as paramount leader, it seemed that China aimed to abandon isolationism, embrace economic reform, and become a normal country, or something close to it. This renewed interest in China during the 1980s by Western governments, investors, and intelligence agencies. That interest became more intense after the collapse of the Soviet Union in 1989. But by then, the MSS and the CCP's other intelligence agencies had already honed their foreign operation methods and had their spies and agents of influence well placed abroad. As Western agencies and those of allies in countries like Japan and Taiwan began to unearth MSS spies in their midst, it became apparent that they were dealing with a very sophisticated organization. Immediately obvious was that the MSS was following classic espionage tradecraft and placing its agents among accredited Chinese officials abroad. These included diplomats, business people, commercial and military attachés in Chinese embassies and consulates, scientists and other academics visiting foreign universities and other institutions, and students and journalists, especially those working for the state-controlled Xinhua. Spies in other legal positions, and thus with a degree of diplomatic immunity, have been found in the Chinese People's Friendship Association, several trade unions, the International Liaison Department, and especially the United Front Work Department.

A major purpose of all intelligence agents working abroad is to recruit local informants and place spies in positions that will provide useful intelligence. China follows this creed very successfully. Agents without any diplomatic cover are known as "illegals," and if caught they face imprisonment and, in some countries, the death penalty. They will also be interrogated, a word whose meaning runs the gamut from lengthy, detailed, and persistent questioning all the way to outright torture. Even so, Chinese illegals have been found planted in all the major American weapons laboratories, including the Lawrence Livermore Laboratory, Los Alamos, Oak Ridge, and Sandia. The CCP's haul, according to the 1999 House of Representatives' Select Committee on U.S. Nation Security and Military/Commercial Concerns with the People's Republic of China, included the design information on all the United States' most advanced thermonuclear weapons, classified information on seven types of American nuclear warheads (including the five currently deployed), and design information on an enhanced radiation weapon, commonly known as the neutron bomb. In addition, Chinese spies obtained information on nuclear warhead re-entry vehicles, the hardened shells that protect the weapons during their return from the edge of space when enormous heat is generated. Mastering this technology is critical to being able to deploy a reliable and accurate nuclear weapon. The committee judged that the penetration of the American weapons laboratories "spans at least the past several decades and almost certainly continues today."

The United States is the motherlode for CCP spies hunting for weapons and other technologies, including vast amounts of data on industrial, manufacturing, and communications systems. But spies for China have in recent decades been unmasked all over the world, with clandestine operations exposed in Africa, Europe, Asia, and Latin America.

As well as Chinese diplomats and other officials posted abroad, the MSS recruits informants and spies among students going to colleges and universities overseas. There were 523,700 Chinese students studying overseas in 2015. Of those, 119,335 were in Canada and 260,914 in the United States. Students are recruited or coerced to gather skills and technologies needed by China. However, most pilfered corporate technology is acquired by means of purchase through Hong Kong-fronted companies. The MSS's most productive way of getting hold of highly protected technologies is to send scientists to foreign universities and colleges on scholarly exchange programs. It was visiting Chinese scientists who acquired plans for the neutron bomb at the Lawrence Livermore Laboratory in California in the 1980s. There are also examples of the MSS placing professional intelligence officers with enough scientific knowledge to pass muster among groups of visiting scientists. These officers are tasked with keeping an eye on the other members of the group, gathering general information on the institutions being visited, and picking out people among the host scientists who might be recruited.

The MSS uses delegations of Chinese business people in much the same way. Since China opened for business in the mid-1980s, thousands of such delegations have travelled abroad every year looking for investments and trading partners. State security agents are planted in these groups, both to keep an eye on the other members and to scout out opportunities to acquire technology. The CCP and MSS have become especially adept at arranging the purchase of foreign companies that own technologies banned from being exported because of their military or associated uses. Again, the United States is the most fruitful target for this form of technology acquisition, but Canada is also an important target for the MSS, as are Australia and several European countries. As will be described in greater detail later, this issue flared in Canada in 2017 with the decision by the government of Prime Minister Justin Trudeau to reverse the blocking by the previous Conservative government of the sale of a Montreal high-tech firm, ITF Technologies, to a Chinese company, and to allow the sale of a British Columbia-based military communications company, Norsat International, to the Chinese company Hytera Communications.

FROM ITS FOUNDING in 1931 as the Red China News Agency, Xinhua has been the eyes and tongue of the Chinese Communist Party. Its reporters are propagandists for the party, printing and broadcasting accounts of daily events that promote the CCP's view of the world. At the same time, its reporters are intelligence agents. Every day, they produce a series of internal journals for limited distribution among CCP officials. These journals increase in accuracy and candour depending how high up the CCP food chain the intended audience is. Mid-level CCP officials get *Reference News*, which includes half a dozen or so pages of candid reports by Xinhua journalists as well as some foreign news. Even more sensitive is *Internal Reference*, which is read only by CCP members at ministerial level or above. Occasionally, Xinhua will produce highly classified reports on issues of the moment for the members of the Politburo Standing Committee. These special reports deal with matters like the 2002 SARS outbreak and public reaction to environmental pollution. The Xinhua reporters' task in situations like these is to give the CCP leaders an accurate and in-depth assessment of the public's mood. Implicit in these reports is judging how much of a threat these issues present to the regime.

Xinhua's overseas bureaus follow much the same formula of producing propaganda pap for public consumption and more accurate reports for the higher levels of the CCP hierarchy. Indeed, some Xinhua foreign bureaus are so large that the bulk of their staff has little to do with journalism. For example, the Xinhua offices in both Hong Kong and the Portuguese colony of Macau were major instruments of intelligence-gathering, influence-peddling, and quiet contacts with the local administrations before the two territories were handed back to Beijing's rule in 1997 and 1999 respectively. In both cases, the Xinhua offices served as quasi-diplomatic missions because there were no other consular links. Indeed, the Xinhua office in Macau was so large that its staff outnumbered the Portuguese colonial civil service; with Portuguese agreement and connivance, it had more or less taken over the administration of the territory well before the handover in December 1999.

The Chinese Communist Party sees its overseas population of Chinese emigrants and foreign residents, generally reckoned to total about 50 million people, as an asset to be marshalled in the promotion of China's political interests. Many other governments, including those of Israel, France, the United Kingdom, and Germany, also have formal departments charged with overseeing relations with their diasporas. None of these governments, however, has established formal structures and networks to manage and influence their diasporas on the scale of the CCP.

The Overseas Chinese Affairs Office of the State Council (OCAO) was established at the very beginning of the People's Republic of China in 1949 as the Committee of Overseas Chinese Affairs. New Zealand scholar James Jiann Hua To, in his 2009 doctoral thesis on Beijing's management of the overseas Chinese (OC), estimated that tens of thousands of Beijing's civil servants are employed in this work. "The Overseas Chinese Affairs Office has attachments in PRC embassies, consulates, and representative agencies in almost every country to personally liaise with local oc communities," To wrote. One of the main objectives of the OCAO is to sustain a useful level of patriotism among overseas Chinese by keeping them connected to their homeland and the towns and villages from which they or their ancestors originated. To that end, there are OCAO district offices at all levels of local government in China, right down to the township level in rural villages. These local officials promote links with the diaspora through sport, trade, and cultural groups, as well as families and hometown associations. The central OCAO department has a substantial budget to pay for these groups to travel abroad to promote their particular interests and reinforce relations with the OC. In his study of the operation, To judges that "despite a sometimes turbulent relationship with the OC, Beijing's intention was always to retain their trust, and access to their political and economic resources for facilitating its domestic development, extending its foreign policy, challenging political rivals, and boosting its international image."

A turbulent relationship is to be expected. In Canada, the United States, and Australia in particular, the vast majority of Chinese immigrants are there because they no longer wish to live under CCP rule. Even so, some emigrants are open to appeals to racial patriotism, the tug of the mother country, or the benefits of financial favouritism.

Coupled with the OCAO is another, largely covert, network aimed at influencing and, when possible, controlling foreigners both abroad and in China. The external policies intended to target non-ethnic Chinese are known as *waishi*, an abbreviation of *waijiao shiwu*, meaning "diplomatic matters." Several scholars and academics have found that at the heart of the *waishi* system is the cultivation of foreign friends. New Zealand Sinologist Dr. Anne-Marie Brady struck a sweet spot in the opening up of China's internal workings in the 1990s and was able to get access in various libraries to internal *waishi* documents that had previously been classified. Since then, the shutters have come down, especially since Xi Jinping came to power in 2012. Brady's work sets out a clear picture of an elaborate and long-established organization within the Chinese state, the sole purpose of which is to identify and recruit friends and agents of influence among foreigners who have contact with China.

The CCP's early philosophy toward dealings with foreigners, beginning in the 1930s, was inherited from the Soviet Union. This was based on projecting a benign international image of the Soviet revolution in order to blunt opposition and win support or acquiescence from non-communists and shielding the Soviet population from outside influences. The CCP adopted these objectives and strategies. These goals were made both simpler and more intense during the 1930s and early 1940s, when the CCP was an outlawed revolutionary army. There were many foreigners in China during those years, but few who had any contact with the CCP or who supported its cause. Those who did gained the undying gratitude of the CCP. People like Canadian doctor Norman Bethune, New Zealander founder of industrial co-operatives Rewi Alley, and several American writers, principally Edgar Snow, became heroes of the revolution and cherished friends. Among these early friends of the CCP were several Canadian missionaries and members of their families who went on to play significant roles in the creation of Canadian foreign policy both in regard to China and more broadly in the 1950s and 1960s.

After the CCP took power in 1949, most foreigners were driven out of China. Only a few who had established strong bonds of loyalty to the CCP, such as Rewi Alley and Mao Zedong's American interpreter, Sidney Rittenberg, remained. The new CCP regime, however, was desperate for foreign expertise. In the early years, it was the Soviet Union and the communist-dominated countries of Eastern Europe that supplied the scientists, teachers, engineers, medical personnel, military advisers, technicians, propagandists, translators, and administrative experts the regime needed. There were exceptions, but access to China by foreigners remained tightly controlled until the death of Mao in 1976. In her exploration of *waishi* handbooks and files, Brady found a passage in a 1995 publication that set out the objectives of the policy: "The more friends we have the better, yet we also have to be selective. We especially want to make friends with foreigners who are friendly to us, have some social prestige, have economic power, or academic achievements, or have political influence;

this will be most advantageous for the achievement of a peaceful international environment and to support our nation's economic construction."

Brady found there are a number of rankings of foreign supporters. Lowest in the hierarchy is "foreign friend," which is often used interchangeably with the "international friend." Next up the scale is "old friend of the Chinese people." The top rank is reserved for people described as "internationalist fighters." This is an exclusive pantheon and includes people like Norman Bethune, Rewi Alley, and Indian doctor Dwarkanath Shantaram Kotnis, whose volunteer work with the Communist guerrillas in the 1930s was similar to that of Bethune. More notable these days are the "old friends," who have remained strong foreign contacts and advocates for Beijing and the CCP regime through thick and thin. This rank includes people like former U.S. Secretary of State Henry Kissinger, the man who negotiated diplomatic recognition between Beijing and Washington. Then there's Sir Percy Cradock, the former British ambassador to Beijing who died in 2010. Sir Percy was a central figure in the negotiations in the mid-1980s for London to return sovereignty over Hong Kong to China. He remained highly influential at Whitehall even after his retirement and was publicly critical of the efforts by the last British governor of Hong Kong, Christopher Patten, to embed democracy in the colony before the 1997 handover. Another "old friend" is former French president Jacques Chirac, who has been described as a "lifelong China addict." Chirac's passion for Chinese culture and history expanded into blocking international criticism of the CCP's human rights record, promoting arms sales to Beijing, and supporting the CCP's efforts to cow Taiwan into submitting to Beijing's sovereignty.

Western commentators have tended to see the foreigners on whom the CCP lavishes its friendship as politically naive and unaware that they are being used by the regime. Brady disputes this. She points out that so far as the CCP is concerned, "friend of China" is a job description more than it is an honour, and she believes that most of the foreigners who take this role do so knowingly, willingly, and often eagerly. "To be a friend has implications of moral superiority over other foreigners in China," she wrote in her 2003 study *Making the Foreign Serve China.* "The rewards for those who have conformed to such controls are high, both in terms of status, access to information, and in the current era, for many of China's high-profile former politician friends, monetary, in the form of consulting fees paid to them by firms who hope to use their connections to do business in China."

The proof that the "honour" is actually a job description is that there are penalties for refusing to perform the duties required of a "friend of China," ranging from negligible to severe. Invitations to lavish banquets will suddenly stop. Phone calls to important Chinese officials will not get through. Academics may find that the access on which their scholarly reputations are built suddenly ends. Business people who try to sever the bonds of friendship can even find themselves imprisoned, expelled from China, or denied visas. "The CCP's political friendship is a deliberate strategy, an integral part of the People's Republic of China foreign affairs system," wrote Brady. "It is very different from the genuine friendships formed from ordinary human interaction. China's political friendship is clearly an application of United Front principles to divide the enemy by focusing on contradictions and uniting all forces that can be united around a common goal."

The United Front is a unique Chinese Communist Party operation. In their book *Nest of Spies,* former Canadian Security Intelligence Service officer Michel Juneau-Katsuya and journalist Fabrice de Pierrebourg explain that the United Front manages a plethora of dossiers concerning foreign countries. "These include propaganda, the control of Chinese students abroad, the recruiting of agents among the Chinese Diaspora (and among sympathetic foreigners), and long-term clandestine operations." Since the book was published in 2009, the mandate of the United Front has become broader and more intense under China's president Xi Jinping. He has redesigned the United Front as a movement for the whole party. This means the United Front now has people assigned to posts at the top levels of all departments in the party and state. The department's staff is said to have expanded to forty thousand in the last few years.

"Enemy forces abroad do not want to see China rise and many of them see our country as a potential threat and rival, so they use ploys and a hundred strategies to frustrate and repress us," says a United Front manual acquired by the British *Financial Times* newspaper, which was the subject of a report published in October 2017. "The United Front … is a big magic weapon which can rid us of 10,000 problems in order to seize victory," the manual continues. This thought was underlined at a rare news conference given the same month by Zhang Yijiong, the executive vice-minister of the United Front. "If the Chinese people want to be powerful and realize the great rejuvenation of the Chinese nation, then under the leadership of the Communist Party we need to fully and better understand the use of the 'magic weapon,'" she said.

A key part of the expansion of the department is that almost all Chinese embassies and major consulates abroad now have staff working for the United Front. "The unity of Chinese at home requires the unity of the sons and daughters of Chinese abroad," says the United Front manual acquired by the *Financial Times*. The comment underlines that even though more than 80 percent of the estimated 50 million overseas Chinese have taken the citizenship of the 180 countries in which they live, the CCP still regards them as potential fifth columnists. The manual suggests a number of ways United Front staff can gain support from overseas Chinese targets. One is making simple appeals to racial and cultural ties to the motherland. Another is a more ideological call to participate in the "great rejuvenation of the Chinese people." But the *Financial Times* reported that the main thrust is to use more crass offers to fund or give other resources to overseas Chinese groups and individuals that the CCP sees as most able to promote its interests. All overseas Chinese "friendship associations" are under the wing of the United Front and are often the agencies through which people are lured into the department's grasp.

Higher up the chain of influence, the manual points with approval to the success of overseas Chinese in elections in Toronto. The manual is unclear about which candidates ran for which posts, but it appears to refer to municipal elections in the Greater Toronto Area and says that in 2003, six people were elected from among twenty-five ethnic Chinese candidates, while in 2006 the number jumped to ten elected from among forty-four ethnic Chinese candidates. "We should aim to work with those individuals and groups that are at a relatively high level, operate within the mainstream of society and have prospects for advancement," says the manual.

The United Front now has nine departments. The first branch is the Parties Work Bureau, which deals with the eight non-communist political parties in China. These parties are fabrications of the CCP, designed to give the appearance of a multi-party democracy, and this branch of the United Front places representatives of the fake parties in various branches of government. Similarly, the second branch is the Minorities and Religions Bureau, which oversees the fifty-five recognized national minorities in China. The aim is to manage these groups so that they do not become separatist organizations and to ensure they understand their cultures and religions are subservient to the CCP.

The third branch is a major operation, and the one of most concern to Canadians. The Hong Kong, Macau, Taiwan and Overseas Liaison Bureau has the historic function of maintaining loyalty to the CCP in Hong Kong and Macau, the former British and Portuguese colonies that are now special administrative regions once again under Chinese sovereignty. The bureau's work in Taiwan is aimed at building alliances with local people with the purpose of undermining the islanders' dedication to their independence. The ultimate objective is to prepare the ground for Beijing to seize Taiwan and its twenty-three million people when the time is ripe. Also within the third branch are the offices dealing with cultivating loyalty among the fifty million overseas Chinese, both to enhance Beijing's reputation abroad and to establish a coterie of agents of influence who can be called on when needed to promote the CCP's interests.

The fourth, fifth, and sixth branches deal with training United Front cadres, working to maintain support for the CCP among poor people left behind in China's economic revolution, and cultivating support among artists, intellectuals, and other people who are influential but who are not affiliated with the CCP.

The seventh branch deals with Tibet. This bureau not only works to suppress Tibetan separatism, undermine the influence of the Dalai Lama, and control the succession when he dies, it is also, confusingly, charged with winning the hearts and minds of Tibetans.

The eighth bureau addresses the CCP's new problem of a rising middle class that has become economically secure in the years of socialist capitalism, and which therefore has little loyalty to the Communist Party. It is the rise of this group that many Western governments and observers have believed for years will change China by demanding political and social reforms. The aim of the New Social Classes Work Bureau is to ensure this does not happen.

The ninth bureau is the newest and is responsible for overseeing the occupation of Xinjiang in northwestern China in much the same way as the seventh bureau operates in Tibet. The bureau is charged with cultivating loyalty to the CCP among the Uyghur, Kazakh, and Tajik peoples who live in Xinjiang, while also suppressing separatist movements and limiting their observance of the Islamic faith.

The United Front has always tried to convey a benign and comforting image. But as its operations in Tibet, Xinjiang, Hong Kong, Taiwan, Canada, Australia, New Zealand, and elsewhere show, it is an iron fist in a silk glove.

The first United Front was created at the urging of the Soviet Union in 1922. Moscow told the nascent CCP that it should join forces with its enemy, the Kuomintang, then led by Sun Yat-sen. Moscow argued that this would be a way for the CCP to protect itself from annihilation. It would also allow the party room to grow like a parasite in the body of the ruling party and would enable the communists to eventually take charge. This alliance lasted only five years. After Sun's death in 1925, Chiang Kai-shek took control of the Kuomintang and, in April 1927, launched a purge of communists, first in Shanghai and then across China. Hundreds of thousands of suspected communists were killed, but key members of the CCP, such as Mao Zedong and Zhou Enlai, escaped. By 1935, the communists had re-established themselves in and around Yan'an in northern

Shaanxi province. After the Japanese invaded China from their enclave in Manchuria in July 1937, Kuomintang leader Chiang Kai-shek was reluctantly persuaded to form a second United Front with the CCP in order to defeat the Japanese. This uneasy alliance held firm until the end of the Second World War in 1945. The front then collapsed as victory over the Japanese morphed seamlessly into the civil war that the communists won in 1949.

The experience of the first two United Fronts was valuable for the CCP. The party learned how useful and profitable temporary alliances with non-communist organizations could be. It learned how easily these alliances could be fashioned and manipulated so long as the CCP displayed a friendly face and underplayed its objectives while maintaining strict internal discipline. Building on this experience, Mao adapted these strategies after the CCP took power. He calculated that only about 10 percent of the population was violently opposed to the new regime. The bulk of the population, he judged, was open to being suborned. The United Front Work Department was established as a major agency under the control of the Central Committee of the CCP, the third level of power in the party hierarchy. Its initial task after 1949 was to convince the bulk of the Chinese population that the CCP represented progress, unity, and democracy, while the Kuomintang embodied the past, corruption, and authoritarianism.

The policy was successful enough to get the CCP firmly established in power before the onslaught of Mao's disasters (the Great Leap Forward and the Cultural Revolution). After Mao's death in 1976, the new paramount leader, Deng Xiaoping, revived the United Front as an essential tool in his efforts to open up the Chinese economy and establish a market system "with Chinese characteristics." The United Front continued to be responsible for managing China's minority ethnic groups, a few ersatz non-communist political parties, and authorized religious groups. But under Deng, the United Front became an important arm of CCP foreign policy. The department was first used to lure overseas Chinese and other friends of China to assist with the economic reform and development initiative. As well as the prospect of making vast profits from getting in early on the reform process, overseas Chinese were tempted with honours such as membership in the Chinese People's Political Consultative Conference, a body of nearly twenty-four hundred people. The CPPCC was placed under the management of the United Front and is now put forward as a forum through which the CCP listens to suggestions from non-communists, including overseas Chinese. The honour of belonging to this organization is diminished, however, by the reality that two-thirds of its members come from the CCP to ensure that the CPPCC doesn't acquire any independent political legitimacy or come up with any resolutions that might embarrass the regime.

The overseas network of the United Front has expanded greatly in recent years. A sign of this is that in 2007, the Central Committee of the CCP increased the United Front's budget by US$3 billion. The department manages a cornucopia of soft power foreign relationships, including a multitude of friendship societies. The Canada-China Friendship Society, for example, was founded in Ottawa in 1976 to foster understanding between the two countries. In its early years, the society focused largely on cultural activities, such as calligraphy, photography, and tours of China. In 1980, however, the society expanded into the Federation of Canada-China Friendship Associations. Its first members included such key figures in early Ottawa-Beijing relations as Chester Ronning, Dr. James Endicott, and Professor Paul Lin. An indication of the group's stature is that later that same year a delegation visited Beijing, where they saw Soong Ching Ling, the widow of Sun Yat-sen and a relative of Paul Lin. The federation now has six branches, in Victoria, Toronto, Calgary, Ottawa, Winnipeg, and Vancouver. The United Front also keeps a close eye on a multitude of professional associations linking China with foreign countries, including Canada.

In the 1980s, the United Front oversaw the creation of a plethora of new groups worldwide, many of which seemed to duplicate the work of the Friendship Associations. One such is the China Association for International Friendly Contact. This was set up in 1984, but it is not in fact a duplicate organization. It is a front for the International Liaison

Department of the People's Liberation Army General Political Department. The primary purpose of this association is to gather military and security intelligence through innocuous-sounding subsidiary groups like the China Painting Academy, the Centre for Across-Cultural Communication, the Centre for Peace and Development Studies, and the Centre for International Network Information Exchange.

One of the United Front's most blatant and least successful operations has been the financing of Confucius Institutes in schools, colleges, and universities in Canada, the United States, Australia, and elsewhere around the world. Although the Confucius Institute program ostensibly comes under the quasi-governmental Office of Chinese Language Council International, its first director was Liu Yandong, a former head of the United Front. In 2009, the CCP propaganda chief Li Changchun described the institutes as "an important part of China's overseas propaganda setup." Initially, many universities, colleges, and high schools in Canada and elsewhere jumped at the chance of joining the China studies bandwagon with Beijing paying most of the bill. By 2014, there were 480 institutes in 123 countries, and managers hoped to have 1,000 institutes worldwide by 2020; however, it quickly became clear to the host schools that the institutes were in fact espionage operations. Many of the host academic institutions in Canada and elsewhere have ended their relationships with the Confucius Institutes.

An essential element of the *waishi* philosophy was that contact with foreigners should be a one-way street. The aim is to steal information and gain influence in foreign countries without allowing China to be infected with ideas and philosophies that would undermine the one-party state. The Tiananmen Square protests in Beijing in 1989 following the death of moderate CCP leader Hu Yaobang — during which the demonstrators demanded political liberalization, more openness about economic management, and prosecution of corrupt party officials — showed that the barriers to foreign ideas were not working. The CCP pulled out its old ideological lexicon and called the protests a "counter revolutionary rebellion." This signalled a sharp turn to the left in party ideology, a course it has followed ever since. The hope among many Western countries, and the justification offered by many Western politicians for doing business with a repressive regime — that economic development would inevitably lead to political reform — died with the protesters on the flagstones of Tiananmen Square. The CCP invoked martial law and sent in the army against the demonstrators in Beijing and those at similar protests they had inspired in over two hundred cities across China.

The Tiananmen Square massacre was a major setback for the international image of China as an eager friend and willing partner to Western countries that had been fostered by Deng Xiaoping and his expansion of the *waishi* program in the 1980s. Most Western countries responded to the massacre by imposing trade and other financial sanctions on China, cancelling state visits to Beijing by their leaders, and withdrawing invitations to Chinese leaders to visit their countries. For about a year after the massacre, the CCP hunkered down and accepted its new isolation without objection. This was in part because the party was consumed with rooting out and re-educating or eradicating the many people within its own ranks who had sympathized with the Tiananmen protesters and who opposed martial law. This internal turmoil was all the more intense because it coincided with the collapse of the Soviet Union. The shattering of the Soviet Empire and the implosion of Russian political life was a constant reminder to the CCP of the fate that awaited them if they played their cards wrong.

It was not until late in 1990 that the CCP began to try to restore its international links and test the strength of the foreign friendships established in the previous decades. Brady quotes *waishi* documents from 1990 saying China's president and CCP secretary general Jiang Zemin instructed all the organization's personnel to step up their links with their foreign contacts. Former U.S. secretary of state Henry Kissinger and former U.S. president George H.W. Bush are cited in several papers as being especially helpful in blunting the effects of sanctions at this time. With essential investment slowed to a trickle in the wake of the Tiananmen Square massacre, the CCP first turned to neighbouring countries in the Far East and Southeast Asia. Several of the countries of Southeast Asia were untroubled by

Beijing's moves to crush dissent. They did it themselves all the time. Others, such as Japan and South Korea, saw an opportunity to expand their manufacturing companies in China's cheap labour market while the big Western players were kept out of play. And most countries of Southeast Asia have elite entrepreneurial classes of overseas Chinese. Many of these people were open to having their patriotism appealed to, especially if it came with mouth-watering monetary inducements. By the early 1990s, China had become too important to the West, its investment firms, and its multinational corporations for the political outrage over the Tiananmen Square massacre to dominate the discourse.

As in other major industrialized nations, the Canadian government of Conservative Prime Minister Brian Mulroney had expressed instant outrage at the Tiananmen Square massacre: an emergency session of Parliament was held on June 5, 1989, sanctions were imposed, and the ambassador to Beijing, Earl Drake, was recalled. The sanctions focused mostly on discontinuing programs in China financed by the Canadian International Development Agency, halting all high-level government-to-government meetings or visits, and, in a move that particularly outraged Beijing, making all Chinese nationals in Canada, most of whom were students, eligible for landed immigrant status and therefore future citizenship. Department of External Affairs briefing papers say that 80 percent of the Chinese nationals in Canada took up the offer. Fred Bild, who took over as Canada's ambassador to Beijing in 1990, has said in his various writings about this period that Beijing's outrage at what it saw as the theft of some of its best and brightest young people was one of the most difficult issues he had to deal with when he took up his post.

There was very little in the list of Canadian sanctions that was directed at trade, and it was not necessary to do so. Canadian investment dropped through the floor, and many Canadian companies with establishments in China shut up shop, fearing the Tiananmen Square massacre would generate widespread and ongoing civil unrest. The companies that opted to stay on found it very much worth their while. Fred Bild recounted in his essay in the 2011 book *The China Challenge*, "Executives from the relatively few Canadian firms that had remained active in China during these troubled times were delighted to find that, with less that forty-eight hours' notice, I could take them to call on virtually any Chinese minister to make representations on whatever venture they were encountering difficulties with. Years later, when things had returned to 'normal,' they referred to this period as the 'halcyon' days."

Since the aftermath of the 1989 uprising, *waishi* activities in Canada and other countries of particular interest to the CCP, such as the United States, Australia, Europe, and the countries of Southeast Asia, have gone from strength to strength. In Canada, blandishments continue to find receptive audiences among politicians, officials, and business people, often more so than in the other countries of interest to Beijing. To see why that is so, it is necessary to take several steps backwards and explore the influence of people called the "Mish Kids."

THREE

CHINESE BUILD CANADA; CANADIANS SAVE CHINA

Bringing in Chinese,
Bringing in Chinese,
We shall come rejoicing,
Bringing in Chinese.

— SONG OF CANADIAN MISSIONARIES IN CHINA, SUNG
TO THE TUNE OF "BRINGING IN THE SHEAVES"

IN THE 1880s, Canada was bringing in Chinese both literally and figuratively, both at home and in China. It was at this time that substantial numbers of Canadians and Chinese discovered each other's countries, but the attractions that each felt could hardly have been more different. For the seventeen thousand or so Chinese (mostly Cantonese from the Pearl River Delta region of Guangdong province) who settled in British Columbia in the 1880s, the appeal was money. A few hundred Chinese had travelled up from California in the 1850s to join the Fraser River Gold Rush, and they created Canada's first Chinese community, Barkerville. But between 1880 and 1885, another fifteen thousand Chinese came from China and California to work as labourers building the British Columbia section of the Canadian Pacific Railway. The contractors favoured hiring Chinese, who quietly accepted pay of only $1 a day, a third of what white, black, and Native workers were paid. The Chinese also bore without complaint the appalling living accommodations provided, which were inadequate and often dangerous even by the standards of the time. Despite these drawbacks, Chinese immigrants, almost all of them men at this point, kept coming in the hopes of earning enough to improve the lives of their families back home in China. The size of the influx became so worrying to the authorities that in 1885 the Chinese Immigration Act was passed, which levied a head tax of $50 on each Chinese person coming to Canada. That didn't stem the flow, leading to a progression of increasingly draconian measures, culminating in the Chinese Immigration Act, 1923, known colloquially and accurately as "the Chinese Exclusion Act." This not only banned further immigration from China but also formalized the non-citizenship of those Chinese people already in Canada. That did not end until the act was repealed in 1947, after hundreds of young Chinese men had volunteered for the Canadian forces in the Second World War, demonstrating beyond any conceivable doubt their right to citizenship. Ethnic Chinese living in Canada were granted citizenship the following year, 1948.

The infatuation with China by a segment of Canadian society was a different matter entirely. Also beginning in the 1880s, first dozens, then scores, and finally hundreds of Christian missionaries from Catholic, Anglican, Presbyterian, Methodist, Lutheran, and Baptist sects went off to the Chinese hinterland to, in their eyes, save souls. In many cases, several generations of Canadian missionary families stayed in China through the murderous upheavals of the Boxer Rebellion, the collapse of the Qing Dynasty in 1911, the chaos of the warlord period in the 1920s, the invasion by Japan in the 1930s and 1940s, and the civil war after the Second World War that brought the Chinese Communist Party to power in 1949. The effects on Canada and its relationship with China right up to the present day are profound. To a significant degree, that was because of the lack of any other major Canadian involvement in Asia. In *Reluctant Adversaries: Canada and the People's Republic of China, 1949–1970*, Peter M. Mitchell wrote: "Canada's low level of political and economic involvement in the Pacific magnified the missionaries' influence on official and public images of China and its Asian neighbours in Canada. The missionaries were Canada's only substantial community in Asia, supported by home constituencies in all regions, to which they regularly reported by circular and private letters."

Thus, the missionaries and their offspring brought up in China, fluent in the languages and cultures — the so-called Mish Kids — were instrumental in shaping public support for the early recognition of the People's Republic of China after the Chinese Communist Party took power in 1949. Sympathy for the CCP among the Mish Kids stemmed from two sources: antipathy toward the neo-fascist Kuomintang and politically left of centre interpretations of Christianity among Methodists and the United Church of Canada. The Mish Kids and other scions of the Methodists, in particular, had a significant presence in the Department of External Affairs in the 1930s, 1940s, and 1950s. They also played major roles in the evolution of Canada's independent foreign policy after the Second World War.

The belief that activism for social improvement was an important aspect of religious life was a central factor in missionary zeal among Christian communities in the last decades of the nineteenth century and the first decades of the twentieth century. One of the results of this was the rise of the Student Christian Movement (SCM) in many Canadian universities. Often it was membership in the SCM at university that led young men and women into the missionary life. Other SCM members who did not have the missionary calling went on to play formative roles in the construction of Canada's independent federal institutions, especially Global Affairs Canada, which has had many names in its lifetime. What was then called the Department of External Affairs became an agent of the social gospel in 1925 — the year that some Methodist and Presbyterian churches amalgamated into the United Church of Canada — when Queen's University Dean of Arts and Science Oskar D. Skelton was appointed the deputy minister. His tenure coincided with the passage of the Statute of Westminster in the United Kingdom in 1931, which announced that it was time the "white" Dominions — Canada, Australia, New Zealand, and South Africa — took responsibility for their own international relations.

Skelton was the architect of the modern Global Affairs, and as he hunted for staff he naturally turned to people who shared his religious and social ethics. Among his recruits were future Liberal prime minister Lester B. Pearson; Canada's first native-born governor general, Vincent Massey;

and Hume Wrong, who first as a senior Canadian diplomat and then as ambassador in Washington in the 1940s and 1950s was a leading stone-mason of the post–Second World War global order. All of these men came from the same United Church and SCM background as Skelton. Support for the China missionary movement was an essential thread in this community's network. Indeed, when Skelton's daughter, Sheila, married in 1943, it was to a young man she had met at Harvard, Arthur Menzies, who had joined the Department of External Affairs in 1940 as its Far Eastern Affairs officer. Menzies had been born in China, the son of fabled Presbyterian minister and archaeologist Dr. James Mellon Menzies, who discovered and first understood the value of the "oracle bones." These were three-thousand-year-old turtle and sheep bones etched with China's first written language. Arthur Menzies became one of the diplomats responsible in the 1950s, 1960s, and 1970s for the development of an iden-tifiable Canadian character on the international stage. His last post, from 1980 to 1982, was as Canada's first ambassador for disarmament. But per-haps the summit of Menzies' career came in 1976, when he was appointed Canada's ambassador to Beijing. He was the third Mish Kid to hold that post after Ottawa's diplomatic recognition of the CCP regime in 1970. (The first two children of missionaries to become ambassadors to Beijing were Ralph Collins and Charles John Small.)

The Canadian national attitude toward the world that these men and women fashioned during and after the Second World War was framed to a significant degree by the missionary experience in China in the late nineteenth and early twentieth centuries. There were two main centres of Canadian missionary work in China: the isolated and poverty-stricken western Sichuan province, where the Methodists dominated, and Henan in northeastern China, which was the preserve of the Presbyterians.

The early years of Canadian Christian missionary work in China were a haphazard business. The first missionary from Canada can only just be counted as a Canadian. The Reverend William Chalmers Burns was sent to Canada from Scotland in 1844 to lobby for support for the Free Church in the wake of theological and communal disruptions in the Presbyterian

Church. Burns proselytized among the Presbyterians of southern Ontario for two years before feeling the call to confront the more rigorous task of saving souls in China. He arrived in the Portuguese colony of Macao in 1847. Over the following years, Burns worked his way along the southern China coast, opening missions first in Guangzhou (then known as Canton), Xiamen, Shantou, and then north to Shanghai and Beijing, before ending his missionary pilgrimage in Manchuria.

Burns's success as a missionary was minimal. It was seven years before he made his first conversion, and the small number of souls he saved for Christ was won after a huge expenditure of effort. He did, however, have a lasting effect by guiding through rural China a young British Protestant missionary, James Hudson Taylor, who became one of the most celebrated missionaries of the age and the founder in 1865 of the China Inland Mission.

As so often happens in human history, Canada's missionary experience in China happened in large part because of chance. In the summer of 1888, James Taylor decided to use the newly opened Canadian Pacific Railway to shorten his journey back to his home in China after a visit to Great Britain. Taylor was at first adamantly opposed to suggestions that he establish a North American branch of his China Inland Mission to provide funds and missionaries for his endeavours. "The Lord has given me no light about it. I do not think it is his purpose thus to extend the work," author Alvyn Austin quotes Taylor as saying. But from Canadians, Taylor got a very different message. After a couple of weeks in Canada, Taylor observed "such deep wellsprings" of missionary enthusiasm that he set up a North American branch of the China Inland Mission with headquarters in Toronto.

Taylor's visit coincided with a generational change in Canadian religious communities that saw the advent of an era of militant evangelism coupled with a strong belief in the Christian responsibility to promote social reform. As Taylor preached at a succession of meetings and gatherings across southern Ontario, he found audiences "intoxicated with the joy of giving." An audience in Niagara was so enthralled by Taylor's description of the opportunities to convert China's vast population to Christianity that it donated enough money to support eight missionaries in China for one year. Taylor viewed the money as a blight: "To have money and no mission-aries is very serious indeed. We have the dollars, but where are the people?" He got his answer at his next stop, a Young Men's Christian Association Bible study session in Hamilton. Seven of the young men had decided they wanted to be missionaries in China. Taylor took six. By the time he continued his journey back to China, Taylor had received forty-two applications and chosen fifteen people to accompany him. On a damp September evening, about a thousand young people carrying torches marched down Toronto's Yonge Street to Union Station to see off Taylor and his band of Canadian missionaries. Over the course of the next sixty years, approximately five hundred Methodist missionaries went to live and work in western China. Their children remain active to this day through organi-zations such as Missionary Kids and The Canadian School In West China.

Meanwhile, the Presbyterians had stolen a march on the Methodists. In 1881, the Reverend George Leslie MacKay, on a furlough home from his work as a Presbyterian missionary in Taiwan (whose western seaboard was then administered by China), preached a sermon in Ingersoll in southern Ontario. In the congregation was a young man, Jonathan Goforth, age twenty-one, who was about to go to Knox College in Toronto. Goforth was inspired by MacKay's sermon, and he even applied to the China Inland Mission before deciding he was too much of a Presbyterian to be able to go to China on a Methodist ticket. Goforth set about raising sponsorships from various Presbyterian missionary committees and regional divisions. The Canadian Presbyterians had established a mission at Henan in north-eastern China in 1886, and reports of famine there helped open coffers for Goforth. He raised enough to be able to set off in January 1888, accompanied by his new wife, Toronto socialite Rosalind Bell-Smith, and a friend from Queen's University, medical student Frazer Smith.

Canada's missionary ventures in China and their subsequent philo-sophical effects on Canadian foreign policy were substantially a United Church affair. The Anglicans preferred to extend their missionary zeal to proselytizing among Native Canadians in the Northwest Territories and subscribing to the missionary efforts of the mother church in Great Britain.

The first Canadian Catholics sent to China were two nuns, who went in 1902 to replace French nuns who had been killed in the Boxer Rebellion in 1900. Two Franciscan priests joined them a few years later, but substantial Canadian Catholic missions to China did not begin until the 1920s. They were, naturally, dominated by French Canadian religious orders, and by 1950 about four hundred French Canadian missionaries were working in China. Thus, the Canadian Catholic missions tended to reflect the solitudes of the time in Canada.

From early on, there were significant social, theological, and political differences between the Methodist missionary establishment around Chengdu in Sichuan province and the Presbyterians in Henan province. Sachiyo Takashima, in his 2001 paper on the politics of missionaries in China, puts some of those differences down to social class. He argues that the culture of the two missions was influenced by the dominant families who staffed them — the McClures in Henan and the Endicotts in Sichuan — and that these families came from very different social classes in Canada. James Endicott Sr. had emigrated from Devon, a politically radical part of England, to Manitoba in 1882, at age seventeen. He studied at Wesley College in Winnipeg and became a Methodist minister in 1893. The Prairies were poverty-stricken at the time, and when Endicott moved the following year to the Methodist mission at Chengdu with his wife, he took with him the tenets of the social gospel movement. Thus, the Chengdu mission became one that focused on poverty, social injustice, and education. By some accounts, when the Chengdu mission recruited local teachers to staff its schools, it was young communists who flocked to take up the positions. This culture blossomed and was embodied in the life and work of the third of Endicott's five children, James Gareth Endicott. James followed his father as a missionary in China, became closely associated with Mao Zedong's deputy, Zhou Enlai, in the 1940s, and aided the CCP in its war with Chiang Kai-shek's Kuomintang.

The Methodists went on to make great strides into the other usual missionary venture: healthcare, clinics, and hospitals. The West China Hospital, founded in Chengdu in 1892 by the Methodists, survives to this day. It has beds for forty-three hundred in-patients and is one of China's largest hospitals. Another Methodist missionary foundation, the West China Medical Centre of Sichuan University, is now one of China's most highly regarded medical schools.

In contrast, the Henan mission had an upper-class medical missionary culture from the start. The China Inland Mission had a sanatorium at Chefoo (now Yantai) on the coast of neighbouring Shandong province, and also a highly rated school for missionaries' children when Jonathan Goforth, his wife, Rosalind, his friend Frazer Smith, and a nurse, Harriet Sutherland, arrived there in August 1888. Indeed, Chefoo was regarded as something of plush expatriates' enclave.

The emphasis in both missionary centres on building and running hospitals and colleges gave the Chinese a more favourable view of Canadians than of the Europeans and other foreign interlopers who were set on acquiring commercial privileges and establishing semi-colonial enclaves. In that regard, York University history professor Peter M. Mitchell has written, "Many Chinese benefited from the training provided by Canadians in hospitals and universities in China, and the majority in later years were not practising Christians. This suggests an impact far beyond the simplistic dismissal often accorded mission influences under the logic of cultural imperialism. It also suggests that not all favourable Chinese images of Canadians derived from the legendary exploits of Norman Bethune."

The beginning of the end of the Henan mission was in 1931, when the Japanese invaded Manchuria in China's northeast, renamed it Manchukuo, and set up Puyi, the last Qing emperor, as its puppet monarch. Chiang Kai-shek and the Kuomintang refused to accept Japan's occupation of Manchuria, but Chiang was far more concerned about Mao and the communists and did nothing to confront the Japanese. That changed after Chiang was kidnapped in April 1936 by the warlord controlling much of northern China, the "Young Marshal" Zhang Xueliang. Zhang kept Chiang prisoner at his capital in Xi'an until the Kuomintang leader agreed to form a United Front with Mao and the ccp and focus on ousting the Japanese from China. Tensions between the two forces built during the following year, and in July 1937, the Japanese sparked what became known as the Marco Polo Bridge Incident. This clash was the opening of Japan's unambiguous invasion of China. The Canadian missionaries in Henan, along with much of the local population, fled south ahead of the Japanese advance.

By the end of 1938, the Japanese advances forced Chiang Kai-shek to move his capital from Nanjing to Chongqing in Sichuan. James G. Endicott in Chengdu had come to believe that the Kuomintang were fascists at heart, but the arrival of Chiang and his administration in Chongqing pulled Endicott into the governing circle. In an effort to give the regime some kind of moral legitimacy, both with the Chinese population and with American politicians and donors, Madame Chiang Kai-shek had founded the New Life Movement. This was aimed at delivering social services and infusing traditional Chinese cultural practices with some of the Methodist Christian values of her upbringing. To this end, she began looking around Sichuan for a foreign Christian missionary who would give her movement credibility both at home and abroad. She fixed on Endicott, and, with the agreement of the West China Mission, he was seconded to the New Life Movement early in 1939.

Initially, Endicott was charmed by Madame Chiang, as were many men. He was deeply impressed by her dedication and by her work on the front lines of the social services network. Endicott was caught up in the daily drama of delivering aid as Chongqing came under ever more intense air attacks by the Japanese in 1939 and 1940. But Endicott's early concerns about Kuomintang fascism began to return in 1940, when he noticed the unexplained disappearance of secretaries of the New Life Movement's Women's War Service Clubs. The women had disappeared only after waging successful campaigns to end corruption and subsequently being accused by local magistrates of being communists. When Endicott confronted Madame Chiang about the disappearances, she said that the missing women were indeed communists and that they had been transferred elsewhere by the CCP. However, Endicott was not convinced, and he later found the women had been arrested, tortured, and then killed by police on the personal order of Chiang Kai-shek. Over the following months, Endicott's conviction grew that the Kuomintang's New Life Movement contained disturbing similarities to some of the Nazi German organizations and that Chiang was far more intent on defeating Mao's CCP than the Japanese. After a series of blistering arguments with Madame Chiang, Endicott resigned and, in July 1941, flew to Hong Kong with his family. The family then travelled to Canada, where Endicott spent most of the rest of the war years.

Japan's attack on Pearl Harbor in December 1941, and Canada's entry into the War in the Pacific, beginning with the defence of Hong Kong later that month, changed conclusively the position of the Canadian missionaries in China. Those who had stayed in Japanese-held territory, especially the Quebec Catholic missionaries, now found themselves enemy aliens and were interned. Some managed to make it to Free China, after perilous journeys across the war zones. Meanwhile, in Ottawa, Prime Minister William Lyon Mackenzie King came under pressure from the Department of External Affairs to appoint an ambassador to Chiang's besieged regime in Chongqing.

King was parochial by instinct and not much interested in China (or Asia in general). His first instinct was to appoint a missionary as ambassador to Chongqing, but instead King picked Brigadier-General Victor Wentworth Odlum. After his military career in the Boer War and First World War, Odlum had become an insurance executive, newspaper editor, member of the British Columbia legislature, and, in 1941, Canada's high commissioner to Australia. Odlum arrived in Chongqing early in 1943 with, by his own admission, little interest in or knowledge of China. He saw his job as preparing the ground for a beneficial trade relationship with China after the war by providing as much aid to the Kuomintang regime as feasible. Odlum may have been out of his depth, but he was surrounded by Mish Kids who were very much at home. Odlum's third secretary was Ralph Collins, a YMCA missionary's son born in China who became Canada's first ambassador to the People's Republic of China in 1970. Odlum's translator was Dr. Leslie Kilborn, son of medical missionaries. The embassy counsellor was Dr. George Patterson, who had been a Methodist missionary in Japan and was later general secretary of the Canadian YMCA.

To a significant degree, the history of the Canadian missionary movements in China up to the closing months of the Second World War was a prologue to the opening of links between the Mish Kids and the CCP. Since his return to Canada in 1941 ahead of Pearl Harbor, James Endicott had spent much of his time travelling and giving speeches in support of Free China. At the same time, Endicott's social evangelism had evolved into socialism and a growing attraction to Marxist communism. Endicott returned to China in July 1944 to teach ethics and English at the West China Union University in Chengdu. The campus had become a hotbed of questioning the Kuomintang and was on the verge of becoming a CCP enclave. In speeches to the students and faculty, Endicott avoided directly criticizing Chiang Kai-shek and his regime, but only just.

Endicott had another life during this period. As a result of meeting several American officers on the ship back to China, he had become an agent for the Office of Strategic Services — the forerunner of the Central Intelligence Agency — in its efforts to establish a working military relationship with Mao and the CCP. What troubled the Americans was Chiang's evident unreliability as an ally in fighting the Japanese. The Generalissimo, as he was known, was allowing the United States and other allies to carry the brunt of the fighting against Japan, while saving his powder to crush the communists after the war was over. It was equally clear that local resentment against Chiang in Sichuan was mounting, and Endicott was instructed by the OSS headquarters in India to provide information and assessments about the opposition to Chiang and its potency. This work brought Endicott into contact with communists at the village level. Late in 1944, his friend Ruth Weiss, a former missionary then working part-time as a journalist and secretary at the Canadian embassy, introduced him to officials at the CCP headquarters in Chongqing. One day in January 1945, Endicott attended a press conference given by Zhou Enlai, the head of the United Front delegation in Chongqing and Mao's right-hand man. Zhou's interpreter stumbled over a question from an American journalist, and Endicott butted in with a deft translation. Zhou invited Endicott to stay behind, and the two had a long philosophical and political exchange. Endicott explained the work he was doing for the oss, and Zhou said he hoped the Canadian would report fully and accurately because "we want America to know everything about us; we have nothing to hide." Endicott asked if a channel could be set up to allow him to regularly pass information from the ccp to the oss, and Zhou agreed.

From then on, Endicott's reports gave increasingly accurate information about the strength of the communists and their support among ordinary Chinese. He warned repeatedly that if the United States didn't do more to ensure that Chiang and the Kuomintang introduced an honest, efficient, and democratic government once the war was over, it would only be a matter of time before there was a communist uprising. At around the time of the death of Franklin Delano Roosevelt in April 1945, there was a change in attitude among the American officials on the ground. They lost interest in dealing with the ccp and instead decided to try to make Chiang and the Kuomintang so strong that opponents would be cowed and social and political stability would be assured. It didn't work. Chiang became ever more repressive. A breaking point came in November 1945, when students in Kunming, capital of Yunnan province, held a rally calling for the creation of a coalition government and the guarantee of fundamental freedoms. Chiang's army dispersed the students, four of whom were killed in the melee. The following month, about five thousand students from five Christian universities in Sichuan province attended a rally at West China Union University to pursue the campaign that had started in Kunming. In an apparent attempt to stop the rally, about thirty police surrounded the stage. Endicott gambled they would not try to stop a foreigner, so he brushed by them and delivered a speech, to the cheers of the crowd. Endicott said the four Kunming students "were given the death penalty at the hands of brutal men for the crime of asking for peace, unity, and democracy."

This incident was the climax of Endicott's disillusionment with the prospects of the Kuomintang forming or wanting to form a democratic and accountable government. Endicott's increasingly firm conviction that

China was heading for a revolution created friction between him and the Canadian ambassador. Nevertheless, Endicott continued to keep in regular touch with the Canadian embassy, and he was regarded as useful by Odlum because of his contacts with senior Kuomintang officials and businessmen whom he had taught English.

Endicott was also considered an asset by his old friend Lester B. Pearson, now the under-secretary of state in the Department of External Affairs. Endicott sent regular reports to Menzies on the China desk. These analyses were circulated widely through the department, including to Pearson, who valued them and wrote asking that the flow continue. Endicott painted a very different picture of current events and the likely future in China than did the ambassador. Odlum, like generations of Canadian business people since, believed that the answer to China's political problems was industrial modernization and the development of trade, for which he saw Canada as a logical partner and beneficiary. The ambassador had no time for Endicott's view that the Kuomintang was failing to deliver the kind of society the majority of Chinese wanted and that the country was heading for a victorious peasant uprising led by the Communist Party. Odlum believed the communists had only a phantom army and were no match for the Kuomintang. Endicott, however, had a major supporter in the Canadian embassy in Odlum's deputy, first secretary Chester Ronning. Endicott's biographer, his son, Stephen, reprinted a confidential letter from Ronning to Pearson in Ottawa dated May 13, 1947:

What Endicott says about the possibility of an agrarian revolution is worth noting. I know of no foreigner in China who is in closer touch with the common people and who has wider contacts outside of official circles. There most certainly is a rising tide of resentment in China against governmental authorities who are not only taking terrific toll from the people to carry on civil war, but are guilty of greater corruption than has been known since the days of the warlords and the Manchus.

There is no doubt that what Endicott says about the ability of the Communists to organize this growing discontent into an effective agrarian revolution is correct … The Kuomintang have driven out of its ranks all effective liberals and revolutionaries. Today, these leaders are in the Communist Party, and have twenty years of experience, and are supported by an army of trained organizers. Conditions are ripe for a revolution."

Ronning was yet another Mish Kid, though of a different stripe from the United Church missionaries and their offspring who had dominated the quilt of China-Canada relations thus far. When Odlum asked in 1945 for a Chinese-speaking first secretary for the embassy, Ronning happened to be available, and he was the perfect man for the job. Over the following two decades, Ronning became a central figure in the often slow and awkward pas de deux that led eventually to mutual diplomatic recognition and Ottawa's acknowledgement of the CCP as the legitimate government of China in 1970. As a senior Canadian diplomat in the 1950s and 1960s, Ronning had a close view of the machinations that the governments of Louis St. Laurent, John Diefenbaker, Lester Pearson, and Pierre Trudeau went through before the deed was done. Ronning recounted much of what he witnessed in his autobiography, *A Memoir of China in Revolution.*

Chester Ronning was born in Hubei province in central China in 1894, the son of Norwegian American Lutheran missionaries Halvor and Hannah Ronning. After his mother's death in 1907, Chester and his older brother, Nelius, were sent to live with their aunt in Iowa. After a year, their father and five younger brothers and sisters returned from China. Halvor moved the family to Alberta, where he set up a Norwegian settlement called Valhalla Centre north-west of Grande Prairie. Chester Ronning completed his education at the University of Alberta and then went back to China as a Lutheran missionary from 1922 until 1927. He returned to Alberta as the principal of Camrose Lutheran College, but he got involved in politics as a member of the United Farmers of Alberta and was elected in a by-election for the provincial legislature in 1932. Ronning transferred his political allegiance to the fledgling Co-operative Commonwealth Federation —

forerunner of the New Democratic Party — and was defeated in the 1935 general election. Ronning led the Alberta CCF from 1940 until 1942, when he stepped down. He ran for the party in Camrose once again in the 1945 election and was defeated. Thus, he was available when Odlum put out his call for a Chinese-speaking second-in-command.

After his nearly two decades of experience in left-wing Canadian prairie populist politics, Ronning arrived back in China with strong sympathies for the revolutionaries. Only a few days after his arrival in Chongqing, Ronning and Odlum were invited to dinner with Mao's representative to the United Front, Zhou Enlai. Ronning was eager to meet the famous revolutionary about whom he had first heard from students at university in Beijing in 1922. Zhou had gained fame as a leader of the reform movements that had sprung up after the First World War. He had been in prison, and in 1920 he had gone on a work-study program to France, where he had continued his communist revolutionary work among fellow Chinese students. Zhou returned to China in 1924 as the official in charge of political training at the new Wampoa Military Academy being run by Chiang Kai-shek. Zhou's tenure at Wampoa came to an end when Chiang expelled communists from the academy in May 1926. Zhou was assigned by the CCP to Shanghai, where he worked at recruiting cadres and embedding the organization in local society. When Chiang launched a reign of terror and massacred the Shanghai communists in 1927, Zhou managed to escape to Hankou, now part of the megacity Wuhan. For the next few years, Zhou operated underground as a party organizer and intelligence agent. He even returned for a while to Shanghai, but in December 1931 he moved to the revolutionary collective established by Mao in the Jiangxi Mountains. It was there that a political partnership was established between the two men that would last until Zhou's death. Zhou survived the Long March, which started when eighty-four thousand communist soldiers and civilians broke out of the Jiangxi base as it was encircled by Chiang's troops in October 1934. It was after the Xi'an Incident in 1936, when Chiang was kidnapped by the Young Marshal and forced to agree to form a United Front with the Communists against the

Japanese, that Zhou, who negotiated with Chiang during the incident, became Mao's consummate diplomat dealing with the Kuomintang and the Westerners supporting China.

Ronning was keen to meet Zhou, and he recorded, "I was not disappointed. He was a confident, modest man. His bearing was almost that of a Chinese gentleman-scholar. His language, however, was very direct and forceful, with none of the pretentious, polite old Chinese clichés."

During this first meeting there was an amusing echo of Zhou's first encounter with Endicott. Ronning thought that the interpreter had softened considerably some of the language in a discussion between Odlum and Zhou. Zhou must have noticed something in Ronning's expression, because he asked the Canadian for his rendering of the conversation, and, as with Endicott, this was the start of a good relationship.

Meanwhile, the clash of personalities between Odlum and Endicott had continued to simmer. At one point, Odlum commented bitterly that Endicott was a "fiery evangelist" whom the Communist leaders regarded as "one of their great foreign friends." Endicott was indeed becoming a good deal more vociferous and extreme in his teaching, preaching, and public speeches. The immediate cause was his observation of the campaign by the Kuomintang, through its Youth Corps, to suppress dissent on campus. When Endicott complained to the university's missionary administration about the activities of the Kuomintang Youth Corps, his allegations were denied and dismissed. It was the beginning of Endicott's separation from the United Church and his shift to becoming a full-time activist for the CCP.

Endicott's crisis in religious belief was neatly summed up in a note in his journal in 1944. "Funny," he wrote, "but there seems to be a direct connection between reactionary imperialism and fundamentalist religion." That's a thought that echoes down the decades.

The breaking point came when Endicott spoke at a rally in Chengdu that was part of a nationwide student protest against the Kuomintang. A few days later, the Chinese Ministry of Education gave the West China Mission formal notice that unless Endicott left China within a month, he would be deported as an undesirable alien. Endicott moved first. On

May 5, 1946, he wrote to his masters in Canada, resigning from both the West China Mission and his position as a minister in the United Church of Canada.

Endicott set off from Chengdu for Shanghai in late May, en route to Canada. But as he went through Nanjing, by this time again the seat of the Kuomintang government, he got a message that Zhou Enlai would like to see him. Zhou told Endicott that he believed the United Front between the Kuomintang, the Communists, and the assortment of democratic parties was about to collapse. Civil war was imminent, Zhou said, adding, "Will you postpone your return to Canada and help us with publicity work?" Endicott agreed, broke his journey in Shanghai, and set about preparing to write and publish an underground newspaper, the *Shanghai Newsletter*.

The first edition of the *Shanghai Newsletter* appeared on June 19, 1946. The editorial line was drawn up during clandestine weekly meetings between Endicott and a member of Zhou Enlai's staff and was carefully crafted to present a classically Western democratic view of current events in China. Even though the print run and circulation of the journal were small, it quickly became an important source of information in Shanghai and further afield. Canadian government archives show it was read in Ottawa. Endicott's son, Stephen, quotes a senior CCP official saying years later: "It was immensely valuable to us. Its circulation was not large but it put us into contact with many influential quarters and won us many new foreign friends. Those were very difficult days in Shanghai — we had no foreknowledge that the Chiang regime would collapse so rapidly and therefore we needed all the sympathy and support which we could get in order to frustrate the attempt by Chiang to involve the Americans more deeply in the war against us. Jim was our comrade-in-arms in this struggle."

Although the moderate tone and political stance were essential elements in the strategy of the *Shanghai Newsletter*, Endicott could not control his editorial instincts for long. The journal became more and more radical as the months passed, to the extent that friends starting warning him not to be "too Red." In March 1947, an old friend of Endicott's from his days working in Chiang's New Life Movement, Chang Chu, invited him to lunch. But as discussion of the gathering political crisis developed, Chang looked Endicott in the eye and said, "Jim, I think you had better go back to Canada as soon as possible."

Endicott had no doubt that this was a warning that Chiang's death squads were out to get him. On June 19, 1947, Endicott and his wife, Mary, left Shanghai aboard the S.S. *General Meigs*, an American troopship used to evacuate refugees. This was not the end of Endicott's service to Zhou and the CCP. In January 1948, he began publishing in Canada a monthly journal called the *Canadian Far Eastern Newsletter*. The journal was published for three decades, and for the first twenty-two years a constant theme was that Canada should recognize the People's Republic of China and establish diplomatic relations with Beijing.

While Endicott was going through his crisis of conscience at the beginning of 1946, Chester Ronning was arranging to move the embassy from Chongqing to Nanjing, once again the Kuomintang capital of China. Odlum left China at this time to take up the ambassadorship to Turkey and was replaced by Thomas Clayton Davis, a lawyer and judge. A ceasefire in the civil war between the Kuomintang and the communists, arranged by General George Marshall, Harry Truman's personal envoy to China, was crumbling. Ronning judged that defeat of the Kuomintang was inevitable. "The Nationalists are defeating themselves," he wrote in his journal on June 6, "by the colossal corruption and greed which has infiltrated the whole political structure and much of their military structure. Truly, the state of affairs in China is a sorry mess." This view contrasted dramatically with reports that Ronning was getting of the situation in areas "liberated" — his word, and indicative of where his loyalties lay — by the Communists. In his journals, reprinted in his 1974 book *A Memoir of China in Revolution*, Ronning notes a meeting with a Canadian doctor who had just been on an inspection tour of hospitals in the Communist-liberated areas:

He was critical of the Communists before he visited them, but came back with glowing reports on the way they are conducting affairs compared to the Nationalists (Kuomintang). He says that going into their territory is like going into a different country. The people are well treated and give support to the People's Committees established in each community. He says there is no graft or "squeeze," that the Communists are friendly to Protestant missionaries, that their hospitals are exceptionally well managed, that they give people free medical attention, that they control food prices, that the people are not over-taxed, and that there is no starvation.

This strategic charm offensive by the CCP was highly effective both at home and abroad. As the Communist armies became increasingly dominant during 1948 and the Kuomintang collapse gathered momentum, victory by Mao and the CCP began to look inevitable. But chaos in the interim was also a certainty. In October 1948, Ottawa decided to evacuate women and children from the Canadian embassy in Nanjing, and the diplomatic staff was cut back. Ronning was one of the diplomats persuaded to stay on. Throughout 1949, cities across China fell to the Communists. Beijing was occupied by the People's Liberation Army in January when the Kuomintang commander, Fu Zuoyi, agreed to hand over the city. After a series of intense battles, the way was open to Nanjing. The Kuomintang capital fell to the PLA on April 23.

"I hope our government will recognize the new government here soon as it is formed and that the civil war will finally come to an end," Ronning wrote in his journal.

Mao declared the creation of the People's Republic of China from the top of the Forbidden City's Tiananmen Gate in Beijing on October 1, 1949. The same day, Chinese officials summoned members of the diplomatic corps in Nanjing to a meeting and announced that the People's Republic of China was being formed in Beijing, which would be the capital. The official insisted foreign governments must recognize the PRC and move their embassies to Beijing. Ronning's immediate advice to Ottawa was that it should give formal recognition to the CCP regime. "The Government of the People's Republic of China was in control of all Mainland China, thus fulfilling the accepted international criterion for recognition," he wrote.

But Ottawa hesitated. On November 16, 1949, the Cabinet agreed in principle to recognize the PRC, but the ministers wanted to get a clearer picture of what demands might be made on Ottawa by the CCP in a recognition agreement. Ronning received instructions from the Department of External Affairs to get details from the Chinese about the procedures leading to diplomatic recognition. Would Ronning be allowed to go to Beijing to discuss details of the move? When Ronning put this to the Chinese, the Foreign Nationals Bureau replied that Beijing would welcome these discussions if Ottawa would first "formally indicate" its desire to recognize the CCP government of China. Ronning recommended to Ottawa that it do this, but the Canadian government balked, interpreting Beijing's reply as a pre-condition and not direct acceptance of the Canadian position. Ottawa, to Ronning's evident frustration, decided the matter required further consideration. "In my opinion, the Chinese reply had been an acceptance of the Canadian proposal, not a counter-proposal," he noted in his journal, adding that he suspected the delay was "due more to American influence than any other single factor."

Finally, on June 25, 1950, Ronning got the go-ahead from Ottawa to start negotiations with Beijing on formal recognition. But it was too late. Canadian hesitation was overtaken by another event: the outbreak of the war in Korea. It would be another twenty years before the two countries established formal diplomatic ties. Even so, the CCP had established, largely through the Mish Kids, a bridgehead of supporters in Canada who would keep the issue of recognition high on the public agenda. And during the coming two decades of an often vitriolic contest for the establishment of diplomatic ties, the network of CCP friends and agents in Canadian society grew and spread, especially into the business and academic communities.

FOUR
WANTED AND UNWANTED FOREIGNERS

Talk to me about China, Ronning.
— PRIME MINISTER JOHN DIEFENBAKER TO CANADIAN
DIPLOMAT CHESTER RONNING, 1959

IT IS BETWEEN the founding of the People's Republic of China in October 1949 and Ottawa's recognition of the Beijing regime in October 1970 that volatile questions about the roles played by various personalities and their motives began to become important for Canada. Who is a "friend of China"? Who is an "agent of influence"? Who is an "espionage agent"? Where are the lines between these roles? What separates a spy from an agent of influence? When does someone wanting to stimulate good relations between Canada and China because of affection for both countries step over a line and become an agent of influence or a spy? Perhaps those lines are best drawn in relation to the Chinese Communist Party's degree of expectation of returns. A genuine Canadian friend of China is someone who simply wants to foster good relations out of personal regard for both countries. But, as has already been described, when the Chinese Communist Party bestows the honorific "friend of China" on someone, the accolade is not so innocent. The CCP considers "friend of China" to be a job description, an appointment as an influence peddler in Canada for Beijing. As previously described, the CCP's leverage is that agents of influence have something to lose if the favour of the Chinese regime is withdrawn because they have failed to adequately promote its interests in Canada.

When it established itself in power in October 1949, the CCP was faced with a question that had troubled its leaders for a while: What would a Chinese version of Marxism look like, and how would it work? Mao

Zedong and the other leaders had already confounded the Marxist-Leninist purists by showing that a successful communist revolution could be launched by rural peasants. Marx and his Russian acolytes had been certain only urban factory workers could destroy capitalism. An equally important difference was that, unlike Russia, China had been buffeted, battered, and humiliated since the 1840s by the imperial incursions of European powers, together with Japan and the United States. In the CCP's eyes, its victory was just as much a war of liberation from foreign imperialism as it was a revolution against China's aristocratic capitalists.

Thus, an immediate task for the CCP was to put muscle behind Mao's declaration at the First Plenary Session of the Chinese People's Political Consultative Conference on September 21, 1949, that "The Chinese people have stood up." To that end, the CCP considered it essential to show that the party dominated foreigners in China. It needed to smash the image of the intrinsic superiority of foreigners that had taken root in the Chinese psyche since the British began the wholesale European scramble for access to China in the 1840s. At the same time, the party intended to follow Mao's much-quoted dictum, "While China is putting its house in order, it is undesirable for guests to be present." In order to preserve the carefully constructed image of the party as a benign movement for agrarian reform, the CCP didn't want too many foreign witnesses as it slaughtered or dispatched to re-education camps much of China's land-owning and rich peasant classes, as well as the urban bourgeoisie. Yet in 1949, there were about 120,000 foreigners living in China, according to a 1996 article in *Far Eastern Affairs* describing information passed to Soviet officials by a visiting CCP delegation in 1949. Among all these thousands there were Canadian missionaries, doctors, and teachers. They hung on in the hope that what they had interpreted as the CCP's expressions of support for the missionary establishments remained true.

They were wrong. With remarkable speed after it secured power, the CCP introduced and enforced a bureaucratic system for the registration and assessment of foreigners. Expatriates were required to go to their local police station or CCP office to explain their reasons for being in China.

British Quaker William Sewell, a lecturer at West China Union University in Chengdu, records in his book *I Stayed in China* that in the beginning, foreign teachers were asked to continue work after the CCP came to power and were assured they were welcome in the new China. They were, however, warned, "any subversion would be met by immediate strong action." They were also strongly advised that the university "must no longer be foreign in outlook." It was not long before an American senior professor at the university was arrested and kept in prison for several months for exhibiting a "bad attitude" toward the new regime. Sewell wrote that what the professor had done "appeared quite trivial, but it seemed that the authorities welcomed this chance to show to the people that they had power over Westerners, who previously had been regarded as above the law."

Yet even as the CCP was expelling the foreigners left in China, it realized that it needed foreign technical and managerial expertise to propel its development plans for the nation. The CCP naturally turned first to their brothers in Marx, the Soviet Union. Mao went to Moscow in December 1949 expecting open-handed aid for the rehabilitation of Chinese industrial plants damaged in the wars and both financial and technical assistance in a new drive for industrialization. Instead, Soviet leader Joseph Stalin established Moscow's ideological superiority by purposefully humiliating the Chinese leader. Stalin only grudgingly approved assistance programs that were never near what the Soviets could have offered or what China needed.

The rude and dismissive treatment dished out to Mao in Moscow made it even more imperative for the CCP to draw on the expertise in the diaspora. So one of the first acts of the CCP on coming to power was to establish the Committee of Overseas Chinese Affairs, a high-level body with the right of direct access to Premier Zhou Enlai. The office had four departments dealing with international liaison, foreign affairs, propaganda, and the United Front. A few years later, in June 1956, another office, the All-China Federation of Returned Overseas Chinese, was established to help integrate the *huaqiao* (overseas Chinese) into life in their motherland, a necessity because for many of them it was a very distant motherhood.

One Canadian for whom the motherhood of China was a generation removed was Paul Lin, who became the CCP's most influential agent of influence in Canada. Lin was yet another Mish Kid, but from a very different background. Lin's father, Lin Zuoran, was born in 1882 in China's Guangdong province. Lin Zuoran had a strong natural intelligence, and he received a solid basic education in the Confucian classics. But his family did not have the money to finance his further education to prepare him for the usual route of advancement in Qing China, the scholar-official examinations and a post in government. In his autobiography, *In the Eye of the China Storm*, Paul Lin says his father was persuaded by relatives already in Canada to join them so that he could make a living, learn English, and see first-hand the skills and technology that made the Western countries so powerful. "So, with a smattering of English, and only enough money to pay the head tax of fifty dollars, Father arrived in Victoria, British Columbia, Canada, on March 9, 1897, aboard *Empress of India*. The colonial authorities registered him as George Lim Yuen (Lin Ran), an abbreviated English transliteration of his Chinese name," wrote Lin.

Like many Chinese immigrants of this period, Lin's father's early years in Canada were a scramble to survive and prosper. The elder Lin worked in salmon canning factories and as a houseboy, but he learned English by attending Anglican Church evening Bible classes. Lin Zouran's intellectual talents were noticed by the Anglican Church's Diocese of New Westminster, and in 1907 he was asked to take charge of the church's mission on Homer Street in Vancouver's Chinatown. That led to the church funding his enrolment at Latimer Hall at the Anglican Theological College of British Columbia. He was appointed a deacon in 1912 and was ordained as the first Chinese Canadian Anglican priest in 1920.

In October 1912, the elder Lin was able to afford to bring his wife, Chiu Mon, and their first child, a daughter, from China. Four other children were born, of whom Paul Lin was the youngest, and the family settled in Vernon, in the Okanagan Valley, where Lin Zouran ministered to the scattered communities of Chinese labourers. Paul Lin recounted that even as a young child, he noticed that his father laced his Sunday sermons with "patriotic cultural nationalism" by weaving the philosophy of Confucius and Mencius into Anglican Christian doctrine. "These teachings of Confucianism and cultural nationalism nurtured in me a passionate attachment to the values of my Chinese ancestry," wrote Lin. But while Lin's education, friends, and teachers made him feel socially, culturally, and linguistically more Canadian than Chinese, he started to become aware of anti-Chinese racism. "I empathized with the suffering experienced by so many first-generation Chinese immigrants. Canadians did not understand that these Chinese came from a country with a long and glorious history," he wrote. "They were discriminated against because China was sick — dominated and bullied by nations with superior military power. My hope then was for China to become strong one day, so that Chinese everywhere could regain their dignity. This intention, cultivated by my patriotic and morally demanding father, became my mission in life."

Natural talent and his father's demands for hard work led Paul Lin to a Governor General's Medal in high school and a place at the University of British Columbia in 1938 to study engineering. "Once I had my studies under control, I began to participate in campus activities, especially those focused on the political issues of the day," Lin wrote. "For me, that meant China under Japanese siege." Lin became an active and eloquent speaker at conferences across Canada of student organizations dealing with international affairs, Japanese imperial militarism in particular. His education at UBC lasted only a year. In 1939, he received a scholarship to take an engineering degree at the University of Michigan in Ann Arbor. Lin said he felt compelled to attend the American university by a desire to find a community of native Chinese students from whom he could learn Mandarin and get first-hand knowledge of what was happening in China. The University of Michigan had welcomed Chinese students since 1893, and there were eighty Chinese there when Lin arrived. He soon became a pillar of this small community, and he supplemented his meagre income by using his blossoming skills as an orator to give speeches organized by the university's extension department on China and the war with Japan.

After two years studying engineering, Lin suffered a crisis common to many students: he realized he didn't want to be an engineer. "I thought that international law, which could be used to defend China's interests, might suit me and also be 'serious enough' to satisfy Father," wrote Lin. He got backing from his academic adviser, Dr. J. Raleigh Nelson, who wrote a powerful letter to Lin's father, lauding his student's skills and whole-heartedly supporting the change in scholastic direction. Lin Zouran wrote to his son, giving him permission to change courses and saying, "Most importantly, is to study something solid that will be useful to the world, and benefit others as well as yourself."

Paul Lin's course was set, and events opened the path before him. Japan's attack on Pearl Harbor on December 7, 1941, leading to the entry of the United States into both the Pacific and European wars, added to Lin's currency as a speaker, and he was in increasing demand.

Around the same time, Lin legally changed his name to Paul Ta-Kuang Lin. *Ta-Kuang* means "Advancement of Light through the Forest." He explained, "Having a proper Chinese name, spoken in Mandarin, was a major step in confirming my identity as a modern Chinese intellectual." He graduated from the University of Michigan with an honours degree in January 1943 and was awarded two scholarships for post-graduate studies at the Fletcher School of Law and Diplomacy, jointly administered by Harvard and Tufts universities. There, Lin began work on a doctorate on the Far Eastern policies of the United Kingdom and the problems of security on and around the Pacific Ocean between the wars.

However, Lin's pro-China activism began to overtake his academic life. Financial necessity prompted Lin to defer his doctorate and to take the paid job of general secretary of the Chinese Students' Christian Association of North America (CSCA). A major part of this job was assisting the large influx of student refugees from the civil war in China between the Kuomintang and the CCP. Many students joined the CSCA in order to attach themselves to a Chinese community. He organized events for them, including on one occasion a speech by Canadian missionary James G. Endicott, whose vehement criticisms of the corruption of the Chiang Kai-shek regime began to influence Lin's thinking. By the time Lin returned to Harvard in 1948 to complete his doctorate, he was totally disillusioned with the Kuomintang. This attitude was reflected in the public postures of the CSCA, which became increasingly critical of the Kuomintang and American support for Chiang Kai-shek. Lin began to be publicly identified in the United States as a subversive.

By early 1949, Lin's political activism had smothered his desire to finish work on his doctoral thesis. Lin was preoccupied with the emergence of the new China under Mao and the CCP's rule. More than that, he didn't want to just write about it. He wanted to be part of it. "I resolved to seek out my ancestral roots and to participate in China's historic transition," he wrote in his memoir. On October 2, 1949, the day after Mao Zedong declared the birth of the People's Republic of China, Lin, his Chinese-born wife, Eileen, and their two young sons flew to San Francisco and boarded a freighter of the Danish Maersk shipping line for the thirty-five-day voyage to Hong Kong. "Had I not left when I did, I might have been swept into Joseph McCarthy's security hearings and been persecuted. I struggled with the decision to leave the United States, but knew in my heart it was time to 'go home' and offer my skills for my people's future."

While Lin and his family were travelling to Hong Kong, the Canadian chargé d'affaires in Nanjing, Chester Ronning, was struggling with conflicting pressures. On one side, he had Chinese officials insisting that Canada recognize the People's Republic, close its diplomatic establishment in Nanjing, and set up an embassy in Beijing. On the other, his superiors in Ottawa were unwilling to make a decision. Ronning himself advocated recognition, but Prime Minister Louis St. Laurent and Secretary of State for External Affairs Lester Pearson had become preoccupied with consulting other members of the Commonwealth before deciding what to do. St. Laurent and Pearson hoped Commonwealth members would defer decisions on whether or not to shift recognition from the Kuomintang's Republic of China to Mao's People's Republic of China until they had discussed the issue at the group's Heads of Government Meeting in January 1950 in Colombo, Ceylon (now Sri Lanka). They were disappointed. India recognized the People's Republic of China on December 26, 1949, Pakistan did so on January 4, 1950, and the United Kingdom on January 6, 1950.

Ronning finally got the go-ahead from Ottawa on June 25, 1950, to start negotiations with Beijing on recognition, but even as the message arrived it was irrelevant. On that day, North Korea invaded South Korea and quickly pushed Seoul's army and its allied American forces back to an enclave around the southern port of Busan (then known as Pusan). Canada immediately signed up to be part of the United Nations intervention force mandated three days later, which eventually included twenty-one countries, though 88 percent of the military personnel came from the United States. For several weeks, it looked as though the besieged South Korean and American troops in the Busan enclave would not be able to hold out and the entire Korean peninsula would come under Pyongyang's rule. But on September 15, about forty thousand United States Marines and nearly five thousand South Korean troops landed at Incheon, on the coast just west of Seoul. It was a brilliant move, planned by UN Commander-in-Chief General Douglas MacArthur, and it changed the course of the war. The UN forces struck north, and by the end of October they were close to the Yalu River border with China.

Soon after the Incheon landing, China sent a message to Washington via the Indian ambassador to the United Nations, warning that if the American-led forces crossed the 38th parallel — the dividing line between the two Koreas at the end of the Pacific War — China would feel compelled to intervene. The American authorities either didn't understand or failed to take the message seriously. On October 8, Mao re-designated the People's Liberation Army's North East Frontier Force as the Chinese People's Volunteer Army. On October 25, after secretly crossing the Yalu River ten days before, this unofficial Chinese army of at least 300,000 soldiers and perhaps as many as 450,000 attacked the UN forces. By January 4, 1951, the Chinese and North Korean soldiers had pushed back the UN forces, and Seoul was captured for the second time in the war. There followed months of hard fighting around the 38th parallel. But by the end of May these battles had become a stalemate, and in July negotiations started on an armistice agreement, which came into effect on July 27, 1953.

As a participant in the war on the UN side, Canada was in effect at war with China because of Mao's intervention. Ronning recorded Ottawa's attitude at the time; unsurprisingly, "It was felt that in the prevailing circumstances, it would not be appropriate to open negotiations with Peking (Beijing). Rather than make a decision against recognition, however, Canada decided to defer the question of proceeding with negotiations until the immediate crisis in Korea was over."

It was also in this period of the Korean War and the years immediately after that Canada's relationship with the United States began to play an influential part in the story of the push and pull of Canada's relations with China. For the CCP and its agents, these years provided a master class on the subtleties of Canadians' complex feelings for the United States: the admiration, affection, jealousy, and pervasive sense of moral superiority that can spill over into disdain. The CCP learned in this period that anti-Americanism in Canada could be a useful tool that is easily aroused and fairly simple to manipulate. This played out in the broader context of the start of the Cold War and fears in the United States of communist subversion in government and other institutions that found its inevitable expression in the witch hunts of Senator Joseph McCarthy.

The indiscriminate anti-left wing campaigns in the United States, which inevitably hit a number of Canadian targets, bred disquiet and suspicion in the political and diplomatic establishments in Ottawa. But Canadian political leaders could not allow anger to outweigh the necessity of sustaining a broadly supportive and functional relationship with the United States. By early 1954, with the ceasefire in Korea holding, Prime Minister Louis St. Laurent again began contemplating seeking mutual diplomatic recognition with the CCP regime in Beijing. Nothing came of it, however, because of vehement and very public opposition from the United States any time any of its allies contemplated recognition of the communist People's Republic of China. The closest Canada came in this period was in 1956. St. Laurent and his foreign minister, Lester Pearson, thought it was time to establish formal relations with Beijing, but beforedoing so they decided to tell President Dwight Eisenhower. They purposefully decided to talk to Eisenhower rather than his emotional secretary of state, John Foster Dulles, figuring they would get a more thoughtful reception. They were mistaken. Ronning recounts, "The President blew up and asked how Canada could think of recognizing 'Communist China, whose hands were dripping with the blood of Americans killed in Korea.'" If Canada took this action, Eisenhower continued, other American allies would follow our lead, resulting in Beijing taking China's seat on the Security Council at the United Nations. With American public opinion firmly against the CCP, Eisenhower continued, Washington would be forced to withdraw from the UN, leading to the inevitable collapse of the organization. This was a deft card played by Eisenhower. Pearson had played a central role in the creation of the UN, and both he and a substantial segment of the Canadian public regarded the organization as his baby. St. Laurent and Pearson dropped the whole idea of making overtures to Beijing.

Many previous assumptions about China were swept off the table when John Diefenbaker and the Conservatives came to power in 1957. For much of the twentieth century, the Liberals had been the party of power. Since the 1880s, the most substantial Conservative government was that of Sir Robert Borden, which was elected in 1911 and survived for ten years. Borden's successor as Conservative leader, Arthur Meighen, survived as prime minister only a few months in the fall of 1920 and again in the closing months of 1926. R.B. Bennett did better and held office from 1930 to 1935. But the overall picture was that the Conservatives held office only when the Liberals were exhausted. As well as defying the Liberal grip on power, Diefenbaker was a prairie populist from Saskatchewan, and his election broke the monopoly hold on the prime minister's office since Confederation by central Canadians (plus one Maritimer). Among the entrenched attitudes Diefenbaker wanted to sweep aside was excessive deference to Washington. With that went unwillingness by the Conservatives to be dictated to by the United States on dealings with China. But, like St. Laurent and Pearson before him, Diefenbaker and his first secretary of state for External Affairs, Sidney Smith, went to talk to Eisenhower about recognition of China before taking any firm action. Chester Ronning recounts that, if anything, Eisenhower's reaction to Diefenbaker was even more outraged than had been his response to the Liberals.

Diefenbaker was not as easily dissuaded as St. Laurent and Pearson had been, but he came at the question of exploring possibilities with Beijing from a very different perspective. His interest was trade, not diplomacy or worries about giving moral backing to what the Americans had deemed a repressive regime. As a leader from the Prairies, which had a glut of wheat from bumper harvests and not enough markets, there were political and practical sides to the question of relations with the CCP that were more pressing than the morality of giving succour to a communist regime. Beijing bought a small amount of wheat from Canada in 1958, and Ottawa became aware that there was a major demand in China for imported food grains, though the government had no inkling as to how much or why. China had managed to hide from all foreigners the extent of the famine propelled by Mao's Great Leap Forward. About forty million people are now believed to have died of starvation between 1958 and 1962. But on the basis of what Ottawa did know, in the autumn of 1960, at the request of the new minister of agriculture, Alvin Hamilton, the Department of Trade and Commerce sent two officials to China to scout out the possibility of selling wheat to Beijing. The pair returned with a favourable report of the market possibilities. Hamilton recalled in an interview with his biographer, Patrick Kyba:

Almost before I finished reading the report ... in late November 1960, I got this telephone call from the clerk at the Queen Elizabeth hotel in Montreal saying there were two Chinese gentlemen at the desk asking for me. Apparently they had flown on Canadian Pacific Airlines ... which took them to Montreal. They got to this hotel and asked for me and he [the desk clerk] had enough sense, bless his heart, to call me directly ... I said, well, if they are from China it must be in response to the wheat sales pitch. So I told the chap on the phone to give them the best suite, put it on my account, look after them, and I had those fellows on a plane as fast as I could to Winnipeg where the Wheat Board was because only the Wheat Board could negotiate the deal.

History, unfortunately, does not record the name of that extraordinarily prescient clerk at the Queen Elizabeth hotel.

The Chinese officials rapidly agreed to buy 28 million bushels (76,000 tons) of wheat and 12 million bushels (26,000 tons) of barley for CAD$60 million, cash. Based on the ease with which this deal went through, Hamilton believed China could be a long-standing and dependable market for Canadian grains. Early in 1961, he sent the chief commissioner of the Wheat Board, William Craig McNamara, to Beijing to investigate the possibility of further sales.

As a result of McNamara's report, Hamilton began negotiations with Beijing on a long-term agreement. Washington's financial sanctions against the CCP proved a problem, however. It was difficult for Beijing to gather enough hard currency to be able to pay Canada for its wheat and other grains. Beijing proposed a cheeky solution: Canada would lend China the money for a two-and-half-year program in which 5 million tons of wheat and 1.28 million tons of barley worth CAD$422 million would go to China. Hamilton agreed to the deal, commenting that, with its thousands of years of civilization, China was a trustworthy bet. With that, Hamilton won himself accolades with the CCP as a friend of China and the affection of Premier Zhou Enlai, who said on one occasion that the agriculture minister had supplanted Norman Bethune as the quintessential Canadian in the eyes of the Chinese people.

Diefenbaker's Cabinet was not quite as overjoyed as Hamilton with the idea of lending the CCP Canadian money to buy Canadian wheat and barley. Some ministers pointed out that bank loans required government guarantees, which meant that Ottawa was giving de facto recognition to the People's Republic of China. Indeed, it can be argued that this wheat and barley agreement was the moment when Ottawa formally accepted the CCP as the legitimate government of China, though the legal niceties and exchanges of diplomats were yet to come.

The cereals agreements saw Canada-China trade expand from about CAD$9 million in 1960 to over CAD$147 million two years later. Through the 1960s, the volume fluctuated between CAD$100 million a year and nearly CAD$200 million. More important for the future, however, it established a paper trail of mutual trust in doing business that prepared the way for diplomatic recognition.

Hamilton's relationship with Beijing outlasted his status as a minister in the Canadian government. He took seriously his role as a friend of China. After leaving government, he became a promoter within Canada of business with China, contacting Canadian companies and urging them to take advantage of the opening Chinese market created by the wheat sales. When Canadian businesses failed to jump at the opportunity he was showing them, Hamilton turned to other countries in Asia and South America, urging them to welcome business with China.

Early in 1964, the Beijing government invited Hamilton to China to advise it on advancing their country's international trade. He was given lavish hospitality, far more lavish than he felt was warranted over discussions about trade. The response Chinese officials gave Hamilton offers two insights. His hosts told him that the country had been shattered by the famine induced by the Great Leap Forward, though this was still being blamed on bad weather. "Just at the moment when we were in the midst of this tremendous national effort thinking we had no friends, you came selling wheat," Hamilton recalled being told. Not only did this indicate what a physical and psychological disaster the famine had been, it also suggested the CCP was regretting its isolation from the rest of the world. A subsequent conversation with Zhou Enlai confirmed Hamilton's impression. "After ninety minutes I realized that he was trying desperately to tell me that the one thing he wanted to do before he finished his political life was to bring the United States and China back into some form of harmony."

Meanwhile, as a means of defending himself against criticism for his management of the Great Leap Forward and the resulting famine, Mao launched the Cultural Revolution in 1966. Paul Lin had been close to the centre of the CCP revolution for fifteen years at this point. But as he observed the mounting social upheaval around Mao's latest campaign, Lin decided it was time to avoid the coming onslaught and return to Canada. He returned to Vancouver in September 1964 as a talented and skilled front man for the Chinese Communist Party.

Lin had left for China at the end of 1949 in a fervour of left-wing excitement to see for the first time the homeland he had never known. Lin's experience close to the centre of the CCP regime was profound, and sometimes threatening. After landing in Hong Kong and taking a coastal liner to Tianjin, the port city for Beijing, Lin arrived in China early in January 1950 with a new identity. He discovered very quickly that he was what would these days be called red aristocracy. In truth, Lin's red bloodlines were not of the top order, but they served him well. Soon after his arrival, Lin took the train to Shanghai to see the woman who would open doors and protect him during his fifteen years in China. Soong Ching Ling was the widow of Sun Yat-sen, the republican revolutionary who had launched the overthrow of the Qing Dynasty in 1911 and set in motion the cascade of events that brought the CCP to power. Soong Ching Ling was one of three daughters of American-educated Methodist minister Charlie Soong, who made a fortune in banking and printing in China. All three of his daughters were educated at the Methodist Wesleyan College in Georgia, but as young women their paths diverged dramatically. The eldest sister, Ai Ling, married banker and finance minister in the Kuomintang government H. H. Kung. The youngest sister, Mei Ling, married Kuomin-tang leader Chiang Kai-shek. Ching Ling married Sun Yat-sen, who died in 1925 with his revolution still incomplete. It was said of the sisters throughout their lives that one loved money, one loved power, and one loved China. Ching Ling's love of China was expressed by throwing in her hat with the CCP after the death of her husband, though she was never a member of the party. But the party found her very useful, because her presence gave the CCP legitimacy as the heirs of Sun Yat-sen, a position that should more logically have gone to Chiang and the Kuomintang. The party treated Soong Ching Ling well and gave her a prominent position as a vice-chair of the Chinese People's Political Consultative Conference, the advisory body that included non-communist figures whom the CCP wished to honour by appearing to value their advice.

Lin's family connection to Soong Ching Ling was convoluted, but, in the world of Chinese extended family loyalties, it was solid. Lin's older brother Andrew had married Pearl Sun, the granddaughter of Sun Yat-sen by his first marriage. Thus, Ching Ling was the step-grandmother-in-law of Paul Lin's brother. There was another family tie that made the bond stronger. Lin's wife, Eileen, was the daughter of Chen Xing, the right-hand man to Soong Tzu Wen, Soong Ching Ling's Harvard-educated brother who became a prominent Chinese businessman and politician in the years before the Second World War.

Lin had hoped to be able to make his academic skills in international law available to the new China, but he found that the course had been expunged from the university curriculum in Beijing as an "instrument of imperialism." So he took part-time work as a translator and writer for magazines.

Lin's relationship with Soong Ching Ling bore fruit in May 1950, when she came to Beijing from Shanghai for a meeting of the Chinese People's Political Consultative Conference. She invited Paul and Eileen to a dinner at which she introduced them to a senior official at the Ministry of Foreign Affairs. Qiao Guanhua was the director-general of the Department of Asian Affairs and the director of the China Information Bureau. Qiao offered Lin a job as chief editor of the daily English-language bulletin on international affairs, *For Your Eyes Only*, which had a restricted circulation among government officials and embassy staff. In 1951, Lin became the head of the English-language broadcasting division of the government's Overseas News Department.

Mao Zedong governed by creating turmoil and keeping off balance all those around him who might otherwise have had time to realize that his administration was catastrophic. Lin managed to avoid getting caught up in most of these upheavals, which could be deadly for anyone who found themselves on the wrong side of an invisible political line. But Lin could not avoid the anti-rightist campaign launched in 1957, when Mao used the Hundred Flowers Campaign of the year before, which had encouraged citizens to openly express their opinions on the communist regime, to reveal his enemies. At all levels of the CCP establishment in 1957, there was a panicked stampede by officials to expose rightists before they themselves became victims. One official at the English Section of Radio Peking who scampered to be the first to point a finger was Sidney Rittenberg, an American CCP member who had been with Mao since the days in Yan'an, the wartime headquarters of the party in Shaanxi province. Rittenberg and another CCP member decided they had to accuse someone of being a rightist to save themselves from becoming targets. They picked staff member Gerald Chen, even though he was innocent. "But he was the best we had. His real name was Chen Weixi, but he used the name Gerald, a souvenir of his Western connections. He was the son of a Zhongqing businessman who had cast his lot with the Communists," Rittenberg wrote in his 1993 memoir, *The Man Who Stayed Behind*. "Living in Canada in the home of Dr. James Endicott, a well-known left-wing preacher who once taught school in China, Gerald had grown close to the Canadian left wing and had returned to China after the Communist victory, a patriotic young man who wanted to do some-thing for his country ... The specific action Gerald was accused of was plotting to overthrow the leadership of the English section in favor of the deputy head of the section, the flashy son of a Chinese-Canadian minister and not a party member."

In his autobiography, Lin confessed to being that "flashy son of a Chinese-Canadian minister." Apart from showing what a viper's nest life in Beijing government circles was under Mao, this vignette shows the lasting influence of the Canadian missionary connections.

Lin does not say so directly, but it seems that the incident warned him that his Western heritage and intellectualism might make him vulnerable to anti-rightist witch hunts. Wisely, Lin decided to avoid becoming a victim of vicious office politics by volunteering to become one of the first intellectuals sent into the country to live with and learn from peasants. Lin recounted, "After a year working alongside these simple but honest and diligent peasants, I more deeply appreciated their sufferings and aspirations. When they eventually grew to trust me and treat me as a friend, I was moved."

Lin's self-abasement paid off. When he returned to Radio Peking in 1959, he was promoted to the post of artistic director in the English-language service. But the times were not as favourable for many party stalwarts; within the CCP, condemnation of Mao for his Great Leap Forward and the resulting death toll was beginning to boil over. The tensions that would explode into the Cultural Revolution were starting to be felt in daily life. It was Lin's father's eightieth birthday early in 1962, and the extended family planned a celebration in Vancouver. Paul and Eileen Lin arrived in Hong Kong in February, where Paul picked up the Canadian passport he had left with relatives there twelve years before. Eileen, however, wanted to apply for landed immigrant status in Canada. When she went to the Canadian diplomatic office in Hong Kong to apply, she was subjected to four hours of questioning, mostly about what she and her husband were doing in China. When it became apparent that it was going to take weeks, if not months, for Eileen's travel documents to be approved, Lin went on ahead to Vancouver. He already had an established style when dealing with officialdom of going straight to the top. Lin wrote one letter to Minister of Citizenship and Immigration Ellen Fairclough, and another to Prime Minister Diefenbaker, confronting head-on the obvious fact that he and Eileen had come to the attention of Canadian security. "I have been given to understand that, in reality, approval of my wife's entry is being withheld on the grounds that I hold views which are not unfavourable to the present government of China," he wrote to Diefenbaker. Lin insisted that there were no inconsistencies between his loyalty to Canada and his admiration for "the heroic efforts of the Chinese people to build a better life for themselves."

In the end, it was with the help of the first ethnic Chinese member of Parliament, Douglas Jung, that Eileen was issued a special ministerial permit to visit Canada for thirty days. Through much of their visit, the couple noticed they were being followed by RCMP officers. When they returned to China in July 1962, Lin wrote to Soong Ching Ling, "We found Canada tightly held in the military-strategic and economic coils of the U.S. octopus, and therefore under the sinister shadow of the American Security Council. Nevertheless, there were broad currents of bitter antipathy to U.S. domination at all levels and enormous, albeit poorly informed, opinion friendly to the People's China."

Given that much of the rest of Lin's career involved trying to give Canadians a more friendly and differently informed view of the People's Republic of China, this letter reads in retrospect like a job application.

During the following months, Lin became increasingly aware of the growing turmoil within the CCP and the prospect that Mao was preparing to strike out against his opponents. In 1964, Lin decided it was time to leave China. "I consulted with Madame Soong and told her that I had learned much by living and working in New China, but now felt I could be most useful as a 'friend of the Chinese people' based in Canada. Madame Soong was understanding and supported my decision."

Lin's memoirs are selective, as such documents always are. Missing entirely from Lin's account of his last couple of years in China is his work at Huaqiao University — literally the Overseas Chinese University — at the port city of Xiamen (previously known as Amoy) in the province of Fujian on the southern coast opposite Taiwan. However, a biography of Lin posted online by Baidu, the Chinese version of Google and Wikipedia, which follows Beijing's demands on web censorship, notes that Lin was a professor at Huaqiao University. The university was founded in 1960 with the sponsorship of Premier Zhou Enlai and still comes under the governmental authority of the Overseas Chinese Affairs Office, and therefore the United Front. The purpose of the university is to encourage students from the Chinese diaspora, especially university graduates, to come to China to pursue their studies and impart their knowledge to the mother country. Huaqiao University emphasizes technical disciplines and has all the hallmarks of a place where CCP security officials can identify and recruit young agents of influence and spies before they return to their home countries. According to Huaqiao University's website, since its founding it has produced nearly 160,000 graduates from 39 countries and territories.

The university has alumni associations in all of these countries, including Canada.

By the time Lin got back to Canada in October 1964, he had made the transition from being a friend of China to a man who wanted to be an agent of influence on behalf of the CCP within Canadian society. The intense interest in him and Eileen exhibited by Canada during their 1962 visit, along with Lin's unacknowledged involvement with Huaqiao University, raises the question of whether he was also a spy or a spymaster. Both the RCMP Security Service (the predecessor of CSIS), and the United States Central Intelligence Agency were convinced Lin was a highly placed operative for the CCP regime in Beijing. Lin made no secret about that. Indeed, he played it up and may have exaggerated it to enhance his influence with Canadians. But if an essential element of being a spy is secrecy and deception, Lin does not fit that definition. He made no secret about his loyalties or objectives.

The most credible picture that emerges of Lin is that of a quintessential and highly talented agent of influence rather than a spy or clandestine espionage agent. Even so, the Canadian and American security agencies continued to view him as a dangerous enigma, even if political and business circles in both countries quickly decided he was a very useful asset in their efforts dealing with Beijing.

Upon arriving back in Canada, Lin took a part-time job as a lecturer in the Asian Studies Department at the University of British Columbia. Lin's position at UBC did not last long, however. Soon after his first major lecture, the head of the Asian Studies Department, Bill Holland, asked to see Lin. Holland wanted to know about the nature of his work in China because, he said, a reporter from *The Province* newspaper had threatened to attack the university for "hiring a professor fresh from Red China." Lin said it was made clear to him that his continued presence was a threat to the reputation of the university and the survival of the Asian Studies Department. The atmosphere of threat gathered in the following months. UBC president John B. Macdonald told Lin that *The Province* was preparing to print a story that Holland had been forced to resign as director of the Institute of Pacific Relations in New York after Senator Joseph McCarthy's Committee on Un-American Activities accused him of hiring a Soviet spy. Lin began looking for other posts and with the guidance of Holland, Lin accepted an offer to head up a new Centre for East Asian Studies at McGill University. Lin took up the post as an assistant professor in the history department at McGill in September 1965. He quickly used this position to mount a drive for a new political, diplomatic, economic, and academic relationship between China and Canada.

FIVE
A FRIEND IN AMERICA'S BACKYARD

Surely peace with Washington is more important than praise in Peking. Our policy should not depart too radically from the position established over the years by the U.S. and its allies.

— PRIME MINISTER LESTER PEARSON TO SECRETARY OF
STATE FOR EXTERNAL AFFAIRS PAUL MARTIN SR.,
JUNE 28, 1966.

PAUL LIN'S RETURN to Canada and his taking the helm of McGill University's Centre for East Asian Studies in September 1965 coincided with several shifts in Canadian public life that smoothed the path for diplomatic recognition of the People's Republic of China. One was a generational change in Canadian national politics. The cautious and highly stylized era of John Diefenbaker was coming to a close. Diefenbaker was satisfied with the benefits of wheat sales and saw no further advantage in pursuing full diplomatic relations with Beijing. After the Liberals returned to government in 1963, Prime Minister Lester B. Pearson and his secretary of state for external affairs, Paul Martin Sr., tied themselves in knots over the intricacies of the debates at the United Nations as to who should represent China. Should it be Beijing or Taipei, or both, and which one should sit on the Security Council? Not only did Pearson have paternal angst over the growing pains of the UN, he worried about shattering the unity of the North Atlantic Treaty Organization if Canada recognized the People's Republic of China. This fear was calmed somewhat when France recognized Beijing in 1964 without the sky falling. But Pearson continued to fear serious reprisals from Washington if Canada went out on a limb for China. Changes in attitudes in Ottawa began when Pierre Trudeau came to Parliament in 1965, became minister of justice in 1967, and ascended to the party leadership the following year. Trudeau came to office as the first Canadian prime minister with some experience travelling in China, and he was committed to diplomatic relations with Beijing. For Trudeau, it made no sense to pretend that Chiang Kai-shek and the Kuomintang exiled to Taiwan were the real government of China. Equally important to him, though, was the opportunity to demonstrate that the lacklustre Pearson days were over and revolution was in the air. Trudeau saw an advantage in reinforcing that image by taking a purposeful swipe at Washington and defying the threats from successive American administrations of retaliation if Ottawa recognized the People's Republic of China. Meanwhile, there was a growing interest in academia in the potential of a more open China as a subject for scholarly discourse. University professors were beginning to enjoy opportunities for getting involved in what subsequently became known as Track II diplomacy, whereby non-governmental actors carry on exploratory, unofficial discussions with foreign counterparts. These arm's-length talks allow many potentially divisive issues to be confronted and often resolved before the Track I diplomats and government officials get involved. Paul Lin was a natural master of the art of Track II diplomacy. He also recognized and understood the utility of the growing anti-Americanism in Canada in the 1960s and 1970s. Much of that distaste came from opposition to the war in Vietnam, and Lin was adept at fashioning that into an argument for Canadian recognition of the PRC.

A watershed moment in the evolving relations between Canada and the Chinese Communist Party regime in Beijing came in August 1966, coincidentally the start of the Cultural Revolution in China. In Banff, Alberta, the Canadian Institute of International Affairs held one of its annual weeklong conferences examining current world affairs. The 1966 conference focused on Canada and Asia. The gathering brought together several of the figures who would play major roles in the saga of Sino-Canadian relations. One was retired Canadian diplomat to China Chester Ronning, who had just returned to Alberta after debriefings in Ottawa and

Washington following an abortive mission to the North Vietnam capital, Hanoi. Another was University of Alberta law professor Ivan Head, who had previously been a foreign service officer in the Department of External Affairs. Most significantly, in 1967 Head became legal assistant to Pierre Trudeau, then the minister of justice. That was the start of a lifelong association that saw Head become Trudeau's foreign policy advisor the following year when Trudeau became leader of the Liberal Party and prime minister. One of Head's roles was to be Trudeau's personal emissary at meetings with players in Canada's foreign affairs drama whom the prime minister either couldn't or didn't wish to meet personally. Among those who became one of Head's regular contacts was another speaker at the Banff conference, Paul Lin.

Secretary of State for External Affairs Paul Martin Sr. came to the conference fresh from another frustrating and inconclusive attempt to push toward deciding how China should be represented at the United Nations. The previous autumn, he had suggested to Cabinet that Canada recommend that the UN General Assembly initiate exploratory talks with the Chinese Communist Party on the terms of entry of the People's Republic of China into the international body. This idea was quickly shelved when, on September 29, 1965, China's foreign minister, Chen Yi, denounced the UN as Washington's puppet and made what the Pearson government regarded as impossible demands for China's entry into the organization. In Parliament, Martin said, "It is not for the United Nations to accommodate itself to the views of a single nation, however powerful or populous. It is for Communist China to make that accommodation. Much to the regret of the Canadian government there is no present evidence that she is ready to do so."

Martin's gloom had lifted somewhat early in 1966 when the United States backed a NATO study into how the People's Republic of China might be brought into the UN. Ideas were bounced back and forth to the extent that Martin decided his emissary to Vietnam, Chester Ronning, should return to Hanoi via Beijing in order to sound out the CCP on its real attitude toward the United Nations. Ronning may have established himself as a friend of China, and particularly of the CCP, but he quickly found this did not give him any special entrée. The Chinese regime simply refused to give Ronning an entry visa, and his mission collapsed. Martin's participation in the Banff conference was delivered in a mood again coloured by pessimism. The conference ignored his doubts and issued a consensus report endorsing Canada's immediate diplomatic recognition of the PRC and urging Ottawa to make its best efforts to give the Beijing regime membership in the UN. The delegates to the conference had been inclined to these positions before the weeklong discussions, but Paul Lin's speech undoubtedly helped reinforce those thoughts.

This was Lin's first major outing since becoming established at the Centre for East Asian Studies at McGill. The title of his speech was bland: "China and the West." But it was pyrotechnic stuff. It established Lin in the minds of many at the conference, as well as those who heard about it afterwards, as the most well-connected interpreter in North America on the beliefs and objectives of the CCP. A natural extrapolation of that was to believe that Lin was a useful mailbox for delivering messages to Beijing. And for counter-intelligence agencies like the RCMP Security Service, the FBI, and the CIA, there was enough in his speech to add to their conviction that Lin was an espionage agent for the CCP.

Lin charged into the boiling controversy of the United States' burgeoning involvement in the war in Vietnam. Washington, he said, appeared to Asians to be intent on imposing its will on the rest of the world.

This is an image established in Asian minds not by Communist propaganda, but by the record of nearly two decades of U.S. power plays in Asia.

Asians find the facts to be these: There is not a single Chinese soldier or military base outside of China anywhere in Asia. It is understandable that they [Asians] find it hard to conceive how Washington, thousands of miles away, can be far more certain than they of the Chinese threat to their security. Asians just cannot accept the assumption of evil Chinese intentions, especially while US napalm, gas, defoliants,

and canisters filled with razor darts rain down on an Asian land where
Chinese soldiers are not even present, and while US military leaders
seem eager to bomb them back to the Stone Age. The image of China as
a bloodthirsty, conspiratorial incarnation of yellow peril, simply does not
fit in the Asian view.

This direct appeal to Canadian opposition to the ratcheting up of American involvement in the Vietnam War, and the subliminal tweaking of Canadian anti-Americanism, echoed other speeches at the conference. It did not, however, find universal favour. The *Calgary Herald* lambasted some of the participants for failing to appreciate the broader implications of the situation in Asia. "A case in point was the bitter attack on U.S. Vietnam policy launched by Professor Paul Lin of McGill University. This speaker painted the United States as a war-mongering aggressor, intent on remaking the rest of the world in its own image," read an editorial comment in the newspaper. "Unfortunately, Prof. Lin was careless with some facts. For example, there was the implication that, while the U.S. may maintain a military presence in several Asiatic countries, there is no Chinese soldier or military base outside China. It appears that Prof. Lin has forgotten about an oppressed little country called Tibet."

Lin ended his speech with a call for Canada in its own interests to seek diplomatic recognition with China as soon as feasible: "An important immediate objective would be to formally recognize, for its own sake, the existence of seven hundred million Chinese; to develop friendship and normal relations with them, including expansion of two-way trade and cultural exchange. To be sure, this calls for the most courageous, the most discerning of statesmanship. It calls for a far-sighted view of the stakes involved for Canada and the world."

This appeal to Canadian diplomatic exceptionalism worked. "The conference strongly reiterated to the government the importance of recognizing Beijing," wrote University of Alberta professor of Chinese history Brian L. Evans in his autobiography, *Pursuing China*. Lin, for his part, felt he had been more successful than he had hoped. A few days after the conference, he wrote to his wife, Eileen, "In the end, Paul Martin summed up his position with considerable embarrassment, having to address pointed questions from an audience that by week's end had become overwhelmingly pro-China. Many have told me my speech made a tremendous impact, some sharp disagreements notwithstanding. The interesting thing was that the ambassadors of Indonesia, Burma, and Japan all agreed with my point of view, as did Chester Ronning, Canada's last ambassador to China."

Two months later, in October 1966, a Liberal Party conference passed a resolution calling for the immediate recognition of the People's Republic of China and for Canada to support its being given membership in the United Nations. In this, the Liberal Party was following Canadian public opinion. Throughout the 1950s and the period of the Korean War, polls showed most Canadians opposed to recognition of Beijing. But that shifted around 1964, when samplings of public opinion began to show consistently that a majority of Canadians favoured establishing full diplomatic links with China.

So did the new leader of the Liberal Party, Pierre Trudeau. In May 1968, one month after he took the party leadership and became prime minister, Trudeau announced that his government would move to recognize the People's Republic of China and support its joining the United Nations, while at the same time acknowledging the existence of a separate government in Taiwan. This was not a new or opportunistic stance by Trudeau. He had more first-hand experience of China than any Canadian prime minister before. Trudeau had made his first trip to China in 1949, at the time of the establishment of the CCP regime. He criticized Western countries for "refusing to recognize the existence of those who rule a quarter — soon to be a third — of the human race." He regarded it as political and economic idiocy to fail "to increase trading relations with the most formidable reservoir of consumption and production that has ever existed." Those words tend to support a criticism that was often levelled at Trudeau: that his intellectualism blinded him to the emotions and subtleties that drive the political motives of other people. His biographer, John English, says in *Citizen of the World: The Life of Pierre Elliott Trudeau, Volume One*, that he had an "overly sanguine view of China," coupled with a degree of naïveté about left-wing regimes and a distorted admiration for some of the CCP leaders, master manipulator Zhou Enlai in particular. English sees Trudeau's views on China as an expression of the anti-establishment attitudes that had been part of his character since his youth, mixed with a genuine desire to break down the antipathy between East and West in the nuclear age. English adds that Trudeau had many misgivings about the CCP regime he did not express in public. Trudeau's ambivalence about the Beijing regime does come through in many passages of the book he wrote with his friend Jacques Hébert after their 1960 tour of China, *Two Innocents in Red China*. But logic prevailed, though it is interesting that when Trudeau and his foreign policy adviser, Ivan Head, wrote about the recognition of China in 1995 in their book *The Canadian Way: Shaping Canadian Foreign Policy, 1968–1984*, the old missionary moral fervour bubbles through:

> *A China open to the world would be subject to the same diplomatic persuasion as other countries, and could be expected over time to adjust its political, economic, and social practices to bring them into harmony with international norms.*
>
> *For all China's seeming fragility, however, the two of us shared in common the unshakeable belief that [China] would in future become one of the two or three most influential countries in the world. For that reason it must not be allowed to assume that it was without friends, or without responsibility to the international community at large. Canada's influence, as always, was limited, but it should continue to be exerted with that future in mind.*

The thought process justifying recognition may have been logical and obvious to Trudeau, but the process to set it motion was not. Officials in the Department of External Affairs and other senior branches of government found themselves confronted by a host of perplexing questions as they attempted to push and pull Trudeau's desire into the shape of a feasible policy. In 1968, with China in the midst of the turmoil of the Cultural Revolution, the first question was whether China had any interest in establishing diplomatic relations with Canada. Attacks on foreign diplomats in Beijing and the return of intense isolationist revolutionary zeal suggested China had little desire to seek new relationships. For Canada to be rebuffed would be embarrassing, especially for the neophyte Trudeau government that was portraying itself as a new broom. Then there was the question of how Washington would react. In the past, the reaction had been angry enough, but in the midst of the Vietnam War, with Beijing seen as a supporter of Hanoi, Washington might become apoplectic and lash out with trade embargoes against Canada. Trade with China, and the survival of Canada's sweet deal selling cereals to Beijing, was another consideration. Inevitably, diplomatic recognition would lead to a broader trade pact with China. Would that benefit Canada or not? Would Canadian industries find themselves competing with imported cheap Chinese goods? Would the CCP open its markets to Canadian investment and manufactured goods as well as to its natural resources?

There were also security implications. It seemed highly likely that the CCP would see the establishment of an embassy with, probably, outlying consulates as bases from which to conduct espionage and subversion operations. This was not only a danger to Canada itself, it might be particularly threatening to Canada's existing community of Chinese immigrants, most of whom supported Chiang Kai-shek and the Kuomintang and who were considered dangerous dissidents by the CCP.

Crucial also was the question of how to deal with the issue of Taiwan. Trudeau had said only that diplomatic recognition must be sought while "taking into account the fact that there is a separate government on Taiwan." What did that mean, and how could it be fashioned into phrases that would be acceptable to the CCP?

Bernie Michael Frolic, in his contribution to *Reluctant Adversaries*, says that if it had been asked, the Department of External Affairs would have advised against seeking formal relations with Beijing, but it followed orders and, by the end of August 1968, had sent a proposal to Trudeau and the Cabinet. There it stalled because of reservations in the Department of Finance and the Wheat Board, both of which worried that if Canada didn't get the attitude toward Taiwan right, the CCP would take revenge by cutting its purchase of Canadian cereals. Frolic recounts:

> By the fall of 1968 these considerations had been incorporated into a formula which was presented to the minister [of foreign affairs, Mitchell Sharp]. Canada would recognize the Peking government as the only government of China, without necessarily accepting China's territorial claims over areas in which it did not exercise jurisdiction. At the same time the Canadian government was prepared to say that Canada considered it desirable and necessary to deal with the government which was in effective control of Taiwan for matters concerning the island. Canada would take the position that such relations were not intended to constitute recognition of Taiwan as an independent state, or to imply any other position as to the status of the territory. The formula also envisaged the possibility that Canada might permit representatives of the Taiwan government to have a trade mission in Canada if they chose to do so, to facilitate Canadian dealings with Taiwan in matters of mutual interest. This constituted de facto recognition of Taiwan, but not de jure recognition.

On January 30, 1969, the Cabinet sent instructions to the Canadian ambassador to Sweden, Arthur Andrew, that he should seek a meeting with his Chinese counterpart with the intention of starting talks on recognition and the establishment of diplomatic relations. In his book *The Rise and Fall of a Middle Power: Canadian Diplomacy from King to Mulroney*, Andrew describes the negotiations in Stockholm as "a textbook affair," though that would appear to be an overly benign description of the following seventeen months.

After the election of Trudeau and the Liberals in May 1968, the CCP in Beijing anticipated an approach by Canadian diplomats; they just didn't know where the connection would be made. Former ambassador to Canada Mei Ping, in the 2010 symposium marking the fortieth anniversary of diplomatic relations, said China's diplomats worldwide were put on alert. "As early as July 16, 1968, the Chinese Foreign Ministry, under the instruction of Premier Zhou, sent cables to all our diplomatic missions abroad asking them to watch out and report immediately if they are approached by Canadian diplomats," Mei said. Even so, it was not a straightforward business for Andrew to get an appointment to meet his Chinese counterpart in Stockholm, Chargé d'Affaires Liu Chi-tsai. The first response Andrew got on February 4, 1969, was a request to call Liu on February 6 in order to make an appointment to meet on February 8. That never happened. In the words of Bernie Frolic, "apparently, the Chinese were waiting [on] guidance from Peking." It was not until February 19 that Andrew finally made contact with Liu and a meeting was arranged for two days later, February 21. The tone of the meeting was reported to have been "entirely cordial," though it concluded with the appearance of a major impediment that dogged the talks for months. Andrew said he had been instructed by Ottawa to arrange with Chinese representatives a time and place to discuss mutual recognition and an exchange of ambassadors. Alongside the diplomatic preparations, Andrew said, the Canadian government wanted officials to consider trade and consular agreements, as well how Sino-Canadian relations might be developed. For his part, Liu told Andrew he wanted to inform the Canadian government of the "three constant principles," which were the basis on which the Beijing government would consider building diplomatic ties. The principles were:

1. A government seeking relations with China must recognize the central People's Government as the sole and lawful government of the Chinese people.
2. A government which wishes to have relations with China must recognize that Taiwan is an inalienable part of Chinese territory and in accordance with this principle must sever all kinds of relationships with the "Chiang Kai-shek gang".

3. A government seeking relations with China must give support
    to the restoration of the rightful place and legitimate rights in
    the United Nations of the PRC and no longer give any backing
    to so-called representatives of Chiang Kai-shek in any organ of
    this international body.

Ambassador Andrew and his team, optimistically, viewed the three
principles as an expression of Beijing's feelings rather than preconditions
for negotiations. With that in mind, Ottawa felt principles one and three
were possible, but two — accepting that Taiwan was an inalienable part of
China — was unacceptable. Second thoughts about the status of the three
principles and whether or not they were preconditions began to creep in
when weeks dragged by without any response from Beijing. Speculation
mounted in the Canadian press and among politicians in both Ottawa and
Washington that the silence was because of CCP indifference to achieving
diplomatic relations with Canada, and perhaps with any other countries,
including the United States. There was not indifference in Beijing, but
there was a good deal of strategic thinking going on. At the 2010 Shanghai
conference marking the fortieth anniversary of diplomatic relations,
former ambassador Mei Ping and another diplomat, Chen Wenzhao, said
they had examined the records of China's Ministry of Foreign Affairs from
1968 to 1970. They found that the decision to proceed with Canada was
the first step toward long-term aims. Other Western countries, principally
Belgium and Italy, were showing interest in establishing diplomatic ties
with Beijing, but after careful consideration, the CCP decided to make an
agreement with Canada the precedent on which subsequent talks with other
countries would be based. Mei and Chen said Canada was chosen because
it was close to the United States, which was already beginning to explore
the prospect of recognizing Beijing. Yet Canada, in Beijing's eyes, was
"somewhat independent" and appeared interested in more than commercial
relations. The CCP's judgment was that Trudeau had a view of the world order
that made it likely he would support the PRC's entering the UN and probably
taking China seat's from Chiang's Republic of China regime on Taiwan.

Paul Lin, now well settled in to his position at McGill University, was by this time feeding perceptions both in Ottawa and Beijing. According to his own account of that time, Lin began receiving regular phone calls from Trudeau's foreign policy adviser Ivan Head soon after the election of the Liberal government in June 1968. At roughly the same time, Lin was contacted by Thérèse Casgrain. She was a friend of Trudeau's and Canada's first female political party leader as head of the Parti social démocratique du Québec. She went on to become a New Democratic Party MP in Ottawa, and subsequently a Trudeau-appointed member of the Senate. Casgrain asked Lin to submit a policy paper on China for inclusion in the Liberal government's review of foreign policy, which he did.

Lin's apparent role as an intermediary between Trudeau and the Beijing government became a controversial public issue early in 1969, even as Andrew and his staff in the Canadian embassy in Stockholm were trying to arrange meetings with their Chinese counterparts. That arose from an opinion piece Lin had written for *The Globe and Mail* on June 21, 1968, headlined, "The Path to Peking is Littered with Obstacles." The piece was commissioned by one of the paper's editors, Norman Webster, who took up the post of China correspondent the following year. The article caught the eye of philanthropist and crusader for world peace Cyrus S. Eaton. Eaton wrote to Lin, inviting him and "any of your friends" to Deep Cove Farm in Nova Scotia. Lin, his wife, and their son went for a weekend in July 1968, and fairly soon after their return to Montreal, Lin got a telegram from Eaton asking him to return for another weekend early in August. This time, other guests included Ted Sorensen, former special counsel, adviser, and speech writer to President John F. Kennedy, and Donald Zagoria, professor of government at Hunter College in New York.

This was the beginning of Lin's role as an intermediary between Washington and Beijing. It started with Eaton proposing in October 1968, at the behest of Zagoria, that Lin use his position at McGill to arrange a conference on China–U.S. relations. Eaton and his American friends felt that holding the conference in Montreal would be far less challenging to both Washington and Beijing than attempting to have a meeting in the United

States. Zagoria envisioned the conference attracting a raft of eminent American academics as well as political operatives like Ted Sorensen, security expert Zbigniew Brzezinski, and the chairman of the Senate Foreign Relations Committee, William Fulbright. The conference was scheduled for early February 1969, while Andrew in Stockholm was still waiting for contact with the Chinese. But then Eaton came up with an additional idea. He suggested that ahead of the conference, a small number of the American delegates meet to try to find a way through the deadlock in Washington-Beijing relations. Eaton asked Lin if he could arrange for a delegation of Chinese business, academic, and science leaders to attend this small meeting. Lin said it might be difficult to arrange such a visit at short notice, but he volunteered to go to Hong Kong "to convey the invitation directly to China's representatives there." It appears from Lin's account of this incident that he planned to go into China to deliver the invitation to the Montreal conference, for which Eaton planned to pay all the expenses. But because of the disruptive effects of the Cultural Revolution, he couldn't get a visa. He returned home from Hong Kong on January 16, and because all seats were booked on direct flights to Canada, he took a Northwest Airlines flight to Seattle, where he planned to change planes for Montreal. In his account of what happened next, Lin wrote:

> After my plane landed in Seattle at 6:30 am, I was pulled out of a group of in-transit passengers by U.S. Customs officials. They forced me to leave the transit area, demanded my passport, and stamped it with a "Temporary Visit" seal, which gave them the authority to conduct a search. I had to relinquish my suitcase, hand over my briefcase, and empty all my pockets. I was so exhaustively searched in Seattle that I missed my connecting flight to Montreal.
>
> Once home, I reported this outrageous abuse of my rights to my friend and colleague Professor Jerome A. Cohen at Harvard Law School. He offered to investigate the matter for me, an inquiry that took nearly six months.

There seems to be little doubt that pulling of Lin out of the transit lounge was an American counter-intelligence operation. A former Canadian diplomat friend of mine met the CIA operatives who said they were involved in the incident, and who chortled as they told the story of Lin's discomfiture. They remain convinced that Lin was an espionage agent for Beijing, a belief that seemed to be confirmed when they found thousands of American dollars in cash in his baggage. The agents' belief was that this money had been supplied by the CCP and was to be used to fund pro-Beijing activities in Canada. My friend was told they confiscated the money. Lin does not mention the money in his account of the affair, but, if it existed, there is another obvious explanation for it. Cyrus Eaton had volunteered to fund the visit of Chinese participants in the Montreal conference, and it would have been natural for Lin to take money with him to Hong Kong to pay those expenses. As he didn't make contact, he would naturally have brought the money back. Whatever the truth, the incident in Seattle was one among a number of blatant moves by American counter-intelligence agents against Lin and his wife, clearly intended to make the couple aware that they were under suspicion and observation.

Knowledge of Lin's trip to Hong Kong began percolating in political circles in Ottawa, though the rumours missed its abortive mission to arrange a quiet Sino-American dialogue in Montreal. Instead, it was pointed to in the House of Commons and subsequently in Canadian newspapers as Lin's "secret mission to China" on behalf of Pierre Trudeau. The spreading of misinformation about Lin's trip has the hallmarks of an operation by intelligence agencies of Chiang Kai-shek's Kuomintang regime. The rumours claimed that as a result of Lin's secret mission, Trudeau had moved away from his previous guarantees to continue recognizing Taiwan as part of any diplomatic recognition deal done with Beijing. Lin denied to various newspapers that he had been an emissary for Trudeau. "I am an academic and am not involved in political manoeuvres," he was quoted as saying in the *Montreal Gazette*, an interpretation that stretched the truth to breaking point.

Meanwhile in Stockholm, matters were proceeding at a snail's pace. On April 3, 1969, Chinese officials called at the Canadian embassy, and it was agreed that the negotiations on diplomatic recognition would take place in the Swedish capital and that the talks would be conducted in English, even though the counsellor at the Canadian embassy, Robert Edmonds, was a Mish Kid from the West China Mission and spoke Chinese. At the next meeting on April 10, they began to get into practical issues like establishing a Canadian embassy in Beijing and a Chinese embassy in Ottawa, telecommunications, travel restrictions, and the extent of diplomatic immunity.

The Chinese could not ignore that the Canadians were doing everything they could to avoid talking about the three principles, fearing these would turn out to be pre-conditions for negotiations. When the Chinese delegates mentioned this, Andrew and his team said the principles, of course, would be discussed when they got into substantive negotiations, and the Chinese side appeared to accept this.

In the nearly a year since the Liberals had returned to office, the Trudeau government had made distinct shifts in its position on Taiwan, and Paul Lin's influence on those changes is obvious, though they did not go as far as Lin wished. Trudeau had come to office believing that a "one-China, one-Taiwan" position was the answer to the conundrum: Canada would recognize the CCP as the government of China, but would also recognize Chiang Kai-shek and the Kuomintang as the administration of a separate country, Taiwan. Trudeau's position was entirely logical, especially as it remained the position of the United Nations — and, indeed, the United States — that there should be a referendum among the island's people on whether they wanted internationally recognized independence or some form of political union with China. Then, as now, there is no doubt that the Taiwanese would have opted for independence. But Trudeau's position was trumped by the vehemently held belief of both Mao and Chiang that Taiwan was part of China. Chiang held to this position even more fervently than Mao. As an exile still holding China's UN seat and claiming to be the real government of China, it was essential to

Chiang's crumbling political legitimacy that Taiwan be considered part of China. Thus, over his early months in power, Trudeau, along with Secretary of State for External Affairs Mitchell Sharp, modified Canada's position to a more nuanced suggestion. Canada would "de-recognize" Chiang's Republic of China as the government of China, maintain only unofficial relations with Taipei, and establish all formal diplomatic ties with the People's Republic of China in Beijing. However, Trudeau adamantly refused to accept the CCP's claim that Taiwan was an intrinsic part of China. The Chinese side, according to the Ministry of Foreign Affairs records now available, was somewhat bemused by what it called Canada's "blurred position" on the Taiwan question, but decided it had to be taken seriously. The CCP was reluctant to back down because dogged insistence on adherence to political principles was built into the party's Leninist and Maoist DNA. It was Canada's refusal to give a clear statement of acceptance of Beijing's claim to own Taiwan that did the most to drag out the negotiations in Stockholm over seventeen months and eighteen meetings. By mid-1970, the Canadian negotiators came up with the words that would eventually break the logjam: Canada would "take note" of Beijing's claim to Taiwan, a phrase that did not imply recognition of China's claim. When it later came time for Washington to grasp this nettle, it "acknowledged" China's claim, a word that Beijing invariably translates as "accepts," causing major problems.

Zhou Enlai, ever the pragmatist, confronted the stalemate when he told the regime's negotiators "we should uphold principle but work it out in a flexible way to achieve success." At the seventeenth meeting in Stockholm, on October 3, the Chinese side accepted Ottawa's "take note" wording to fill the elusive second paragraph, which was divided into two. Thus, on October 10, 1970, Mitchell Sharp rose in the House of Commons to announce mutual recognition and the establishment of diplomatic relations under a four-paragraph agreement that read:

> *The Government of the People's Republic of China and the Government of Canada, in accordance with the principles of mutual respect for*

sovereignty and territorial integrity, non-interference in each other's internal affairs and equality and mutual benefit, have decided upon mutual recognition and the establishment of diplomatic relations, effective October 13, 1970.

The Chinese Government reaffirms that Taiwan is an inalienable part of the territory of the People's Republic of China. The Canadian Government takes note of this position of the Chinese Government.

The Canadian Government recognizes the Government of the People's Republic of China as the sole legal Government of China.

The Chinese Government and the Canadian Government have agreed to exchange ambassadors within six months, and to provide all necessary assistance for the establishment and the performance of the functions of diplomatic missions in their respective capitals on the basis of equality and mutual benefit and in accordance with international practice.

Two days before, on October 8, Zhou had reported to Mao on the outcome of the Stockholm negotiations. Chen Wenzhao, former Chinese diplomat in Toronto, told the 2010 symposium in Shanghai what happened next: "On hearing the good news, Chairman Mao laughed and said, 'Now we have made a friend in the backyard of America!' Canada was America's ally. The establishment of diplomatic relations with Canada broke a hole in the backyard of America. And this was a slap at America's anti-China policy of 'two Chinas' and 'one China and one Taiwan.'"

SIX

ROMANCE MEETS REALITY

The overall return on our investment has not been impressive. There is no evidence that the lustre of the maple leaf or the memory of Norman Bethune have persuaded the Chinese negotiators to opt for sourcing their requirements in Canada unless the price is right.

— CANADA'S AMBASSADOR TO BEIJING RICHARD GORHAM,
FEBRUARY 7, 1987

AS SOON AS diplomatic relations between Ottawa and Beijing were established in 1970, it became apparent that the two sides had very different expectations for the relationship. For China, a door had been opened into the future. For Canada, all too often it was a window into nostalgia. The judgment by Mao Zedong and his premier, Zhou Enlai, that Canada was the best candidate among Western countries for China to seek diplomatic relations with proved to be spot-on. Former Beijing diplomat Chen Wenzhao, in his paper to the 2010 conference in Shanghai on China-Canada relations, said the "Canadian Formula" drew global attention. "That had a huge influence on China's relations with the rest of the world." Acceptance by the People's Republic of China of Canada's simple phrase taking note of the claim to Taiwan led to a wave of negotiations with eleven other middle power Western countries and a raft of agreements over the following two years to establish diplomatic relations. This wave ended the diplomatic isolation that had stunted China's internal and external development for more than twenty years.

Canada was the stalking horse for Washington, as the latching on to Paul Lin by American movers and shakers proves. But Washington's approaches to Beijing were more tentative and drawn out than those of other governments. After the July 1971 visit to Beijing by Richard Nixon's National Security Adviser Henry Kissinger, the president himself went to China in February 1972. In the course of that visit, the two sides issued the Shanghai Communiqué, in which they pledged to work toward normal diplomatic relations. For the time being, they established quasi-diplomatic liaison offices in each other's capitals. Full diplomatic relations were not put in place until January 1979.

For Ottawa and Beijing, the opening of diplomatic relations loosed a mad tumble of efforts to establish business, academic, and personal relationships. Secretary of State for External Affairs Mitchell Sharp was quoted by Paul Evans in *Engaging China* as saying later that the quick expansion of relations with China after 1970 was his most important foreign policy achievement. In August 1972, Sharp led to Beijing the largest commercial delegation that Canada had sent abroad. On a government-to-government level, basic templates were established for diplomatic, political, and commercial contacts. This provided the framework that encouraged Canada to help facilitate the PRC's entry into the United Nations in October 1971, and later into the International Monetary Fund and the World Bank.

Meanwhile, Canadian government agencies began making efforts to advise Canadian businesses on entering the Chinese market. At first sight, the prospects did not look encouraging. As Gordon Houlden, the director of China Institute at the University of Alberta and a former Canadian diplomat in Beijing and Hong Kong, has written, in 1970 the two economies were polar opposites. While the Canadian economy was heavily oriented toward trade, "China, with an economy then focused on agriculture and Soviet-style heavy industry, had not yet emerged from the internal disruption and chaos of the Cultural Revolution." It would not be until after the death of Mao and the coming to power of Deng Xiaoping with his programs of economic reform and plan to open China to state-managed capitalism that Sino-Canadian commercial relations would take off. In the meantime, structures were put in place to take advantage of that moment if and when it came.

Negotiations began for a Canadian-Chinese Trade Agreement, which gave mutual most-favoured nation status. This means that each country applied import tariffs on the other's goods that were as low as for trade with other most-favoured nations. The agreement was signed in 1973, at which time trade between the two countries had already doubled from 1970. Canadian business people had quickly become mesmerized by the size of the potential Chinese market: it required selling goods to only a small proportion of the population to make vast profits. Canadians were soon to learn that their vision of China as a market of over one billion potential customers was largely a mirage. Because of the country's regionalism, its lack of an effective distribution network, and opaque local trade practices and protection regulations, China was more realistically seen as a large collection of markets of about fifty million people each. In 1973, when a Canadian trade fair was held in Beijing, it attracted about six hundred Canadian business leaders and officials. It was also the first foreign trade fair attended by Premier Zhou Enlai. As they signed a trade agreement, the two countries also set up a Joint Economic and Trade Committee as a forum for Canadian and Chinese officials to discuss economic and commercial concerns.

Behind these official bridges for trade, other links were being forged. A CIA file on Paul Lin, declassified in 2010, gives interesting insights into both how Canadian businesses were approaching China and how Beijing was facilitating contacts. The papers present a picture of Lin in June 1973, when his position was established as a one-stop go-between for politicians, business people, academics, officials, and journalists wanting to make contact with the Chinese leadership. The key document is a report, unasked for and apparently unwanted, about Lin by American Mish Kid and advocate of Washington cementing ties with Beijing Harned Pettus Hoose. The three-page memo about Lin's operation in Montreal was sent by Hoose to Brent Scowcroft, then the military affairs assistant to President Nixon. Scowcroft passed it on to Richard Solomon at the National Security Council with a note suggesting it should be passed on to "the Agency for an analysis."

Hoose had been a consultant to Nixon's National Security Council in the early 1970s, was involved in some of the planning for the 1972 visit to China, and had become a promoter of business with China. He clearly valued his past attachment to the world of security intelligence and was keen to keep the association by freelancing. It is clear from the memo that he had visited Lin in Montreal around June 1973 and had been to both Lin's home and his office at McGill University's Centre for East Asia Studies.

The Hoose memo starts with a brief description of Lin's office. "Substantial mail and memoranda from PRC and from PRC embassy," it says. "Bookshelves include Chinese and English editions of Marx, Engels, Mao and similar works. Well thumbed 'little red book' on desk." The description of Lin's home, an apartment in a "luxury complex" on Nuns' Island, is much more detailed. Hoose notes the layout of the apartment, that it is "furnished in western style," and that it has on display many Chinese artifacts "of excellent quality." The memo goes on to list some of the photographs on display showing Lin and his wife, Eileen, with Zhou Enlai and Soong Ching Ling.

Hoose then describes Lin's study. The context of this section suggests the American had gone to see Lin to get assistance in making contact with Chinese officials. He says there were two telephones on Lin's desk, one a standard dial phone and another on which "Dr. Lin speaks ... directly with the PRC embassy staff, apparently in Ottawa [but not confirmed as to city], without assistance of operator and without dialing." On Hoose's behalf, Lin picked up the second phone and was put through to the commercial consul, Fang Yin. "Dr. Lin's manner and speech with Fang Yin and others was courteous but mandatory, e.g. 'Wo yao ni chien ta, yeh pang ta-ti mang' [I want you to meet him and assist him]." As a Mish Kid, Hoose spoke Mandarin. Hoose also made notes about the pictures in the study, including "what appeared to be original brush-strokes, directed from 'Mao Tsetung' to 'Lin Ta-Kuang.'"

The memo continues with a hodgepodge of observations and conclusions. Lin, Hoose wrote, using quotes to indicate phrases that Lin had said to him, is "a close friend of Premier Chou En-lai," had "assisted" in arranging

Canada's recognition of the People's Republic of China, and had "assisted" Canadian Pacific Airways to get landing rights in China. "He is 'very close' to 'the highest authorities' in many of China's 'governing circles,' including 'State Council,' 'China Council for the Promotion of International Trade,' 'Bank of China,' and others."

Hoose continued, "Dr. Lin appears to have relatively substantial sums of money on his person. E.g., a wallet unusually well filled with Canadian bills, displayed at restaurants and similar places.... He has intervened on behalf of Canadian firms, as to entry to PRC and as to the Canadian Industrial Fair in Peking."

He observed, "He is capable of sending (or causing the sending of) written materials to Peking via diplomatic pouch, and is capable of communicating (or causing communication) with Peking via means 'other than cable or mail' (diplomatic pouch?)."

Lin's speeches, wrote Hoose, "are the straight Chinese communist line, delivered without subtle indirection. However, he always refers to PRC and Chinese as 'they,' and takes the position that he is a Canadian educator, delivering his scholarly analysis." But, Hoose insisted, Lin was not a benevolent operator. "The word is out among some U.S. firms involved in seeking trade with the PRC that Dr. Lin can assist in establishing contacts. He does so, variously for a consulting fee or for a grant for his studies."

Hoose ends with the comment that Lin "is far more than a professor, and is substantially involved with and quite possibly a powerful member of the PRC 'governing circles.' He should be regarded as a total PRC supporter, probably having PRC functions in North America. He can be useful to some U.S. companies in establishing contact with PRC trading officials and for related purposes, but should be regarded by the U.S. as potentially very dangerous."

The response of Richard Solomon, the National Security Council official to whom Scowcroft sent the Hoose memo, is noteworthy. "I have talked with CIA people about Harned P. Hoose's 'intelligence report' on Paul Lin, and there is nothing in it not already known to the Agency."

In October 1973, four months after Hoose sent his memo to Scowcroft, Prime Minister Pierre Trudeau, his wife, Margaret, and an entourage of friends and associates visited China to mark the third anniversary of the diplomatic breakthrough. Brian Evans was attached to the Canadian embassy at the time, and later became professor of Chinese history at the University of Alberta. In *Pursuing China*, he quotes the briefing book prepared by the Department of External Affairs for the visit as describing relations somewhat cautiously as "warm and friendly" and "active but not intensive." There was, said the briefing book, a "fund of goodwill" toward Canada which was generally seen as a "well-meaning and sincere power with a generally benign influence in the Western alliance." It warned, however, that visitors should not believe that Canada had a privileged status in China. Whatever positive views there were of Canada among Chinese citizens and the Chinese government arose almost exclusively from the fact that Canada was the first significant Western country to recognize China. Canada, the briefing paper warned, could easily "close out the emotional debt."

Ottawa was far less restrained in its ambitions for the Trudeau visit. This was to be the Canadian Camelot taking to the road, complete with Margaret Trudeau (expecting a second Christmas Day baby), an exhibition of Group of Seven paintings, a tour by a Canadian hockey team, concerts by the Vancouver Symphony Orchestra, and, more practically, a delegation of university chancellors and presidents. More than two dozen reporters were in the prime minister's entourage, and extraordinary arrangements were made to ensure their videos of Trudeau's visit got back to Canada in time for the evening television news every day. Material could not be sent directly from China, and it was considered too expensive for the Trudeau team to set up its own satellite link. So a system was devised for recorded television reports to be flown to Guangzhou in Guangdong province and then taken by taxi to the border with Hong Kong, where they were delivered to the news outlets' local correspondents. The reports were then dispatched by satellite back to Canada in time for broadcasting the same evening, local time.

Although the Trudeau visit was an elaborate piece of political theatre, several important relationships were established that gave the Chinese

Communist Party access to and influence in Canada for decades to come. One theatrical moment occurred as Trudeau and his entourage arrived at the airport in Beijing. Paul Lin had taken a sabbatical from his post at McGill in August 1973 in order to travel back to China and write a memoir of his experiences. During this visit, he spent time with his old mentor Zhou Enlai. In his memoir, Lin describes at length conversations with Zhou about the Cultural Revolution, but he does not mention any discussions about Trudeau's pending visit. This is a glaring blank. Lin by this time was well established as the CCP's premier agent of influence in Canada. And as Lin said in his memoir, he had regular conversations with Trudeau's foreign policy adviser, Ivan Head. It defies belief that with Trudeau's visit in the offing, Zhou would not have quizzed Lin about his views on the political situation in Canada. Nor would it be surprising if Trudeau and his officials used Lin, in addition to the Chinese embassy in Ottawa, as a sounding board for the reception they were likely to receive in Beijing. Lin recounts that when the Trudeau entourage arrived in October, he went out to the airport in Beijing with visiting Canadian friends architect Arthur Erickson, his partner, Francisco Kripacz, Moshe Safdie, and his wife, Nina. There was quite a crowd to greet Trudeau, and Premier Zhou, who had met him at the steps of the aircraft, led his visitor over to the enthusiastic gathering. Zhou saw Lin in the crowd and apparently said, "Professor Lin, welcome to China." Lin recalled, "Trudeau followed and also shook my hand, saying: 'Paul Lin, it is good to see you in China.'"

Trudeau and Lin saw each other again a few days later when Arthur Erickson arranged a private lunch for Pierre and Margaret, Lin and Eileen, and the Safdies at the Summer Palace. This extraordinary request had to be approved by Premier Zhou and involved the reservation of the Ting Li Pavilion next to Kunming Lake. It was there that the Empress Dowager Cixi, who controlled the declining years of the Qing Dynasty from 1861 until her death in 1908, listened to the birdsong of orioles. Erickson served a menu of Cixi's favourite dishes, much to the delight, said Lin, of the guests of honour. Lin said in his memoirs, "Later that evening, I received a phone call from the premier's office, inquiring about the menu that had so impressed the Canadian prime minister that he was almost late for his afternoon meeting with Premier Zhou!"

It was a visit bracketed by banquets. Zhou greeted Trudeau and his party with a banquet in the Great Hall of the People on the west side of Tian anmen Square on October 11. Trudeau responded with a banquet on October 13 before leaving by train for the south accompanied by the newly rehabilitated Vice-Premier Deng Xiaoping, who had been condemned and exiled to the countryside during the Cultural Revolution. Between those two lavish meals, Trudeau spent many hours talking to Premier Zhou in three formal meetings. Much of the conversation was about political philosophy, in which both men took great delight, but they also discussed more pragmatic subjects. Zhou at one point noted pointedly that the bilateral trade balance was heavily in Canada's favour and that a more equitable commercial relationship should be created. They also signed a landmark agreement allowing for the reunion of family members in China with their parents or children living in Canada. This would see the first immigration from China to Canada in a generation and prepared the ground for an influx of people into Canada from both Hong Kong and China in the decades to come.

After his final meeting with Zhou, Trudeau was taken off by himself to see Mao Zedong, who by then was only semi-functional and had been carefully prepared by his medical attendants to be able to manage a brief encounter with the Canadian visitor.

An important product of the Trudeau visit was an agreement for an exchange of university students between Canada and China. This remains an essential element in the relationship between the two countries. The vast majority of the Chinese students who come to Canada do so wishing to advance their scholarship and ability to contribute to society. Most of those who take advantage of the route to Canadian citizenship that student visas offer do so because they genuinely want to become Canadians. But the movement of Chinese students to Canada, now running at about 120,000 a year, is also a major channel for infiltration into Canada by the CCP's intelligence agencies and the United Front.

On the Canadian side, the student exchange program grew out of an experiment that had been launched soon after setting up the embassy in Beijing in 1970. Because the Department of External Affairs did not have enough officers with experience of China, it was decided to appoint Canadian academics trained in Chinese studies to the post of cultural officers at the Canadian embassy.

The first Sinologist-in-residence was Professor William Saywell of the University of Toronto, who took up the one-year post in July 1972. After returning to academic life in Canada, in 1993, he became the president and chief executive of the Asia-Pacific Foundation of Canada, a business-oriented research and analysis institute.

The arrival of the first group of Canadian students in China was scheduled to coincide with Trudeau's visit. Evans recorded in *Pursuing China* that the students gathered in Hong Kong in November 1973. "I went to Hong Kong to meet them and to accompany them through the border crossing and on the flight to Beijing. They were an interesting group with a broad range of interests, including poetry, traditional Chinese medicine, history, politics, and film," he wrote. "There were ten women and ten men, representing most regions of Canada and having a range of political views from conservative to Maoist. The Maoists had a mentor in the person of Professor Paul Lin of McGill. They expected to share accommodation in Beijing with Chinese students [at the Peking Language Institute] and to participate fully in the Cultural Revolution experience."

Divisions grew between the Maoists and non-Maoists in the Canadian group. The Canadian Twenty arrived when the institute and most of Chinese society were in the turmoil of the Cultural Revolution. "Some among the Canadians felt they should be as active as possible in emulating their Chinese neighbours, and in participating in the life of the Institute," Evans wrote. "Others eschewed togetherness, no matter for what reason. The Chinese Institute authorities, faced with so many national groups, preferred to deal with them as groups, although they did not favour full foreign student participation in Chinese life. Here, indeed, was a contradiction which the Canadian group was never able to resolve."

The Chinese side was much more careful about ensuring there were no contradictions as it selected its students for the exchange. Ira Basen, now a CBC radio producer, was a student at Ottawa's Carleton University in the summer of 1973. He got a summer job helping the nine Chinese students acclimatize to Canadian life and prepare for their year at the university. These were the first students from the People's Republic of China ever to be allowed to study in North America. Basen wrote in an article for the CBC website, which was published on May 30, 2008, that he believed they were assigned to Carleton University "so they could not stray too far from the watchful eye of the [Chinese] embassy in Ottawa." He added, "Clearly, their selection had not been random. They were all bright, reasonably proficient in English and had participated in the Cultural Revolution, spending time working in the countryside with 'the people.' But they were also modest, unfailingly polite, eager to learn and, while supportive of their government, relatively apolitical and candid about the failings of their own economy."

The stimulus for Basen's article was that by 2008, one of the nine Chinese exchange students from 1973, Lu Shumin, was back in Ottawa, this time as China's ambassador to Canada. Lu had been posted to Ottawa in 2005 after rising rapidly through the ranks of the Chinese diplomatic service. Lu arrived in Ottawa shortly before the election of the minority Conservative government under Stephen Harper and his announcement that he would not sell out human rights "to the almighty dollar." Lu's tenure coincided with the most distant period in relations between Ottawa and Beijing since 1970. Harper railed against Beijing's suppression of dissent in Tibet and Xinjiang and the persecution of Falun Gong. The prime minister also declared in Parliament that there were a thousand CCP agents in Canada engaged in industrial espionage. Lu pushed back strongly against the charges by Harper and his government. The ambassador vehemently denied all the allegations of human rights abuses and, unusually for a Chinese ambassador, held several news conferences with Canadian journalists. Behind the scenes, a major lobby operation was mounted using the CCP's agents of influence in business and academia to get the Harper government to change its attitude toward China. For better or worse, the lobby was successful, and some of that success must be credited to Lu's experience and understanding of Canadian society.

Insights into the early years of Canada-China student exchanges are provided by an examination of the program made by the Canadian International Development Research Centre (IDRC), published in 1983. The report was written after conducting extensive interviews with students from both countries and with the academic administrators involved.

Canadian Academic Relations with the People's Republic of China Since 1970 demonstrates the very different approaches and attitudes toward the exchanges the Canadians and Chinese took. The twenty-five hundred Chinese students who came to Canada between 1970 and 1983 took a clear-sighted and pragmatic approach to the opportunity. In the first six years, from the 1973 agreement until a broader pact on academic exchanges was concluded in June 1979, most Chinese students came to Canada to take non-degree courses in English, with a small minority taking French. They also audited courses in technical subjects. The picture that emerges is of the Chinese students and their mentors grabbing the most immediately useful gain on offer — language — and sizing up Canadian universities' capacities in science and technology in order to plan for future exchanges. It was an entirely rational approach. Once the door to Canadian academic institutions opened wider after 1979, the majority of Chinese students headed straight for the sciences, especially electrical engineering, computer science, mechanical engineering, chemistry, and physics. The Canadians, in contrast, were still brimming with the romanticism born of missionary culture. The report notes, "[T]heir proportional distribution among specializations is strikingly different from that of Chinese academics visiting Canada." One-third of the one thousand Canadian academics and students who went to China in the same thirteen-year period, by far the largest group, opted for arts courses, particularly Asian studies, education, and languages.

Unlike the Chinese coming to Canada, a significant number of the Canadians (13 percent) were faculty members going to China for three principal reasons. About a third of them were what the report politely calls "academic tourists." From their complaints about the packed and rushed sightseeing itineraries, these people had clearly grabbed the opportunity for a subsidized holiday in China. Another third were visiting lecturers at Chinese academic institutions, and 20 percent were Canadian university administrators in China to negotiate future exchange relations with Chinese counterparts.

Canada's unfocused and blithely generous approach to the student exchange program inevitably led to the whole thing getting out of hand very quickly. The Chinese swiftly realized that they were on to a good thing and that the Canadians had no real process in place to monitor or regulate what was happening. A bureaucracy set up under the Council of Ministers of Education of Canada was meant to oversee the placement of the Chinese students and academics in Canadian universities and colleges. But, says the IDRC report, "this system came under increasing strain as a growing number of potential visiting scholars clearly indicated their Canadian institutional preferences or even asked individual Canadian professors with whom they had already corresponded to obtain 'official' sanction for their placements."

The Canadians were getting a crash course in *guanxi*, the essential Chinese survival tool of using every available connection to game the system. The IDRC report says that by 1980 the situation had become chaotic, as "most Canadian universities were unprepared for these diverse Chinese initiatives and lacked a co-ordinated approach to academic relations with China." As a result, no one in the universities or in the responsible government departments had any clear idea of how many Chinese researchers were in Canada, which university departments they were attached to, or what they were doing. The report said, "As one harried administrator indicates '... It is very difficult to pin down who is going where ... all in all it's a very ad hoc procedure ...'" The system was slowly brought under control, largely through an infusion of federal funding for university administrations in 1982. But a glaring omission in the IDRC report is any consideration of the security implications for Canada of this unregulated and evidently uncounted wave of Chinese researchers descending on Canada's science faculties.

Pierre Trudeau's 1973 visit to China, the associated trade fair in Beijing, and the bilateral trade agreements that flowed from them paved the way for the creation of a non-profit organization to foster trade relations. A November 2008 briefing paper for the Library of Parliament entitled *Canada's Trade Policy and Economic Relationship with China* says the Department of External Affairs established the Canada-China Trade Council in 1978. Success has many fathers, and this appears to be a case where everyone wants to claim parenthood of a body that has become not only a driving force behind bilateral trade but also the club of the men who have created Canada-China policy for much of the past forty years.

Paul Lin has an account of the founding of the organization, later renamed the Canada-China Business Council, in his memoir. In 1977, Paul Desmarais of the Montreal-based Power Corporation approached him to help arrange for a group of Canadian businessmen to attend the massive annual Chinese trade fair in Guangzhou (the old Canton). This Lin did, and as a follow-up he organized a conference in December 1977 hosted by his own McGill University Centre for East Asian Studies together with the Faculty of Management. The conference sponsors were a gathering of Canada's corporate aristocracy: the Royal Bank of Canada, the Bank of Montreal, the Bank of Nova Scotia, the Aluminum Company of Canada, Inco, Canadian Pacific, MacMillan Bloedel, and Desmarais's Power Corp. About sixty people attended the discussion on the Chinese economy and the prospects for Canada-China trade. Lin wrote that as a result of the success of the conference, Desmarais and Maurice Strong of Petro-Canada pushed for the establishment of a permanent Canadian trade presence in China before Washington agreed to terms of diplomatic recognition with Beijing and American business people started flooding into the Chinese market. The ten founding companies and financiers of the Canada-China Trade Council in 1978 were gold producer Barrick, BMO Financial, Bombardier, the China Trust and Investment Corporation (CITIC), Export Development Canada, Manulife Financial, Power Corporation of Canada,

Sun Life Financial, and SNC Lavalin. This collection of Canada's business elite became a persuasive lobby for enhanced relations with China, for which the benefits of trade were held to be of paramount concern.

The creation of the council marks one of several pinnacles in Lin's career. He retired from McGill in 1982, and in 1986 he was appointed rector of the University of East Asia in Macau, then still a Portuguese colony. Lin was instrumental in conferring honorary Doctors of Law on both Henry Kissinger and Pierre Trudeau while he was at the helm in Macau. He resigned in 1988 in a dispute over academic freedom. He settled in Vancouver and became honorary professor at the Institute of Asian Research at UBC. Despite his dedication to China and the CCP, Lin could not accept the Tiananmen Square massacre and became a vocal critic. He was made a member of the Order of Canada in 1998. He died in 2004.

Lin's account of the founding of the Canada-China Business Council tallies with that of retired Senator Jack Austin, a close associate and friend of Trudeau who was heavily involved through much of his career in developing the Canada-China business relationship. In an interview with *Business in Vancouver*, published on February 13, 2018, Austin added a colourful vignette to the story of the council involving Power Corp., founding chairman Paul Desmarais, and CITIC. Austin said it is often forgotten that after drawing CITIC into the business council, Desmarais set in motion the beginnings of investment in Canada by Chinese state-owned companies. He offered to sell CITIC a fifty percent share in a paper mill owned by Power Corp. in Castlegar, B.C. It was the CCP's first experiment in foreign investment. "CITIC got its first big domestic credibility through this Canadian effort," Austin told the newspaper. "It was a major moment of prestige and significance in the relationship between China and Canada."

Power Corp. was and is especially influential because of its close ties to the Liberal Party, both as an employer of past and future prime ministers and through close family ties. Paul Desmarais was an adviser to Pierre Trudeau when he was establishing himself in the federal Liberal Party and when he became prime minister. After his retirement from politics,

Trudeau became an international adviser to Power Corp. Another prime minister, Brian Mulroney, worked as a labour lawyer for Desmarais before entering politics. Paul Martin Jr. was president of Canada Steamship Lines Inc., Power Corp.'s Great Lakes shipping subsidiary, in 1974 before going on to become prime minister in 2003. Jean Chrétien, prime minister from 1993 to 2003, had even closer ties to Power Corp. Chrétien's daughter, France, is married to André Desmarais, the son of Paul. André Desmarais took over the China file from his father when he became president and co-chief executive officer of Power Corp. with his brother in 1983. André Desmarais took over the chairmanship of the Canada-China Business Council, remains the body's honorary chairman, and is also a member of what his official biography calls "several China-based organizations." Among these, he was on the board of the Chinese state wealth fund, CITIC Pacific, from 1997 to 2014.

In Canada, Power Corp. was the premier gatekeeper of this country's formal relations with China. A measure of their influence can be seen in a story told to me by a friend who was a senior government official immediately after the Liberals returned to power in 1993 after nine years of Conservative government. Among the junior ministers in the new government of Jean Chrétien was a first-time MP from the Vancouver suburb of Richmond, Raymond Chan. Chan was made the secretary of state for Asia-Pacific affairs under the Department of Foreign Affairs and International Trade. He had been born in Hong Kong, the son of Kuomintang refugees from China after the CCP's victory in 1949, and had immigrated to Canada in 1969. His riding, Richmond, was heavily populated by other immigrants from Hong Kong who had come to Canada ahead of the territory's return to Chinese sovereignty in 1997. Chan was the first Chinese Canadian to be appointed a minister in a Canadian government.

As Chan and his new staff were putting together their office in late 1993 and working to set out their objectives and priorities, they got a pointed piece of advice from an official in the department. "You'd better go down to Montreal and see André Desmarais," they were told. An appointment at the Power Corp. offices was arranged. When they arrived, they were given a tour of the impressive antiques and art — Krieghoff, Group of Seven, Riopelle. One picture, however, was out of context. Desmarais explained that the painting had been given to him by his good friend Li Peng. It was Li who, as premier of China, had declared martial law on May 20, 1989, leading to the storming of Tiananmen Square the night of June 3. Intentionally or not, this moment made an impression on Chan's team. Three years before, Chan had been expelled from China after demonstrating in Tiananmen Square on the first anniversary of the massacre. My friend told me, "We left the Power Corp. offices feeling we'd been told in no uncertain terms where Canada's China policy was made."

Whether that comment was entirely accurate or not, what was evident was that during the late 1970s and the 1980s, Canada's policies toward China were driven by efforts to secure a commercial relationship that would continue to grow. When the old missionary goals of Canada's moral duty to push the CCP toward political and social reform and improvement of its human rights record did arise, they were usually answered from a business perspective. This was the well-worn argument that as China's economy grew through trade, a middle class would be created that in time would demand a representative government and all the civil rights flowing from the rule of law.

The arrival of the Progressive Conservative government in June 1984 did not change that attitude. Brian Mulroney's passionate pursuit of the end of the apartheid regime in South Africa led some people to hope he might deploy similar enthusiasm toward human rights in China, but they were mistaken. On October 11, 1985, Mulroney told Parliament, "I have indicated to the House of Commons, to the premier of China and the president of China the fact that the intention of this Government is to pursue the policy set out by my predecessor, Mr. Trudeau, with which I agree. We have honoured that in all circumstances."

Mulroney took seriously his bequest from Trudeau of ripening relations with China. Two-way trade stood at $2 billion when Mulroney came to power. In 1993, when he left office, it was at $4.78 billion. However, the trade gap had widened in China's favour, as it has done ever since the opening of diplomatic relations. By the time Mulroney retired from Parliament, Canada was selling China $1.68 billion each year but was buying $3.10 billion.

In 1986, Mulroney made his first official visit to China. In his book *Engaging China*, Paul Evans, whose research material included declassified government files, quotes the prime minister as he wrote in his diary on the flight back to Canada: "Much remains to be done in expanding the relationship but persistent work by successive Canadian prime ministers, principally Pierre Trudeau, is clearly paying off. I think the extent and quality of my meetings with Chairman Deng, the premier, the president and the general secretary indicate the value of this highly advantageous relationship."

In the briefing book for Mulroney's visit, quoted by Paul Evans, the prime minister was advised not to make a big deal in public about the CCP's human rights record. Mulroney followed this advice while in China, but when he returned to Ottawa, he instructed Secretary of State for External Affairs Joe Clark to order a major review of Canada's China policy. The aim was to create an "effective, dynamic, coordinated course for bilateral relations with China." According to Paul Evans's account, the department came up with glowing predictions for Canada's future ties to China. This preliminary paper argued that China would continue to be of growing importance because of its cultural achievements, geopolitical strength, and significance as a market. The paper also judged that Canadian public support for a deeper and broader relationship with China was "intense," particularly if it resulted in the creation of more jobs in Canada.

In response to this draft paper, the Canadian embassy in Beijing threw a bucket of cold water over the more fanciful expectations for relations with China. "Canada appears mesmerized with China but we should discourage this in favour of a more realistic attitude," was the embassy's response. "Dialogue will not produce Chinese recognition of Canada as a world mover and shaker." China, continued the memo, remained a Marxist-Leninist state "with more in common with the U.S.S.R. and Eastern Europe than

its Asian neighbours. China's relations with the outside world are characterized by much of the same selfishness and self-centredness to be found
in Soviet and Eastern European relations with the outside, amplified by
historical Middle Kingdom attitudes of sublime superiority."

The embassy's memo also noted that there must be real concerns about
Chinese espionage in Canada as relations intensified. Thirty years later,
the very same message could be written with even more emphasis and
urgency.

The embassy's cautions appear to have had minimal effect on the policy
drafters in Ottawa. The final paper, *A Canadian Strategy for China*, was
approved by the Cabinet Committee on Foreign and Defence Policy on
March 31, 1987. It said Canada should capitalize on Canadians' fascination
with China in order to secure a relationship for the time when China
became a major world power, which it prophesied would be around the
year 2000. The policy went on to set out nineteen steps to secure that bond,
based on programs and agreements already in place. But the strategy also
said the period of Canadian "romanticized interest" in China was over
and needed to be replaced with a hard-nosed attitude that calculated the
"real potential benefits for Canada." The paper explained that Canada
needed to cultivate a better understanding of China and of its management
practices in government and to strengthen the lines of communication and
consultation between the two governments. Significantly, the paper also
promoted aid programs for China that focused on development, not politics.
Human rights were not mentioned.

But even as Mulroney, his ministers, and officials were musing about
future relations with China, discussions between London and Beijing over
the future of the British colony of Hong Kong were setting in motion
events that would change the Sino-Canadian relationship forever.

SEVEN
REALITY BITES

Those goddamn bastards! Who do they think they are, trampling on sacred ground like Tiananmen so long?! They're really asking for it! We should send the troops right now to grab those counter-revolutionaries, Comrade Xiaoping! What's the People's Liberation Army for, anyway? What are martial law troops for? They're supposed to grab counter-revolutionaries! We've got to do it or we'll never forgive ourselves!

— VICE-PRESIDENT WANG ZHEN TO PARAMOUNT
LEADER DENG XIAOPING, JUNE 2, 1989

Yesterday, I saw with my own eyes that they do not care about the people. They care only for their own power. They killed ordinary people in cold blood. They are worse than the fascists.

— EMPLOYEE OF THE CANADIAN EMBASSY,
BEIJING, JUNE 5, 1989

MUCH OF CHINESE family and social culture has been shaped by the terrible truth that in the five-thousand-year history of the nation, it has not produced a government the people could trust. Chinese people have therefore developed an intricate network of relationships, starting with family bonds, to protect themselves from the depredations of those in power. Beyond the family, the network extends into clans and associations of people with the same family name. This is simplified somewhat by the assertion that there are only the "Old Hundred Names" in China. Then there is *guanxi*, often translated simply as "connections," which many foreign business people see as the key to their enterprises in China.

The Chinese diaspora and Chinese business people travelling abroad have taken many elements of this protective network with them, even when they live and work in countries where they are not under constant threat from predatory authorities. The port cities of the Pacific Rim all have family name clubs. A Chinese businessman named Chow, for example, can land at Malaysia's Penang International Airport, go to the Chow name club, and immediately have a circle of contacts, even if he's never been there before. There are similar, often invisible, clubs among overseas Chinese people whose families come from the same district or town in China. Canada's immigrant Chinese business community, for example, is now bristling with these hometown business associations.

The central element of all these and many other social associations is the idea that no one can ever have too much protection or too many options for survival when the world descends into chaos, which it often does if you are Chinese. That is why the number of people from Hong Kong pressing to come to Canada and acquire the added security of Canadian residency or citizenship began to increase in the 1960s. At first glance, that seems strange. Why would people want to leave Hong Kong when the territory's post-war boom was beginning to take off? In his 2010 book *How the Chinese Created Canada*, Adrian Ma recounts, "Thousands of Hong Kong citizens began coming to Canada during this social and economic boom, my own parents included. But I wondered — why did people want to leave this amazing city after it rose from poverty and into international prominence? The answer, my parents told me, was that no one was sure if the prosperity and liberty could possibly last."

This was not an irrational fear. Not only was China — just over a border from Hong Kong that could not be militarily defended — engulfed by the Cultural Revolution through much of the 1960s and 1970s, the disruption spilled over into the British colony. In May 1967, a labour dispute grew and mutated into anti-British riots by pro-Communist agitators, some waving Chairman Mao's Little Red Book. The demonstrations went on for three months. Fifty-one people were killed, ten police officers among them, in the upheaval. The riots were clearly influenced by the

Chinese Communist Party. In all probability they were directed by it, too. When, in October 1967, Chinese Premier Zhou Enlai ordered the violence to cease, it stopped immediately.

The riots and unrest came as a shock and a warning to the British administrators in Hong Kong and their masters in the Colonial Office in London. It forced them to think about the future of the territory, which the United Kingdom had begun to acquire in 1841 when the Chinese ceded Hong Kong Island as part of the reparations demanded by London after it defeated China in the First Opium War. The British trading companies, most of them dealing in opium, felt vulnerable and exposed on the offshore island. They wanted to get possession of the Kowloon side of the harbour, which would make their anchorages, warehouses, and all the comforts of the growing settlement far more defendable. That opportunity came in 1858, when the British launched the Second Opium War against China. A temporary lease for Kowloon as a place to encamp British soldiers was arranged with the local Chinese authorities in 1860. When China was again defeated in 1861, the United Kingdom claimed possession of Kowloon in perpetuity as part of the peace treaty. The final pieces of the Hong Kong patchwork were put together in 1898, when the British minister in Beijing, Sir Claude MacDonald, negotiated a ninety-nine-year lease for what became known as the New Territories beyond Kowloon, which included a host of off-shore islands, the largest being Lantau.

The CCP and the People's Liberation Army could easily have swept up Hong Kong when they took control of China in 1949, and there has never been a satisfactory explanation of why they failed to do so. The United Kingdom reinforced the garrison in Hong Kong in anticipation of a PLA assault, but London never believed it could or would put up a serious defence of the colony. The experience of the Japanese invasion in December 1941 had proved military defence was impossible. One explanation put forward for the CCP failure to invade is that even then they saw the value of having Hong Kong as a window onto the world; there is some evidence to support this view, including a 1980 remark by a Chinese State Council official, Zhao Guanji, that during the Korean War Hong Kong was "China's lifeline." Robert Cottrell, in *The End of Hong Kong*, published in 1993, says that during the Korean War, China depended on Hong Kong as a route to import gasoline, chemicals, rubber, motor vehicles, and machinery. This was to avoid embargoes imposed on China by the United Nations and the United States. It is a profound irony that a British colony should have provided a back door to succour China in a war in which British troops were fighting China's People's Liberation Army.

In October 1955, with the Korean War over and the CCP now firmly in control in China, then governor of Hong Kong Sir Alexander Graham made a private visit to Beijing and had an unofficial three-hour meeting with Premier Zhou Enlai. Accounts of what was said vary, but it seems that Zhou said the CCP was prepared to tolerate the British presence in Hong Kong so long as London observed certain rules, including not promoting or allowing the development of democracy in the colony or steering it toward self-government. Foreign powers, which undoubtedly meant the United States, should not be allowed to use Hong Kong as a military base. Chiang Kai-shek's Kuomintang should be prevented from using Hong Kong as a launch pad for subversion in China. Chinese officials in Hong Kong should be protected, and China's economic interests using the colony should not be obstructed. By and large, the United Kingdom followed Zhou's rules of conduct until the last British governor, Christopher Patten, launched a belated and ultimately futile bid to entrench democracy in Hong Kong just before the handover.

When British officials began peering into the mists of Hong Kong's future in the 1960s, the end of that lease was thirty years away, but the timeline was shortening rapidly. The British tried to divine the CCP's attitude toward Hong Kong's future, but without success. China was convulsed with its own problems. The Cultural Revolution withered and died with Mao in 1976, but was followed by an attempt to seize power by his wife, Jiang Qing, and her Gang of Four. The post-Mao intrigue and fighting went on for two years until Deng Xiaoping emerged as paramount leader in 1978. Later the same year, Deng issued an invitation through an emissary for the governor of Hong Kong, Sir Murray MacLehose, to visit Beijing.

The British tied themselves in knots trying to work out a useful approach for MacLehose to take on his mission to the Chinese capital. So convulsive were the internal arguments and speculations that it was not until March 24, 1979, that MacLehose set off for Beijing, accompanied by his wife, a handful of officials, and a senior member of the colonial Executive Council, lawyer and banker Sir Kan Yuet-keung.

MacLehose arrived in Beijing still unclear about how, in what context, and with what end in sight to bring up the subject of the future of Hong Kong when he met Deng. The Chinese leader had no such hesitation. He and other CCP leaders had been quietly discussing the matter among themselves for several months since Deng had won a firm grip on power. They saw Hong Kong as part of their play to try to persuade Taiwan to make some form of political union with the mainland and acknowledge the sovereignty of Beijing. A direct appeal to Taiwan to join China with a guarantee that it would remain largely autonomous had failed. Hong Kong, in the minds of the CCP, was now to be a guinea pig for a policy that became known as "One Country, Two Systems," with the aim of luring Taiwan out of its rejection of Beijing's advances. MacLehose's meeting had hardly started before Deng explained the CCP's policy toward Hong Kong. Deng is recorded in the 1990 book *The Diplomacy of Modern China*, edited by Chinese foreign ministry officials, as saying, "It has been our consistent view that the People's Republic of China has sovereignty over Hong Kong, while Hong Kong also has its own special position. A negotiated settlement of the Hong Kong question in the future should be based on the premise that the territory is part of China. However, we will treat Hong Kong as a special region. For a considerable length of time, Hong Kong may continue to practise its capitalist system while we practise our socialist system."

More succinctly, and in a phrase that delighted the headline writers in Hong Kong's business newspapers, Deng told MacLehose to tell the territory's investors to "Put their hearts at ease." When he got back to Hong Kong, MacLehose said, "It was a most realistic and helpful comment for the record." It was not enough, however, to calm the fears of many

Hongkongers, and the two main barometers of their sense of security —
the Hang Sen stock market index and property prices — were launched
on juddery ups and downs over the following years.

Meanwhile, Deng and the CCP began wooing the *tai-pans* (chief
executives) of Hong Kong's major corporations and conglomerates. The
objectives were twofold. The first was to ensure Hong Kong's continued
value to China as an entrepôt for trade and investment by convincing
its leading business people that they would continue to be able to make
money in a free port with minimal regulations. They aimed to make the
tai-pans, who already had significant power in Hong Kong's legislative
and executive councils, into Beijing's fifth column in the territory and to
use them as tools to pressure the British as negotiations continued. The
second objective was to use the *tai-pans*' business experience and expertise
to energize Deng's economic reforms in China. To that end, cavalcades
of Hong Kong business leaders and other influential figures were invited
to Beijing to be wined and dined and offered privileged entry into the
early opening of the Chinese market in return for their support and
business acumen.

The spring of 1982 saw a lot of this traffic. Most notable, perhaps, was
a meeting on May 21 between Deng and Henry Fok, a billionaire property
developer who already had a long association with the CCP. He had made
his first fortune gun-running for the CCP during the Korean War in defiance
of UN embargoes. Fok was the CCP's most trusted agent of influence in
Hong Kong. He became a member of the drafting committee of the
Basic Law, Hong Kong's post-handover mini-constitution, and in 1993 was
made vice-chairman of the National Committee of the Chinese People's
Political Consultative Conference. On the same day as the Deng-Fok
meeting, Premier Zhao Ziyang met Li Ka-shing, another major property
developer whose conglomerates dominated the Hong Kong stock market.
Li subsequently became one of the most significant figures in the Hong
Kong-Canada connection. He had begun buying property in Canada with
the purchase of a Vancouver West End apartment building in 1968. By
the time of his meeting with Zhao, Li owned several other apartment

blocks in Vancouver as well as a shopping centre, and he had begun to add properties in Toronto to his portfolio. His most important foray, however, came in 1988, when he won the bid to develop for housing 82.5 hectares of provincially owned land, the site of Expo '86 around Vancouver's False Creek. In a portent of things to come, Li beat a local consortium headed by Jack Poole of the BCE Development Corporation, a close friend of British Columbia Premier Bill Vander Zalm, and Jim Pattison, billionaire car dealer and former Expo '86 chairman. Li won by being a good deal more diligent in his research, nurturing political ties, and putting together the most potent development team for what was the biggest real estate development in Canada at the time. Among Li's most important local liaisons were architect Stanley Kwok, the president of B.C. Place, and Craig Aspinall, a former image maker for the ruling Social Credit Party, who has been described as knowing "every crevice of the government's body." Li made his son, Victor, the head of Concord Pacific Development, which oversaw the scheme. In its architectural style, the development is a highly visible link between Canada and Hong Kong. Its apartments were a comfortingly familiar landing place for many Hong Kong immigrants.

In retrospect, it is interesting how little changed in the years of debate and negotiations following Deng's March 1978 meeting with MacLehose. The Joint Declaration between London and Beijing was published in 1984, and the Basic Law was made public in 1990. These spelled out that Hong Kong would become a Special Administrative Region of China. As such, it would keep its capitalist system and marginally democratic government. There were vaguely expressed expectations that this would blossom into full democracy. The leaders of Hong Kong's pro-democracy movement have frequently interpreted these expressions as a commitment by Beijing, but the wording is not definitive. The Basic Law said the territory would keep its independent judiciary and rule of law inherited from the United Kingdom. There is, however, a fifty-year time limit on Hong Kong's retention of its post-colonial institutions. After that, the territory's special status ends.

Not everyone in Hong Kong, whose population then numbered about six million, was convinced this was a recipe for stability in the territory. The flight from Hong Kong that had started with the opportunities provided by greater wealth in the 1960s grew in the 1970s and became a steady stream in the 1980s and 1990s as the sense of uncertainty mounted. And for many among those looking for a safe haven from Hong Kong's murky future, Canada was the favourite bolthole.

A major reason for the attraction to Canada was that it was already well established as a refuge for Hongkongers. Between the years 1968 and 1976, Canada admitted 90,118 Chinese immigrants, most of them from Hong Kong. But not all that migration was to the credit of either Hong Kong or Canada.

When MacLehose took over as governor of Hong Kong in November 1971, one of the glaring problems in the territory was corruption in the Royal Hong Kong Police Force. The force was a classic British colonial creation with similar counterparts all over the world. It was made up of British and European officers, often young men fresh out of school, while the body of the force was constables and sergeants who were recruited from among the local population. The locals were underpaid and had developed the habit of supplementing their inadequate incomes by demanding bribes — "tea money" — of one sort or another. The system had become highly formalized and managed by the senior sergeants in the various police administrative districts. These sergeants became hugely wealthy and at least as powerful in local affairs as the bosses of the criminal Triad gangs, with whom they were often closely associated. The graft was not confined to the local Hong Kong non-commissioned officers. One of the most notorious recipients of bribes was Chief Superintendent Peter Godber, who managed to stash away tens of millions of dollars in overseas accounts and then slip out of Hong Kong and back home to Great Britain before he could be detained and charged.

MacLehose was a bundle of energy and arrived with a list of things he felt needed doing to invigorate Hong Kong. High on the list was cleaning up the police force. This he did by creating the Independent Commission

Against Corruption in 1974. The ICAC was given strong powers, such as the right to pursue people whose lifestyle and assets appeared to exceed their known income. But the ICAC was also imbued with expectations of unimpeachable standards of moral probity. The ICAC was not only very successful in cleaning up corruption in Hong Kong, it also became a model for similar institutions throughout Asia.

At first, the sergeants known as the Five Dragons thought they could ride out this reformist storm, as they had done in the past when the administration made efforts to clean up graft and protection rackets. But it quickly became apparent that MacLehose was not like the placeholders London had often sent before to manage its Chinese colony. He clearly meant business, so the sergeants decided it was time to collect their winnings and head for safer climes. The five sergeants fled Hong Kong ahead of the founding of the ICAC. Canada and Taiwan were their first stops, though all five eventually ended up in Canada. Many other corrupt Hong Kong police officers are reported to have followed the same route. An article in the September 6, 2006, edition of *Asianpost* quotes a report by the RCMP Asian Organized Crime unit indicating that up to forty-four Hong Kong police officers are believed to have sought sanctuary in Canada for fear of being targeted by the ICAC. Many used Canada's Immigrant Investor Program to get permanent resident status.

The *Asianpost* article deals with the story of how the family of one of the Five Dragons, Hon Kwing-shum, returned part of his ill-gotten fortune after protracted negotiations with the Hong Kong government. Hon, also known as Hon Shum and Hon Sum, worked for thirty-one years for the Hong Kong Police Force, during which time his total salary earnings were the equivalent of $35,000. But when he retired in 1971 and subsequently immigrated to Canada, he had assets worth millions, including more than fifty properties and numerous bank accounts in Hong Kong, Florida, Thailand, and B.C. In Vancouver, he owned at least eleven residential and commercial properties, as well as dozens of companies and a restaurant on Robson Street.

The Hong Kong authorities made efforts to extradite Hon, as they did others of the Five Dragons, but they were unable to get Canadian courts to agree to the petitions. The problem was that the legal basis in Hong Kong for apprehending the Dragons — having assets "disproportionate to and unable to be explained or accounted for by his official emoluments, awards, or allowance" — was not a crime in Canada. Even so, after Hon died in Taiwan in August 1999, his family decided to come to an arrangement with the Hong Kong authorities. They handed over all Hon's Hong Kong properties, said to be worth the equivalent of $20 million at the time.

Another of the Five Dragons who benefited from Canadian courts' tight reading of extradition rules was the most successful of the five, Lui Lok, known in popular culture as the "$500-Million Sergeant." Lui became something of an anti-establishment hero in Hong Kong, and several films were made loosely based on his exploits. He retired from the police force in 1968, at age forty-eight, and immigrated to Canada with his wife and eight children in 1973, one year ahead of the founding of the ICAC. Lui's assets in Hong Kong were frozen and then seized by the local authorities, but efforts to extradite him failed. Lui died in Vancouver in May 2010.

Corrupt police and members of the Triads were always a tiny minority of the people from Hong Kong who sought to become Canadian permanent residents and citizens. Statistics Canada figures show that 233,077 Hongkongers immigrated to Canada between January 1990 and March 1997, joining an already large Canadian population of people from the territory. By the time of the handover, about 500,000 immigrants from Hong Kong lived in Canada.

This large movement of people was spurred in part by an aggressive program launched by the Canadian government in 1986 to attract immigrants from Hong Kong, who were seen as well educated, highly entrepreneurial, and, more often than not, wealthy. Ottawa's hunt for Hongkongers far outstripped the efforts of other natural destinations like Australia and the United States. In 1993, the Montreal-born British scholar Gerald Segal accused the Canadian government of pursuing a policy of "immigration without responsibility" for poaching Hong Kong's brightest and best.

Segal did not know the half of it. The program was conceived with either such insouciance or else such crass disregard for its likely ramifications that it is a lasting stain on Canada's reputation. To put it bluntly, the program fostered corruption by creating a climate that encouraged people to seek out and give bribes for false documents or statements to back their applications to enter Canada. About one-third of the people immigrating to Canada during the heyday of the exodus from Hong Kong came via the Immigrant Investor Program. A significant number — though no one has an intelligent estimate of how many — were either not qualified to call themselves entrepreneurs or were criminals. In both cases, the applicants had obtained fraudulent documents from Hong Kong and from Canada to support the fiction that they qualified for entry. The unforgivable truth is that it was Canadian policy-makers and administrators who, knowingly or otherwise, created a situation where corruption was bound to flourish.

Charles M. Campbell, former vice-chairman of the Canadian Immigration Appeal Board, published *Betrayal and Deceit* in 2000, a brutal dissection of decades of Ottawa's immigration policies. Included in his sweeping denunciations is a whole section on the Canadian Immigrant Investor Program, which was first dominated by applicants from Hong Kong and then, during and after the time Campbell's book was published, from mainland China.

The Immigrant Investor Program was the brainchild of the Mulroney government, and when it was wheeled out in 1986 it was intended to provide seed money for Canadian economic growth. This was a misconception to begin with. The Canadian Economic Council said at the time that there was plenty of investment money available in Canada and there was no need to go hunting offshore. At any rate, the deal offered by the government to immigrants was that in return for investing between $150,000 and $250,000 in Canada for three years, the applicant received immigrant status for themselves, their spouses, and their young children. Over the years, both the size of investment required and the net worth of the applicants were raised until, at the time the program was killed in 2014, applicants needed to invest $800,000 and to have assets of $1.6 million.

In the early years, about half the people using this program to immigrate to Canada came from Hong Kong. Campbell notes a 1997 study done by Citizenship and Immigration Canada of successful Immigrant Investor Program applications, which found that very few of them fitted the criteria. Half of them spoke neither English nor French, and many of them were not entrepreneurs or business managers at all. They were mostly retired people from other professions. In addition, "there is little control over questionable financial arrangements, money laundering, the involvement of organized crime and funds from illegitimate activities."

One of the extraordinary failures of the program was that applicants didn't actually have to produce the investment the system required. Campbell wrote that in 1992, the rules were that an Immigrant Investor Program applicant had to have assets worth $500,000 and had to make an investment of $150,000, which went for three years to a designated investment manager in Canada who had control over the money. These Canadian managers often reinterpreted the program so that the immigrant would be liable for only $100,000. Then, to cap that, the investor didn't have to produce the money at all. Instead, they borrowed it from Canadian financial institutions. So the whole justification for the program — that it would bring new investment capital into Canada — was utter nonsense.

The descent from nonsense to farce is set out in a 2014 federal government analysis called *Evaluation of the Federal Business Immigration Program*. This is not an easy read for the average layperson, but what it shows is that a high proportion of the people taking advantage of the Immigrant Investor Program not only avoided bringing new money into Canada but also evaded paying Canadian taxes by minimizing their declared income in Canada. The report shows that in their first decade in Canada, they paid on average only $1,400 in taxes per year. After ten years in Canada, the immigrants were reporting, on average, only $12,700 a year in net self-employment income.

One of the first people to latch on to the money-making possibilities of Hongkongers wanting to come to Canada, even before the Immigrant

Investor Program was introduced, was Toronto lawyer Martin Pilzmaker. He had a one-man practice on Bay Street, but was soon making so much money advising and, as it turned out later, bilking Hong Kong millionaires that he was courted by the big law firms. This is an example of how persistently the Canadian establishment has focused on how much money could be made doing business with China and ignored the morality of how that was being achieved. Pilzmaker joined Lang Michener in 1985, where he is reported to have been paid four times as much as another partner, future prime minister Jean Chrétien. At first all seemed to go well. Pilzmaker brought the firm about $1 million in business in the first year, according to the *Toronto Star*. It didn't last. On June 8, 1988, the RCMP raided the Lang Michener offices at First Canada Place in Toronto and seized Pilzmaker's files. Christopher Moore writes in his 1997 book, *The Law Society of Upper Canada and Ontario's Lawyers, 1797–1997*, that much of Pilzmaker's "practice, it transpired, depended on fraudulently obtaining citizenship for wealthy non-residents and plundering their accounts as well." Pilzmaker's scam was to tell his clients to report the loss of their Hong Kong passports, which he would keep for them in Canada. The clients would be issued new Hong Kong passports, which they would use for their regular travel. But when it came time to apply for their Canadian citizenship, they would produce the old passport cared for by Pilzmaker. These passports appeared to prove that the clients had not left Canada for years. The case also highlighted the reluctance of many immigrant investors to actually live in Canada, though many were happy for their wives and children to do so. The story had an unhappy outcome. Pilzmaker was disbarred and, in July 1989, charged with fifty immigration offences. He was out on bail awaiting trial when he was found dead of a drug overdose in a downtown Toronto hotel room on April 19, 1991. In 1990, the Law Society of Upper Canada found five Lang Michener partners guilty of misconduct for their involvement in Pilzmaker's activities.

From the start, a toxic air hung over the Immigrant Investor Program. The Mulroney government recognized this, but only with reluctance. As will be described in the next chapter, in 1991, an experienced diplomat,

Brian McAdam, was posted to the Canadian mission in Hong Kong as an immigration control officer to examine reports of security problems with the visa program. A more purposeful step was taken after the Liberals returned to power in 1993: the government hired David Webber, a senior forensic accountant with the World Bank, to conduct interviews and look at whether or not the applicants had complied with the regulations. He produced his report in 1998 after a four-year study and concluded that the Immigrant Investor Program was "riddled with fraud." Webber said, "claims made by Immigration Canada about the program's success were a gross exaggeration and that rules introduced by Ottawa ... to combat fraud are completely ineffective." He continued, "I found that in many cases there was no investment at all or that the amount of that investment was grossly inflated. Canadians gave up something of real value — a visa or passport — and received very little in return."

After the handover in 1997, the number of people from Hong Kong seeking to move to Canada via the Immigrant Investor Program dropped off sharply. But as immigration to Canada from Hong Kong subsided, the number applying from China itself grew. And these applicants quickly came to dominate what had been designed as a global immigrant entrepreneur program. When the program was wound up in 2014, there were fifty-nine thousand applications pending, of which forty-five thousand were from mainland China. Among the applicants who were sponsored by provincial governments, the proportion of mainland Chinese was even higher: 99 percent, according to provincial statistics.

As the program matured, corruption and fraud became more deeply embedded. *The Globe and Mail* published articles in February 2011, after its Chinese-speaking researchers, posing as people wanting to immigrate to Canada, contacted immigration consultants in China. The newspaper provided verbatim accounts of these contacts, which showed clearly just how deeply corruption had overtaken the scheme. What stands out, though, is that much of the fraud and deceptive documents were being provided by companies in Canada. In one conversation with an immigration consultant in Beijing, the *Globe* researcher expressed interest in going to Canada via the Immigrant Investor Program. The consultant explained how much money would have to be invested and said that for the federal program, the applicant must be able to show "three years of executive management experience, such as vice-general manager or higher title." The consultant then immediately went on to say, "Our Canadian lawyer in Vancouver will help you find an enterprise and the enterprise will provide the documents for you to immigrate there."

In response, the *Globe* researcher asked, "Do you mean you will find me a company over there to provide the deposit for me?"

"Yes," said the consultant. "In other words, the company hires you as their executive manager, but they're not really hiring you. It costs about 1 million [yuan]." That is the equivalent of about $190,000.

In another approach to another immigration consulting firm in Beijing, the *Globe* researcher said he didn't have executive management experience. The consultant said perhaps he should look at B.C., because the provincial government had its own immigration program for entrepreneurs. "We will help you find a company in B.C. province of Canada, and that company hires you to work as their executive manager," said the consultant. "This company is usually the big one, one of the top five hundred in the world. They urgently need a capable and experienced executive manager." The consultant went on to describe the process. The Canadian company would interview the applicant in China, during which still photos and videos would be taken. The applicant would also have to sign a contract with the company. "And then," continued the consultant, "we hand those materials to the B.C. province's immigrant bureau, so that you can work there. We help you find the proper company, and certainly you need to pay a sum of money to that company. It costs about 150,000 Canadian dollars."

In other words, a lasting by-product of the federal government's ill-considered scheme to lure high-flying investors into Canada was to infect this country with strains of business corruption. Those viruses have grown and spread and made other forms of corruption commonplace in Canada. Huge amounts of money were easily moved into Canada by corrupt CCP officials and members of the red aristocracy in the 2000s and early

2010s. They made Canada internationally notorious as a money-laundering centre. According to the Washington-based anti-money laundering lobby group Global Financial Integrity, 60 percent of the money being spirited illegally out of China during this period was moved through false invoicing. That means that companies in Canada were providing false or inflated invoices to Chinese business partners. This enabled the Chinese partner to get permission to export capital that could then be sorted away in Canada, usually as an investment in either property or business.

For most of the hundreds of thousands of people who immigrated to Canada from Hong Kong in this period, their motives for moving and the bureaucratic routes they followed were entirely legitimate. Among those people were many whose concerns went beyond the simple yet powerful fear of instability in Hong Kong after it returned to Chinese rule. These people believed in the civic values, especially the rule of law and an independent judiciary, by which the British administered the territory. Many had lobbied for those values to be extended into full democracy in Hong Kong. Their decision to come to Canada was driven by a desire to live in a society governed by those values, which they feared would have little chance of being realized after the handover, despite Beijing's promises to move swiftly to full democracy in the territory. But the move did not mean they had given up on political reform in Hong Kong. Vancouver and Toronto remain centres for activists working for democracy in Hong Kong, and that makes those individuals and groups targets for the CCP's intelligence organizations.

Although in 1955, the British had doffed their hats to Zhou Enlai's pointed request that they not foster democratization or independence in Hong Kong, pressures on the ground made a degree of reform necessary. In 1956, some powers were given to the Urban Council, and half of its members were elected on an expanded franchise. The growing demand for independence among the United Kingdom's other colonial possessions echoed in Hong Kong. In the 1970s, the colonial administrators again started coming up against their lack of political legitimacy when trying to govern an increasingly well educated and wealthy community. Formal advisory bodies were put in place to integrate a variety of business and social groups into the colony's decision-making process. This structure also injected into the system a degree of transparency through forums where grievances and contentious issues could be resolved.

The desire among Hongkongers for more political reform and a genuinely representative and accountable system increased as talks between Beijing and London about the handover proceeded during the early 1980s. With both the British and Chinese governments keen to produce an agreement that would ensure Hong Kong's stability as a financial and trading hub of Asia, the Joint Declaration of 1984 contained some flowery language anticipating continued political reform even after the handover. But, as has been all too evident subsequently, the wording had no binding effect on Beijing and the CCP. Even so, the desire among Hongkongers for a more responsive system could not be stifled. In 1985, elections to the Legislative Council (LegCo) were held under a new dispensation. Twelve legislators were elected by nine functional constituencies representing the commercial, industrial, financial, labour, social services, education, legal, medical, and engineering sectors. Among those elected in 1985 were two pro-democracy activists, Martin Lee and Szeto Wah, who would shape much of Hong Kong's political debate over the following years.

In November 1986, there was a moment from which there was no turning back when a mass rally was held that spawned the organization of the pro-democracy movement. In 1988, the group began demanding faster paced democratization and direct elections to LegCo. The CCP was swift to respond to what it saw as a growing threat to the stability of China and its own longevity in power. There was a fashionable notion at the time that by swallowing Hong Kong, the Chinese Communist Party would ingest revolutionary reform in China and poison itself. To forestall any such outcome, the CCP beefed up its operations in Hong Kong, expanding the Xinhua news agency and its United Front offensives. Pro-Beijing candidates were run in elections for district boards, the lowest rung on the municipal administration ladder. But these boards, which dealt with mundane matters such as the positioning of bus stops, had the advantage for the CCP of implanting its agents right at the grassroots level of Hong Kong life.

The CCP's charm offensive, however, collapsed on the night of June 3, 1989, when troops massacred several thousand demonstrators in Tiananmen Square in Beijing. During May, many groups in Hong Kong had sent support of various kinds to the students in Tiananmen Square. For a while it looked as though the democracy movement in Hong Kong might be a beacon whose glow would be cast over China. So the crackdown, matched by attacks in more than two hundred other Chinese cities where similar protests were held, had a profound effect in Hong Kong. On the morning of June 4, Hong Kong was a cold and lonely outpost of free speech and the rule of law. About a million Hongkongers took to the streets and marched in silent denunciation of the CCP's murderous response to the peaceful protest in Beijing.

Horror at the massacre prompted an emergency debate in the House of Commons in Ottawa. Secretary of State for External Affairs Joe Clark called it a "tragedy and an outrage." Hansard quotes him as saying, "We had hoped and believed that China was on the road to extensive and fundamental reform.... Many among us believed that China would somehow manage the pressure for such change by becoming more democratic, more open and more respectful of its own people." The carnage on the streets, said Clark, had also killed those "positive signs of a nation in the process of change."

While the Canadian ambassador to Beijing, Earl Drake, and his team rushed to arrange the evacuation from China of all among the five hundred or so Canadians in the country who wanted to leave, the government in Ottawa was preparing a raft of diplomatic and economic sanctions against the CCP regime. These included the temporary recall of Ambassador Drake, deferment of regular high-level exchanges, and the cessation of bilateral official visits. A new staff position focusing on human rights was created at the embassy in Beijing. Provinces, towns, and cities suspended their twinned relationships with Chinese counterparts. This was a blow to the United Front, which oversees China's twinning relationships and their capacity for developing infiltration relationships in Canada.

On the economic side, Canada's \$2-billion line of credit to China was halted at the end of June, pending a review. Support by the Canadian International Development Agency for several projects in China was suspended, and approval for new projects was put on hold. Nuclear co-operation consultations were suspended, as was a small defence co-operation program. Radio Canada International began broadcasting into China in Mandarin.

While much sound and fury accompanied the Mulroney government's response to the Tiananmen Square massacre, it signified very little. As Paul Evans has pointed out in *Engaging China*, "While these measures sent signals, they did not derail the engagement train. Ottawa did not cut diplomatic relations or trade, impose general sanctions, or terminate the aid program as members of the opposition and angry citizens' groups demanded." Only three months after the Tiananmen Square crackdown, the Department of External Affairs approved an Export Development Corporation loan to China, and Joe Clark reaffirmed his commitment to engagement. There is, he wrote in the *Toronto Star* on August 5, "no gain to the cause of reform in China to be had from a policy which is 'anti-China.' A poorer and more isolated China is not in the broad interest of the Chinese people."

Direct meetings between Canadian and Chinese officials may have been banned, but bumping into one another in the corridors of diplomatic gatherings elsewhere was another matter. Clark met his Chinese counterpart on the fringes of an international conference in Cambodia in September 1989. In 1991, the minister of agriculture visited China. "China," said former ambassador to Beijing Richard Gorham in a memo quoted by Bernie Frolic, "is a sacred cow that eats Canadian wheat." In 1992, the minister of international trade visited Beijing in what had become a carefully calibrated but purposeful program to revive high-level contacts and business. Mulroney set the objective out clearly at a dinner held at the prime minister's residence in May 1993 for Chinese vice-premier and economics expert Zhu Rongji. Canada, Mulroney said, "would be prepared to fully engage with China in the years ahead." But for domestic political reasons, it would have to do so cautiously because of Canadians' concerns about human rights.

In the end, Mulroney left office before the re-engagement came. That fell to the resurgent Liberal Party, led by Jean Chrétien, which won the election in October 1993. Chrétien held considerable experience of China from his previous posts in Cabinet and, most immediately, through his family. Thus, an early initiative of the Chrétien government was to start planning a major trade mission to China for November 1994. For the CCP, this was a welcome signal that its confinement to diplomatic isolation after the Tiananmen Square massacre was over. For the Liberals, it was another demonstration of Canada's supposed special relationship with the People's Republic of China.

Throughout the 1994 Team Canada mission, Chrétien was repeatedly asked whether he had raised human rights issues in his meetings with Chinese president and CCP secretary general Jiang Zemin. "I'm the prime minister of a country of twenty million people," he responded to reporters on one occasion. "He's the president of a country with 1.2 billion. I'm not allowed to tell the premier of Saskatchewan or Quebec what to do. Am I supposed to tell the president of China what to do?" Chrétien did eventually make a strong statement on human rights, but he reserved it for a speech to a hand-picked audience of students at Tsinghua University in Beijing.

David Mulroney was working on the China desk in Ottawa's department of foreign affairs at the time of Tiananmen Square. The Canadian government's action after the massacre "was the right response, and it taught me two lessons," he said in his 2015 book *Middle Power, Middle Kingdom*. "The first is that some partners are so important that, whatever the disagreement, it is essential to leave at least some of the lines of communication open, if only to understand developments that might have an impact on Canada. The second lesson is that, in the public fury to repudiate all aspects of the now-damaged relationship, you have to be careful that you don't end up punishing people who are part of the solution rather than part of the problem."

EIGHT
SNAKEBITE

China remains one of the greatest ongoing threats to Canada's national security and Canadian industry. There is no longer any doubt that the Chinese Intelligence Services have been able to gain influence on important sectors of the Canadian economy, including education, real estate, high technology, security and many others. In turn, it gives them access to economic, political and some military intelligence of Canada.

— SIDEWINDER REPORT

BRIAN MCADAM WAS a thirty-one-year veteran of the Department of External Affairs in 1991 when he was assigned to the Canadian diplomatic mission in Hong Kong. McAdam has told several interviewers in the years since that he was posted to Hong Kong to root out suspected security problems that appeared to have arisen since Ottawa started the drive to attract immigrants from the British colony in the mid-1980s. A subsequent RCMP disciplinary review committee report tagged the concerns to one incident. There was "a complaint by two Hong Kong residents who indicated they had received an offer to expedite the processing of their visa application from two women who identified themselves as employees of the Mission if they were prepared to make a payment of $10,000 through the intermediary of a local immigration consultant. They declined the offer and complained about it in writing to the Mission but received no response and therefore decided to subsequently complain to the RCMP."

McAdam soon became convinced that corruption was not confined to this one incident but was rampant, especially among locally hired staff, and that entry visas and residency permits were being sold to Hongkongers for large sums of money. He found that about two thousand blank visas were missing, and he also found counterfeit stamps, ostensibly from Canadian diplomatic missions in other parts of the world, used to validate visa documents. This trail led McAdam to evidence that several Triad members had obtained Canadian visas and had moved their families to Canada despite their known criminal backgrounds. He also began to suspect that the computer system had been hacked in order to doctor the biographies of known criminals. McAdam started firing off reports — thirty-two in all — to senior officials in Ottawa, setting out his evidence as it accumulated. But there was no response from his superiors. McAdam says he only truly understood what he was up against when he got a phone call from one of his contacts in the Royal Hong Kong Police Force charged with combating organized crime, which involved monitoring the telephones of known Triad leaders. "What shocked the Hong Kong policeman was that the Triad member had phoned someone in the Canadian immigration minister's office in Ottawa," McAdam said in an interview with the *Ottawa Citizen* newspaper in 2008. "The officer commented: 'With that kind of relationship, you've got a really serious problem.'" Then, said McAdam, the Hong Kong police officer described the Canadian official telling the Triad boss, "Don't worry about McAdam. We'll take care of him."

Whether or not the taped phone call was the stimulus, in 1993 McAdam was offered a major promotion to a post in Ottawa. McAdam accepted and moved home, only to find that the job had been given to someone else and that he had been effectively sidelined. In many interviews, McAdam has admitted that he became obsessed with the evidence he had found of corruption in Hong Kong and that his ostracism affected his health. He was on medical leave for two years and then took early retirement at age fifty-one. There is no doubt that McAdam's fixation and his determination to have his charges acknowledged and thoroughly investigated meant he was easy to discredit.

There were RCMP investigations into McAdam's allegations about corruption in the Canadian mission in Hong Kong beginning in 1992. But, according to McAdam's account, every time an investigator started to get close to verifying the evidence McAdam had collected, the Mountie was reassigned. This happened several times until 1996, when David Kilgour, the Liberal MP for Edmonton-Strathcona, who was also the secretary of state for Latin America and Africa and a noted activist on questions of corruption and human rights, responded to one of McAdam's pleas for an investigation. Kilgour wrote to Prime Minister Chrétien asking for a public inquiry into the corruption allegations. Instead, another RCMP probe was begun. A nineteen-year veteran, Corporal Robert Read, was handed the file and went to Hong Kong. Read spent several months in what was still a British colony reviewing McAdam's allegations, and, according to both men, he found evidence to corroborate many of them. Read also found that all the RCMP reports on McAdam's charges, starting in 1992, consistently falsified McAdam's information and dismissed promising leads for follow-up investigations. When Read pointed out these disparities to his superiors, they were dismissed as isolated acts of incompetence by the Mountie investigators. To Read, it started to look much more like systematic corruption and a thoroughly orchestrated cover-up. But when Read started to press this assessment to his senior officers in 1997, he was pulled off the case. Read accused his superiors of obstructing the investigation, and he was fired. The ex-corporal decided that the national interest overrode the oath of secrecy he had taken as an RCMP officer. In August 1999, Read sought out Fabian Dawson, an eminent journalist with considerable experience of Asia and Hong Kong, who at that time was at *The Province* in Vancouver. Read set out the whole story of the malaise in the Hong Kong diplomatic mission and the lack of response from senior government officials, which Dawson reported in a series of stories in his newspaper after verifying the information as far as possible. Among other allegations, Read said that at least 788 files from the Computer-Assisted Immigration Processing System (CAIPS) had been deleted. Read also confirmed McAdam's claim that about two thousand blank visa forms were missing. Read showed Dawson a copy of a top secret report in which he wrote, "The loss of control of CAIPS ... the loss of control over immigration from Hong Kong ... from 1986 to 1992 is a most serious breach of national security." In a comment to Dawson, Read added, "I believe there has been a massive conspiracy to cover up the whole issue."

Read was charged by the RCMP with breach of his oath of confidentiality and taken before an internal adjudication board. The board found Read's action in going to the media to be "disgraceful," and it also castigated him for providing "false information" to the newspaper. "There is not a shred of evidence of cover-up wrongdoing or of illegal conduct that required public scrutiny," was the board's verdict. Read appealed to the RCMP's External Review Committee and got a very different decision. In its judgment, the committee said it would be quite right to discipline Read for violating his oath of secrecy "unless the member acted to disclose a matter of legitimate public concern requiring public debate." After reviewing all the evidence, the committee concluded, "The Force has consistently demonstrated a reluctance to investigate the activities of LES [locally engaged staff] at the mission." The report looked at Read's examination of the relationship between the LES and the Canadian officers at the consulate. This, said the committee "did reveal that the extent to which gifts, money and other benefits had traded hands was far more widespread than the Force had previously been led to believe by DFAIT [the Department of Foreign Affairs and International Trade] and CIC [Citizenship and Immigration Canada]." The committee decided that the RCMP's response to Read's investigation was "preordained" because the corporal's superiors "did not believe there was any merit in Mr. McAdam's complaint." The review committee concluded that despite having a code of conduct violation lodged against him, Read was still motivated by the desire to have the RCMP properly investigate what was going on in Hong Kong. "Regardless, the disclosure would still have to be regarded as a matter of legitimate public concern because it exposed the fact that the Force had, for seven years, failed to take appropriate action to determine if employees at the Mission had engaged in immigration fraud."

Read's victory didn't last long. The committee's judgment was appealed to the RCMP assistant commissioner, who in January 2004 reversed the verdict and said that Read's dismissal from the force had been justified.

During the same period, McAdam, like Read, was fighting to save his professional and personal reputation. It was a hopeless effort. For four years after his return to Ottawa in 1993 and his eventual parting with the civil service, McAdam went through bouts of depression where he hardly got out of bed for days on end. And in several interviews with diverse media outlets, he freely admitted to becoming obsessed with clearing his name. But he has an eccentric personality that is easily dismissed by the men in suits who thrive in the Ottawa establishment. Veronica Alice Mannix, a documentary filmmaker, interviewed McAdam in the early 2000s while preparing a film, *Whistleblower*, on people who had raised the alarm on government actions despite the inevitable repercussions to their careers.

"[He] lives in a bunker-like house he's built outside Ottawa which functions as a complete entertainment centre, office, and research facility. His capacious, womb-like basement is divided neatly into quadrangles representing his various interests — one is devoted to magic, and features a comprehensive collection of magic books, gadgets and assorted parapher-nalia, all meticulously displayed. Another houses his pool table and his sets of Go, a Japanese game of strategy, and chess," Mannix said of McAdam in the commentary of her film. "A third displays the elaborate charts (twelve in total) he has drawn up over the years detailing the web of cor-ruption and conspiracy he has discovered, linking individuals, companies, governments and secret criminal organizations in Canada and all around the world. The fourth area is devoted to his high-end computer, through which he communicates with an elaborate network of contacts in the world of espionage all around the globe."

It was the games room rather than McAdam's communications centre that led to the next stage in the saga of exposing and documenting the Chinese Communist Party's influence in Canada. In 1994, Peter Lund, a junior officer on the Asia-Pacific Desk at the Canadian Security Intelli-gence Service, was introduced to McAdam by an RCMP officer who had also been involved in gathering information on corruption in the Cana-dian consulate in Hong Kong. The two struck up a working relationship, and McAdam began feeding Lund information about Chinese Triad presence and operations in Canada. Late in 1995, Lund introduced McAdam to his boss, the head of the Asia-Pacific desk at CSIS, Michel Juneau-Katsuya. Juneau-Katsuya had begun his career as an RCMP officer in New Brunswick, then joined CSIS when it was created in 1984 to supplant the troubled and increasingly dysfunctional RCMP Security Service. He was an avid student of Asian cultures and had a fascination with the Japanese game Go. The game is believed to have started in China about twenty-five hundred years ago and can be described as a cross between checkers and chess. It is, however, vastly more complex than either of those games. Go, which translates as "the encircling game," is played on a board marked with a nineteen-by-nineteen grid, and opponents have either black or white pieces called stones. The object is to move stones so as to surround the opponent and force him or her into submission. Unlike chess or checkers, there are no clear moves that lead to visible victory. Go is more a game of psychological victories and defeats. It is a game that flows with the philosophy of the Chinese military strategist Sun Tzu, whose seminal book *The Art of War* was written at about the same time as the development of Go.

Juneau-Katsuya became a regular visitor to McAdam's underground den for games of Go. Inevitably, the two men talked about McAdam's investigations of corruption in the immigration system in the Canadian Hong Kong consulate and the methods that had been used to facilitate the immigration into Canada of Triad members. The situation in Hong Kong was of particular interest to Juneau-Katsuya, who was beginning to assess the implications for Canada of the return of the British colony to Chinese sovereignty in two years' time. Juneau-Katsuya focused on the potential dangers posed for Canada by the troika of CCP intelligence agencies, Hongkonger and Chinese entrepreneurs with strong links to the CCP, and Triad gangs that the CCP had publicly called "patriotic organizations." The material gathered and analyzed by Juneau-Katsuya and his staff, working for the first time since the founding of CSIS with RCMP intelligence officers in Operation Sidewinder, was eventually drawn together in a draft report titled *Chinese Intelligence Services and Triads Financial Links in Canada*. The twenty-four-page draft, classified Secret, was submitted to an internal RCMP-CSIS Joint Review Committee on June 24, 1997, just a week before the return of Hong Kong to China's rule.

It transpired later that the submission of the Sidewinder report set off a bureaucratic storm both within and between CSIS and the RCMP. The result was that nothing happened, much to the frustration of agents who believed in the report's theme that the CCP and its various tentacles represented a threat to Canadian security. As so often happens in Canadian public life, attempts by politicians or officials to hide contentious documents give them added currency. Most of the report was leaked to Canadian journalists in the autumn of 1999.

Sidewinder set out an alarming picture of how Chinese intelligence services and others with close ties to the Beijing regime had managed to infiltrate and influence large areas of Canadian corporate and public life. It said that since the 1980s, more than two hundred Canadian companies had come under the influence or ownership of the CCP and its close associates, giving them control of strategically significant Canadian technology and resources. The report noted large investments in Canadian banks by Hong Kong's premier tycoon, Li Ka-shing, and his son Richard. Macau casino tycoon Stanley Ho was the principal shareholder in the Semi-Tech Corporation of Markham, Ontario, a specialist in secure information systems designed for governments, national defence departments, and police forces. Chinese companies, especially ones in Hong Kong, had invested heavily in Chinese-language media and entertainment industries in Canada, said the report. There was also major Chinese investment in real estate in Canadian cities, notably Vancouver, Toronto, and parts of Montreal. "In itself real estate is not an obvious threat to the security of Canada," said the report. "But it becomes an excellent vehicle to gain access to local politicians and their influence and power." Thus, the rapid growth of investment in Canadian companies by Chinese entrepreneurs with links to the CCP is a challenge to national security, said the report. Suspect Chinese investors' "influence over local, provincial and national political leaders has also increased. In the game of influence, several of these important Chinese entrepreneurs have associated themselves with prestigious and influential Canadian politicians, offering them positions on their boards of directors. Many of these companies are Chinese national companies," noted the report, indicating that as state-owned enterprises, they are under CCP control.

The Sidewinder report went on to describe Beijing's placing of agents of influence in Canadian universities. It pointed particularly at the University of Toronto and the University of Western Ontario. Unfortunately, the two sections billed in the index as "Universities and Research Centres" are missing from the published version. The leaked draft picks up with some detailed accounts of how Chinese intelligence services had used the business ties between the two countries as cover for their operations. One incident was the theft of nuclear technology information from Ontario Hydro, which was found to have been sent by fax to China's State Science and Technology Commission. There were examples of officials from China's Ministry of State Security and from the People's Liberation Army travelling to Canada as members of trade delegations in order to mount intelligence operations or to try to acquire sensitive technology.

Perhaps as important as the story set out in the Sidewinder report was the thoroughness with which it was repudiated by Ottawa government officials and institutions. To a significant degree, the pillorying of Sidewinder has shrunk the public and official appetite to examine the degree to which the CCP has infiltrated Canadian society and obtained influence over matters that affect the Beijing regime.

To be fair, Sidewinder was vulnerable to derision. There were several significant holes in the analysis set out in the draft report. A major one was why Canada is a major target of Beijing for information gathering and the creation of a network able to exert economic and political influence. Happily, Juneau-Katsuya provided an answer in the 2009 book *Nest of Spies*, which he co-authored with Fabrice de Pierrebourg after leaving the intelligence agency. Speaking generally, and not just about China, Juneau-Katsuya said Canada is attractive to foreign intelligence services for four reasons. First, Canada is a repository of advanced technology, which he suggests is more easily accessible to spies than in the United States. Second, Canada has a strong economy that provides both natural resources for export and a significant population of consumers to purchase manufactured imports. Third is the perceived need to be able to manipulate Canada's national and international politics, to try to ensure that immigrants, who are probably dissidents, aren't able to undermine the interests of the regime in the country of their birth. And fourth is military espionage. In the days of the Soviet Union, the Russians found that Canada was an inviting window through which to get at American and other NATO secrets. Beijing now has the same view.

There's a similar description of Beijing's objectives in the book *Chinese Intelligence Operations*, in which former CIA analyst Nicholas Eftimiades says, "Overall, China's intelligence activities support its policy interests by acquiring foreign high technology (for military and civilian uses), identifying and influencing foreign policy trends (such as bilateral policy and trade issues), and monitoring dissident groups (such as democracy advocates and Taiwanese nationals)."

Adding to the drama in the Sidewinder report was the claim that a significant part of the CCP's success was because of the close links between the Chinese security services and the sometimes brutally violent Triads. Several of the famous business people, mostly from Hong Kong, such as Li Ka-shing and Stanley Ho, who had appeared on the Canadian corporate scene in recent years had a darker side. The report claimed they also held senior ranks in the Triads. These allegations have been made on many occasions, most notably by United States Congressional bodies, but no compelling evidence has ever been produced. "By using these alliances, the Chinese government is trying to gain influence on Canadian politics by maximizing their presence over some of the country's economic levers," said the report's summary.

The report has an appendix describing the origins of Triads in the seventeenth century. They began as underground resistance groups fighting for restoration of the deposed Han Chinese Ming dynasty against the invading Manchu Qing usurpers. The Triads failed as Ming insurgents and rapidly evolved into criminal organizations that survived by fostering strict internal discipline, a strong hierarchical structure, lifetime loyalty, and a reputation for merciless violence against opponents. This appendix was taken largely from a report called *Triad and Other Organized Crime Groups*, written by Garry Clement, an RCMP officer based at the Canadian diplomatic mission in Hong Kong, and McAdam, when he was an immigration officer at the mission. Hong Kong was at the time the hub for operations by the Triads, and the Clement/McAdam report was prepared with help from the Royal Hong Kong Police Force. Like Sidewinder, the Triad report was leaked to Canadian journalists. There was a copy in the Southam News Asia bureau files when I took over that office in 1993.

The sheer number of immigrants coming from Hong Kong and Canada's sensitivity to charges of racism made a perfect cover for Beijing to slip in spies and agents of influence. As a result, says the Sidewinder report in its conclusions, "the Chinese leadership appears to be today in a position to developing [sic] a potential influence over the international market and particularly on the Canadian economy and political life of the country." The writers say that it is difficult for them to argue against the influx of people from China and their investment money because "most of it has been done legally. If you look at a single individual, the threat does not seem to be there, but because of their associations and their alliances with China, the facts analysed lead to the believe [sic] that a gain of influence is been [sic] the object of a concerted plan and that could constitute a threat to Canada."

The leaked copy of the Sidewinder report ended with seven recommendations to the CSIS-RCMP Joint Review Committee. The first was that an expanded task force be created, including officials from the Department of Foreign Affairs and International Trade, Immigration Canada, and Revenue Canada, as well as representatives of the RCMP and CSIS. This task force would have three objectives. The first would be to assess the actual control of Chinese companies over the Canadian economy. The second would be "to review who the influential Canadian figures are on the boards of the Canadian companies." This appears to be another of the many typographical and grammatical errors in the leaked draft report. These mistakes apparently occurred because it was written in French, while the leaked version is a poor English translation. The report almost certainly meant influential Chinese figures on the boards of Canadian companies. The third objective would be to liaise with the FBI, which had apparently recently done a similar study in the United States.

The second recommendation was that a series of presentations be given to CSIS regional directorates and RCMP divisions "to alert operational managers to the need to investigate Chinese activities the better to grasp the links among the Chinese Intelligence Services, the triads and entrepreneurs in the service of Chinese companies." Similarly, the third recommendation was to produce a series of presentations on the situation for senior members of the Canadian security and intelligence community. The fourth was to make presentations to officials in "government departments affected by the problem, such as Justice and Industry." The fifth was to review companies that had installed security systems for federal government departments and Crown corporations to find out the real owners of these companies and if they represented a risk to Canada. The sixth was to thoroughly research how much money had been given to Canadian political parties by Chinese-owned companies in Canada. The seventh and final recommendation was to explore and analyze the extent of the involvement of the Chinese government and Triads in the entertainment industry and media in Canada.

The Sidewinder report's content and allegations grabbed the public's attention by themselves, but interest intensified when stories began circulating in the media about why the report had been leaked. They claimed that there had been a strong politically driven effort to close down Operation Sidewinder and ditch the report. The implication was that the report threatened the economic interests of those Canadians who had formed partnerships with Hongkonger and Chinese investors. Allegations of attempts to smother the Sidewinder report added force to the argument that Chinese intelligence agencies had gained undue influence over Canadian public life, apparently to the extent that Beijing was now a direct threat to this country's national security. Mixed in with this were allegations that there had been a heated argument between senior officials in CSIS and the RCMP about the validity of Operation Sidewinder and its proper fate. Senior CSIS officers, it was claimed, found the evidence in the report flawed and badly presented. The RCMP stood by the report and thought it should be the basis of a much broader and more thorough investigation into what Beijing was up to in Canada. To cap it all, there were reports that much of the material gathered in preparation of the Sidewinder report had been destroyed.

The suggestions of a rift between CSIS and the RCMP were credible. CSIS had been created because of the failure of the country's previous anti-espionage organization, the RCMP Security Service, to effectively do its job. In the 1970s, there were many allegations of incompetence and illegal operations by the RCMP Security Service, which led to the calling of a judicial investigation, headed by Justice David MacDonald, which reported in 1981. The MacDonald Commission's main recommendation was that a new civilian security intelligence organization should be created. This was done in 1984, with CSIS requiring judicial approval to get warrants for its surveillance work and being subject to inspection of its work by both the government-appointed Security Intelligence Review Committee and the office of the inspector general. SIRC was designed to examine CSIS's past activities and judge their effectiveness and legal acceptability. The inspector general was tasked with looking at current CSIS operations and giving advice to the solicitor general, and later the minister of public safety, on their legality. The office of the inspector general was disbanded by the government of Stephen Harper in 2012. It is expected to be replaced by a committee of parliamentarians who will have top security clearance and will be informed of current CSIS operations.

The removal of domestic intelligence responsibilities from the RCMP and the creation of a new civilian organization were expected to cause a difficult transition. It was inevitable that some of the founding staff of CSIS would have to be former RCMP officers. It was uncertain how they would react to having to give up the protective camaraderie of the brotherhood of the red serge and work with new recruits to CSIS, many of whom would come from academia, the military, and other quasi-intelligence operations. Not only would the new inductees come from very different institutional cultures than the paramilitary heritage of the RCMP, they would also have very different ways of assembling information and judging its importance. RCMP officers tended to make judgments based on experience and instinct. The new young academics at CSIS looked at what could be nailed down as fact and what unchallengeable conclusions could be drawn from those facts. In many ways, it was amazing that it took more than a decade before the two main founding cultures of CSIS clashed in public.

The public and political clamour for an accounting of the handling of the Sidewinder report became impossible to dismiss. The task fell naturally to the Security Intelligence Review Committee. SIRC looked closely at events surrounding the production of the report, its fate, and the differing views of the RCMP and CSIS. The five members of SIRC at the time were the chair, corporate and commercial law specialist Paule Gauthier; lawyer and corporate director James Andrews Grant; former Ontario premier and interim national Liberal Party leader Bob Rae; former Reform Party member of Parliament Raymond Speaker; and former New Brunswick premier and ambassador to Washington Frank McKenna.

The committee published its assessment of the Sidewinder affair as part of its 1999–2000 Annual Report. SIRC's verdict was damning and was expressed in a forceful tone that was clearly intended to close the door on the controversy. The committee found no evidence of political interference or untoward efforts to shut down the project. "Sidewinder was not terminated," said SIRC. "It was delayed when its product was found to be inadequate." The commentary continued that SIRC "found the [first] draft to be deeply flawed in almost all respects. The report did not meet the most elementary standards of professional and analytical rigour." It was entirely appropriate, said the assessment, for senior CSIS and RCMP officers to move to ensure that future joint projects between the two forces were of a higher standard. Equally, SIRC members found no evidence of a substantial rift between CSIS and the RCMP as a result of the disagreements over Sidewinder.

And they saw nothing suspicious in the fact that "transitory documents" that were part of the assembly process had been destroyed.

SIRC was equally dismissive of the central theme of the first draft and almost contemptuous of the quality of the work that had gone into it: "The committee … found it to be deeply flawed and unpersuasive in almost all respects. Whole sections employ leaps of logic and nonsequiturs to the point of incoherence; the paper is rich in the language of scare-mongering and conspiracy theory."

SIRC then went on to make an essential point: "It is apparent to the committee that, at its core, the Sidewinder first draft lacked essential definitional clarity: if one purports to examine the extent of illegal and threat-based activities allegedly taking place alongside entirely legal and benign ones, it is vital to be able to tell the difference between the two. Sidewinder's first draft drew no such distinctions, providing instead a loose, disordered compendium of 'facts' connected by insinuations and unfounded assertions."

SIRC took the logical next step and compared the leaked Sidewinder first draft with the still secret final version, code-named Echo, which was completed in January 1999 after the disagreements between the RCMP and CSIS had been sorted out. The SIRC report notes that they had been told by a senior RCMP officer the force was "not fully satisfied with the final report" because unlike the first draft it "fails to raise key strategic questions and to outline some of the more interesting avenues for research." However, SIRC "has read both Sidewinder versions and the differences between the two are considerable — the quality and depth of analysis in the final version is far higher than in the draft. Clearly a great deal went on between completing the first draft and releasing the final report many months later."

SIRC's final verdict was that it "found no evidence of substantial and immediate threat of the sort envisaged in the first Sidewinder draft, no evidence that a threat was being ignored through negligence or design, and no evidence that the government had not been appropriately warned of substantive threats where such existed." The committee noted that both the RCMP and CSIS continue to investigate threats to Canada's national security coming from Beijing and elsewhere.

One failing of the first draft of the Sidewinder report, along with the evident incompetence of its production, was that it took far too narrow a view of the efforts of the Chinese intelligence services to infiltrate Canada. It undermined its own credibility through overemphasizing the Chinese Communist Party's links with and employment of the Triads. These links undoubtedly exist, but the drama of the claims of a national government using criminal gangs as its espionage foot soldiers obscured the far more subtle and successful means that Beijing uses to ensure its interests in Canada and other countries.

Although the Sidewinder report was discredited by both senior intelligence officials and the review committee, it is clear from what senior CSIS officials and others have said publicly since that the agency believes the major elements within the report to be true. In the years since the report was written and leaked, other public material has emerged to support the thesis that the CCP has worked assiduously to influence Canadian media, academia, businesses, and political life.

Ironically, in the winter of 1998, just as the first draft of the Sidewinder report was approaching completion, CSIS published among its publicly available documents a study that made some of the same points. The study, published as Commentary No. 72, was by Holly Porteous, an Ottawa-based analyst of security issues. It is called *Beijing's United Front Strategy in Hong Kong*, and it describes how the Chinese Communist Party won over non-communist community leaders in Hong Kong ahead of the 1997 handover. This successful seduction, wrote Porteous, calmed fears in Hong Kong about the transition and enabled the Communist Party to take control without any significant adverse reaction from the territory's six million people. That has changed in the years since, as Beijing has reneged on pledges made in the 1984 Joint Declaration. But in the period immediately after the 1997 handover, the United Front was able "to create a widespread consensus of opinion that the People's Republic of China could make good on its promise to preserve Hong Kong's capitalist system under the so-called 'One Country, Two Systems' rubric," Porteous said. To make the point that she was not just talking about Hong Kong, Porteous writes near the top of her commentary, "The significance of United Front work cannot be overstated. To assess the ramifications of United Front work, it is necessary to understand its nature, the institutions supporting its ventures, its targets, and finally, its expected outcomes. In this context, Canada cannot claim disassociation from the phenomenon, if only because of the sheer size of its Chinese community."

She is quite right, though it is very important to remind readers that it is not only ethnic Chinese who are targets of the United Front and its agents. Non-Chinese Canadians are just as likely to be recruited as agents of influence by the United Front and Beijing's other intelligence services. Indeed, because of naïveté, ignorance, or sheer venality, non-Chinese Canadians are often easy recruits for Beijing. Chinese immigrants are more experienced with the regime most of them have come to Canada to escape.

In her paper, Porteous singles out the state-controlled Xinhua news agency as one of the carriages used by the United Front in Hong Kong in the run-up to the handover to recruit or otherwise engage sympathetic groups and individuals to exercise influence on Beijing's behalf. She does not mention it, but this was also true in the Portuguese colony of Macau, where the staff of Xinhua outnumbered the Portuguese civil service.

(I remember spending an evening talking with a senior Portuguese official at the Clube Militar de Macau and asking him how the Portuguese had avoided the confrontations with Beijing that the British experienced in Hong Kong. The official, a department head, laughed. "Because I always check with Xinhua before I announce a decision," he said.)

Since the Chinese Communist Party abandoned Marxism and Maoism as the pillars of its political legitimacy in the 1980s and embraced a rudimentary form of capitalism to boost the Chinese economy, relations with business classes at home and abroad have become of fundamental importance. Porteous notes that this is "essentially an alliance between two highly conservative groups that have a common interest in preserving the status quo." In other words, business people the world over are natural allies of authoritarian regimes. For Beijing, the first steps to developing a mutually beneficial relationship with the previously despised capitalist classes began in the 1980s with approaches to leading Hong Kong tycoons. They were assured their businesses would not be grabbed or destroyed after the 1997 handover. More than that, they were offered free rein to expand their businesses into mainland China in return for sharing their expertise in running market economy businesses.

Porteous also mentions the United Front's efforts to cement relations with the Hong Kong Triads, which were such a strong element in the Sidewinder report. She quotes a former head of the Xinhua office in Hong Kong, Wong Man-fong, saying in 1997 that he was instructed by Beijing to tell Triad "dragon heads" that the Chinese government "was prepared to turn a blind eye to the triads' illegal activities if they could promise a peaceful handover of the territory on July 1." If they didn't do Beijing's bidding, they would be closed down.

Without the help of the diaspora, Porteous said, Deng Xiaoping, the CCP's paramount leader who launched the market economy revolution in the early 1980s, did not believe China could quickly achieve its economic potential. "In reminding its Diaspora of their duty to the homeland, China has sometimes asked for more than just money and sympathetic words," Porteous wrote. "Inducing Chinese abroad, by threat or by appeal to patriotism, to conduct economic and technical espionage is also the aim of the United Front work." She then cites cases from the United States where immigrant Chinese engineers were persuaded to pass details of secret nuclear technology to Beijing, and how the Chinese government had attempted to influence both American and British elections by using front companies to donate money to favoured politicians. But, Porteous warns, pointing to a study by Australian scholar David S. G. Goodman as evidence, no one should assume that immigrant Chinese somehow constitute Beijing's fifth column in their new countries. Goodman's study of the Chinese diaspora found only weak sentiments toward China among most of the people interviewed. There was, however, a clear warning in Goodman's discovery that "the strongest ties [were] felt by a business elite whose enterprises have exploited familial or native-place ties on the mainland to gain a foothold."

At the end of her commentary, Porteous stepped back from the Hong Kong focus of the paper and looked at the Canadian perspective. She judged that, having regained sovereignty over Hong Kong, Beijing would next turn its attention to Taiwan, the independent island nation that the Chinese Communist Party claims is a renegade province. She foresaw Beijing intensifying its efforts among overseas Chinese around the world to support China's claim to Taiwan. "As the divide and rule tactics that characterize United Front work will form the basis of this campaign, Canada must exercise vigilance to ensure that the rights and freedoms of Chinese-Canadians are not threatened," she said.

NINE
CONTROLLING THE MESSAGE

Simply put, the Chinese government is leveraging technology to quietly export its domestic censorship regime abroad and, by manipulating how observers everywhere comprehend its past, present, and future, it is enlisting them without their consent in an alarming project to sanitize the historical record and globalize its own competing narratives.

— GLENN TIFFERT, *PEERING DOWN THE MEMORY HOLE*

FIRST AS A political movement and then as a ruling regime, the Chinese Communist Party has always put a lot of energy and resources into crafting a benign public image and attempting to bury the evidence of its most brutal and unsavoury activities. In the 1930s and 1940s, the aim was to persuade the United States and its Western allies that the CCP was merely an agrarian reform movement, bent on bettering the lives of China's hundreds of millions of oppressed and poverty-stricken peasants. Any suggestion that the party was actually a Leninist-Stalinist organization with class warfare and the eradication of whole sectors of Chinese society at the top of its agenda was dismissed as hateful propaganda fomented by the Kuomintang regime of Chiang Kai-shek. In the last few decades since economic remodelling began in the early 1980s, and especially since the 1989 nationwide protests and Tiananmen Square massacre, the CCP's objectives have been just as pointed. At home, its aims are to remove or carefully tailor all references in media to matters of political reform, human rights abuses, independent movements with political objectives, regional separatism, local uprisings against the state and the party, economic problems, and environmental degradation. Abroad, the purpose is to take direct or indirect editorial control of all Chinese-language media among the diaspora and to get Western media to focus on the CCP's achievements, not the horrors that litter the path to China's economic, military, and political rise.

The Canadian media has been a target for this intense campaign of thought control, as have newspapers, magazines, and broadcasters in other countries with large populations of immigrant Chinese, such as the United States, New Zealand, and Australia. Until the mid-1980s, most Chinese-language media in Canada, as well as the American market to which it was often linked, was based in Hong Kong and Taiwan. There was little or no influence or ownership from mainland China and the CCP. That began to change around 1985, when the CCP became aware that the influx of immigrants into North America from mainland China was changing the demographic of the diaspora. At the same time, the CCP's Beijing administration had amassed enough of a fortune from its manufacturing industries to be able to lavish large amounts of money on buying and influencing foreign media.

In November 2001, the Washington-based Jamestown Foundation published a report by Mei Duzhe, *How China's Government is Attempting to Control Chinese Media in America.* The report focused on the United States, but all the newspapers referred to were also distributed in Canada or had Canadian editions. The report identified four major Chinese-language newspapers: *World Journal, Sing Tao Daily, Ming Pao Daily News,* and *The China Press. World Journal* is based in Taiwan, *The China Press* is directly controlled by Beijing, and *Sing Tao Daily* and *Ming Pao Daily News* hail originally from Hong Kong.

The *Sing Tao* operation fell into the CCP's grasp in the late 1980s when its then owner, Sally Aw Sian, had a corporate financial crisis and turned to Beijing for help. Since then, a majority share in the Canadian operation has been acquired by Torstar Corp., owners of the *Toronto Star.* The arrangement is that *Sing Tao* has the right to translate and publish stories from the *Toronto Star.* However, Torstar does not seem to keep much of an eye on how its material is used, because several instances have been found of *Sing Tao* doctoring stories to conform with the CCP's view of the world. One notable case consisted of reports in 2008 of unrest in Tibet, where the *Sing Tao* versions bore very little relation to the original *Toronto Star* stories, which contained vehement criticism of Beijing.

In the run-up to the return of Hong Kong to Chinese sovereignty in 1997, the CCP wanted to have a newspaper in the territory on which it could rely to present Beijing's views uncritically. It hit on *Ming Pao Daily News*, which in October 1995 was bought by a wealthy Malaysian surrogate for the CCP, Tiong Hiew King. Tiong, a timber baron, owned Chinese-language newspapers throughout Southeast Asia as well as the *Ming Pao* editions in the United States and Canada. He had close business ties with China, and his newspapers exhibited great sensitivity toward the CCP on issues such as human rights and political reform.

The *World Journal* is owned by Taiwan-based United Daily News, the island nation's most influential newspaper group, and is distributed throughout North America from offices in New York, Boston, Chicago, Dallas, Houston, Los Angeles, Philadelphia, and San Francisco. For many decades, it was the most popular Chinese-language newspaper in North America. Editorially, it leaned toward the views held by the Kuomintang and Chiang Kai-shek's exiled mainlanders on Taiwan. As the pro-democracy and pro-independence movements have grown in Taiwan, United Daily News and its offshoots have appeared less and less comfortable with their traditional position as adversaries of the CCP. In recent years, the company has developed business ties with Beijing, and the results show in the editorial stance of *World Journal*. There have been several reports of Beijing's consulates in various North American cities putting pressure on local *World Journal* offices to temper their coverage and not, for example, carry advertisements related to Falun Gong.

In 1990, the CCP launched a series of newspapers for the North American market that were directly under its control. The *China Press* was established in New York, but it has offshoots in Canada circulating in Vancouver, Toronto, and Montreal. Editorially, *China Press* newspapers are cheerleaders for the CCP regime.

As well as these major publications, there is a plethora of minor Chinese-language free newspapers available, more than thirty in and around Toronto and at least ten in the Vancouver area. But most, if not all, avoid printing any editorial content that would offend Beijing. Many of them, however, provide useful insights into the hierarchies within Chinese Canadian communities because they have a habit of publishing photographs of and mentioning business people or other notables who are in favour with the Chinese consulates.

The story of broadcast Chinese-language media is similar. Cable and digital outlets have allowed the CCP's state television and radio broadcasters direct access to the homes of Chinese-speaking Canadians. Many new immigrants from mainland China simply click on the websites of their familiar programs and bypass Canadian-produced Chinese-language material entirely. This changing demographic of immigration from China has exerted pressures on existing operations such as the Fairchild Media Group, which originated among Cantonese-speaking Hongkongers. The arrival of more and more Mandarin-speaking mainlanders has forced Fairchild to change its programming. "There is definitely a shift happening," Joseph Chan, president of Fairchild Media Group, said in an interview with the UBC student newspaper, *The Thunderbird*, published in April 2015. "The Mandarin audience has a lot of potential. If we want to grow, we need to attract this audience." That has meant change not just in the language but also in the slant of news coverage. The *Thunderbird* story quotes several editors and publishers saying mainlanders are not interested in news focused on Hong Kong issues, such as democratic reform, that have been a staple of these outlets' coverage. And mainlanders often don't agree with the pro-reform, pro-democracy stance of the Cantonese, so the broadcast outlets have had to tone down their coverage.

The result of all this media empire building by the CCP is that Chinese Canadians who want news in Chinese have little ability to tune in to anything that is not influenced by the CCP. The only real options are the newspapers and broadcasters linked to Falun Gong, whose main outlets in Canada and other Chinese diaspora centres are *The Epoch Times* newspaper and New Tang Dynasty TV. And while journalists working for these outlets usually make great efforts to act professionally, Falun Gong is in such a daily battle for survival with the CCP that antagonism inevitably affects their journalism.

The CCP's efforts to dominate Chinese-language journalism in Canada have been hugely successful. But this success has come at a heavy cost: dedicated Chinese Canadian journalists have been fired, threatened with physical attack, or otherwise harassed. Sheng Xue, a prominent investigative reporter who has been the target of CCP retribution for her journalism, gave an interview to *The Epoch Times* in August 2015. "Even though we are in Canada or in Australia or Europe, most Chinese media are under the influence of the Chinese communist regime. This is a very sad reality. Sometimes when you talk to Chinese immigrants, they don't even know what is the universal values of Canada — this is very sad," she said. "A lot of people, even though they have lived in Canada for many years, still have the same communist mentality. This is not good for Canada, it is not good for those people, and it is not good for the Chinese community."

Control and monitoring of Chinese-language media in Canada is usually exercised by China's local diplomatic mission, be it the embassy in Ottawa or the consulates in Toronto and Vancouver, the two cities with the largest immigrant Chinese populations. But the CCP has found that publishers of Chinese-language media can easily be encouraged to self-censor. This is done by either offering business advantages in China or, if the publisher proves recalcitrant, threatening harm to his or her businesses in Canada and China or to relatives in China.

For individual journalists, such as outspoken columnists, there is now a substantial record of their being silenced, either by arranging for them to be fired by their employers, who don't want to get into the CCP's bad books, or by direct threats of physical violence. No one in the Chinese-language media in Canada forgets the story of Albert Cheng.

Cheng was born in Hong Kong in 1946 and trained as an engineer. He immigrated to Canada in 1969 and worked in Vancouver as an aircraft engineer for Canadian Pacific Airways. Cheng is an opinionated and restless man with a strong impulse to get involved in civic issues. He was a major figure behind the creation of the Chinese Cultural Centre in Vancouver. Cheng moved back to Hong Kong in the mid-1980s, where he got involved in publishing Chinese-language editions of international magazines such as *Forbes*, *Playboy*, and *Capital*. He was founder and president of the Chinese Canadian Association of Hong Kong. Like many Hongkongers, Chen was drawn into the democracy and reform movement by the Tiananmen Square demonstrations and their aftermath. In 1994, he started co-hosting a groundbreaking political talk show on Asia Television called *New Tease*. A year later he left to host a breakfast show called *Teacup in a Storm* for Commercial Radio Hong Kong. This rapidly became the most popular program in Hong Kong, with a daily audience of over one million people listening to Cheng flay the territory's establishment for its many sins. As *Time* magazine put it in an article published in September 1998, "Freedom of speech has always been regarded as the canary in the coal mine that is Hong Kong's democracy under Chinese rule. Few people have exercised that freedom with as much gusto as Albert Cheng. For the aggressive, abrasive radio commentator, no subject was taboo, no tycoon too rich and no politician too powerful: Cheng attacked everyone, without fear or favor, and with thundering outbursts of laughter."

What prompted the *Time* article was that shortly before its publication, on August 19, 1998, Cheng was outside the offices of Commercial Radio when he was attacked by two men wielding meat cleavers. They were methodical in their attack, slashing Cheng across his back, arms, and right leg. The style of the attack was in a tradition typical of Triads. It was designed not to kill Cheng but rather to disable him as visibly as possible; this served as a warning to others. It took four and a half hours of surgery to rejoin Cheng's broken bones, flesh, and nerves. It then took two years of physiotherapy for him to be able to walk again. Cheng eventually went back to work at Commercial Radio, but in 2004 the station buckled under political pressure while its licence renewal was in doubt. He was fired. Cheng's response was to run successfully for a seat in Hong Kong's legislature, where he became a champion of free speech and civil liberties.

Cheng is not the only Hong Kong journalist to have been attacked by gangsters. In February 2014, Kevin Lau, former editor-in-chief of the Hong Kong edition of *Ming Pao*, was attacked by two men as he walked to his car. The attack was similar to the attack on Albert Cheng: the attackers used meat cleavers and aimed to cause crippling damage rather than death.

Lau had became a *cause célèbre* among Hong Kong journalists after being fired, apparently for being too vigorous in his hard-hitting reporting on China. Former colleagues and other local journalists mounted street demonstrations protesting his firing. These were part of demonstrations against what are seen as efforts by the CCP to exert control over Hong Kong's media and politics. A month later, in March 2014, the vice-president and the senior managing executive of Hong Kong Morning News Group were attacked while they took their lunch break outside the Science Museum. The attack came just before the group was to launch a new independent news publication. So far, journalists in Canada who have fallen afoul of the CCP have only received threats or been fired from their jobs. But the awful fate of Cheng and others hangs over Chinese Canadian journalists every day as they try to do their jobs honourably and professionally.

As noted above, the *Toronto Star* copy is sometimes censored of content deemed offensive by the CCP before it appears in *Sing Tao Daily*. The *Vancouver Sun* had a similar experience when it launched a Chinese-language Internet edition called *Taiyangbao* at the beginning of 2012. As international affairs columnist for the parent group, Postmedia, I had an office at the *Sun* at the time. *Taiyangbao* was aimed at Chinese speakers not only in Vancouver and Canada but also in China. In planning the digital edition, and with the Chinese market in mind, *Vancouver Sun* editors made contact with the Chinese consulate in Vancouver, which showed great enthusiasm for the project and even offered to help arrange translators for the newspaper. The offer was accepted, but fairly soon after *Taiyangbao* began appearing, readers who read both Chinese and English began complaining about the differences between the two versions. At this point, a *Sun* editor came to me to seek advice. I said the first thing to do was to understand exactly what was happening. I put together a team who read both English and Chinese to prepare a log comparing the contents. Within a few days, the team produced reports showing that the consulate-supplied translators were expunging from the *Sun* copy any references unacceptable to the CCP. Armed with these reports, the *Sun* editors fired the consulate's censors and obtained new translators. But within hours, *Sun* editors noted a dramatic drop in the number of hits on the *Taiyangbao* site. I sent messages to friends and contacts inside China, who quickly reported back that Beijing's censors had blocked access to the site from within China. It was a typical and effective piece of retribution against *The Vancouver Sun* for daring to push back against the authority of the consulate and the CCP. There was also a wider message for those seeking access to the Chinese market: access is provided only so long as you play by the CCP's rules.

There have been occasions when both Liberal and Conservative governments have played by these rules and acquiesced in CCP drives to control or intimidate Canadian media. These examples reveal, perhaps, the depth of the psychological infiltration of Canadian public life that has been achieved by the CCP.

In January 2005, reporters and news organizations in the Parliamentary Press Gallery in Ottawa were preparing for Prime Minister Paul Martin's three-day visit to China, part of a nine-nation Asian tour. Essential to the preparation was getting a working visa from the Chinese embassy. To that end, the Prime Minister's Office helped arrange the paperwork with the embassy for the Canadian journalists, as it always does on these occasions. On January 12, David Ren and Danielle Zhu of New Tang Dynasty TV, a Press Gallery member, got a call from the Prime Minister's Office to say that their visas were ready and they could collect their passports from the PMO. But before Ren and Zhu could collect the documents, officials from the Chinese embassy took them back and cancelled the visas.

The Chinese authorities never explained their action, but Reporters Without Borders, the international press freedom organization, had no doubts. In a press release issued on January 18, 2005, RWB said, "The NTDTV network has some 50 stations throughout the world, of which four are in

Canada. The authorities in Beijing accuse NTDTV of belonging to banned Falun Gong religious movement, which they have branded as a 'diabolical sect.' ... Some NTDTV employees are indeed Falun Gong members, but the network offers a wide range of programming including news bulletins with reports that are very different from the propaganda offered by the state television network CCTV."

The RWB statement went on to say it believed NTDTV was also being targeted by Beijing because of its coverage of issues the CCP found sensitive or embarrassing, such as the cover-up of the outbreak of SARS in 2003. Indeed, it was NTDTV that broke the story of the SARS epidemic.

When Prime Minister Martin was questioned about the exclusion of NTDTV from the press corps accompanying his tour, he said it was a "very serious issue" because for his government freedom of expression and press freedom were "part of our values." Those values were compromised, however, when Chinese president and CCP leader Hu Jintao visited Canada in September that same year: both NTDTV and *The Epoch Times* found their access to events curtailed. In particular, their accreditations to report on a speech by Hu to a dinner in Toronto organized by the Canada-China Business Council were withdrawn because of "space limitations." In response to questions from a *Toronto Star* reporter, a spokesman for the council denied there had been any pressure from the Ottawa government to exclude the two news outlets. "We looked at media that would best serve the interests of our membership," council spokesman Victor Hayes was quoted as saying.

There was, however, direct action by the government of Stephen Harper to exclude *The Epoch Times* and NTDTV from public and media events when Hu Jintao visited Canada again in 2010. Susan Delacourt, of the *Toronto Star*'s Ottawa bureau, reported on June 25 that Chinese diplomats demanded that during the four public appearances of Harper and Hu, media contact be kept to a minimum, and that there be no press conference. More than that, wrote Delacourt, Chinese officials insisted that NTDTV and *The Epoch Times* be kept away from all proceedings. Delacourt said that the Prime Minister's Office, "through negotiations with senior press-gallery sources over the past few weeks, made it clear that they were organizing events to keep NTDTV and *The Epoch Times* at some distance from the Chinese president, as their guests were demanding." Delacourt noted that both news outlets were "accredited members of the Canadian Parliamentary Press Gallery, with all the same access rights as the *Star*, the CBC, CTV or any other media outlet."

The *Epoch Times* got the last laugh on this occasion, despite the ban. It obtained a recording of a speech by the first secretary of the education section of the Chinese embassy in Ottawa, Liu Shaohua, speaking to about fifty Chinese students studying in Canada on Beijing state scholarships. The story quoted Liu as saying the embassy was arranging to cover the hotel, travel, and food expenses of about three thousand people being brought to Ottawa to welcome President Hu. "This time," the newspaper quoted Liu as saying, "for you, all expenses will be paid by us. You do not talk about it outside. Do not talk about it to anyone, except to people in this circle."

The *Epoch Times* said the embassy was arranging a large crowd of Beijing backers because opponents of the CCP had dominated previous visits to Canada. "Liu says when Hu visited in 2005 and was met with protesters, officials in China were furious," said the story. "He complained that during that visit, Canadian authorities did not co-operate with Chinese demands regarding the protesters, but this time he says there were some limited guarantees."

Not all CCP pressure on Canadian media has been through diplomatic channels. In September 2010, Tao Wang, an NTDTV reporter who had come to Canada from China in 2007, told *The Vancouver Sun* he had been threatened by agents of China's Ministry of State Security. Wang told the newspaper he had been getting threatening phone calls for about a month, which had become increasingly harsh to the point of death threats.

The pressure began when MSS agents began visiting clients of a medical equipment company he still owned in China. "They told them that I participated in illegal activities in Canada that are harmful to the national security of China and asked them to stop doing business with my company," the newspaper quoted Wang as saying.

The situation escalated on September 2, 2010, when a man who identified himself as an MSS agent passed a phone number to one of Wang's managers in China with instructions for Wang to call, which he did. "I asked him why he interfered with my business and he said, 'You are a smart man; you should know the reason very well.' Eventually he said, 'Your activity in Canada is a threat to China's national security ...' He said I must stop all activities in Canada, which, in my understanding, is my reporting for NTDTV. This is the only thing I do. He said if I don't follow instruction, they will take further action on my company."

The Vancouver Sun reported that two weeks later, on September 17, an MSS agent relayed another message to Wang via one of his company managers in China. This said that Wang must submit a written guarantee that he would not participate in any political activity in Canada. When Wang ignored this demand, he got another phone call from the MSS agents. "They said, 'You actually think there is nothing we can do to you because you are in Canada?' They also mentioned, 'If you ever go public on this, you are — in Chinese words — seeking death.' I believe it was a very clear message." On the same day, said the *Sun*, two MSS agents went to the offices of his company in China and effectively closed the operation down, putting his ten employees out of work.

Earlier the same year, on March 24, 2010, the director of the Canadian Security Intelligence Service, Richard Fadden, gave a speech to the Royal Canadian Military Institute in Toronto. During a subsequent question and answer session, Fadden was asked about foreign interference in Canada. What Fadden said then set off a storm of argument and recrimination that continues to echo around Canadian public life. "There are several municipal politicians in British Columbia and in at least two provinces there are ministers of the Crown who we think are under at least the general influence of a foreign government," Fadden said. "They haven't really hidden their association, but what surprised us is that it's been so extensive over the years and we're now seeing, in a couple of cases, indications that they are in fact shifting their policies as a reaction of that involvement with that particular country."

Fadden did not identify China as the main infiltrator into Canadian political and public life, but that was the assumption made by almost everyone who commented on his remarks when they became public in June 2010. Much criticism was heaped on Fadden for casting suspicion on the loyalty of Chinese Canadians who had been elected to municipal councils or provincial legislatures. As a result, Fadden was questioned by Parliament's Standing Committee on Public Safety and National Security. The committee's report said Fadden had made "unacceptable statements" and recommended that the government renounce those statements and "apologize to the Chinese Canadian community." The committee also wanted Fadden fired and protocols put in place to ensure that "people occupying higher offices, such as the Director of csis, not be permitted to make public statements that cavalierly cast aspersions on select groups of Canadians."

The matter might have withered and died there except that five years later, on June 16, 2015, *The Globe and Mail* published a story identifying Ontario Minister of Citizenship, Immigration and International Trade Michael Chan as one of the people referred to by Fadden. The newspaper emphasized that Chan was not suspected by csis of treason or of espionage, but reported that the agency had taken "the extraordinary step of sending a senior official to raise the matter at Queen's Park." The story said that information from csis was passed up the reporting line of bureaucrats to the office of then Liberal Premier Dalton McGuinty. Chan's position was reviewed by the provincial Office of the Integrity Commissioner, which found he was in compliance with Ontario's legislation and regulations. Chan vehemently denied the implications of *The Globe and Mail* article and launched a libel suit against the newspaper.

In the course of his public reaction to the story, Chan implied that the attention put on him by csis showed the agency was suspicious of all Canadian minorities. On June 26, a freelance writer for the *Chinese Canadian Post*, Jonathan Fon, published a column criticizing Chan for his broad condemnation of csis. The agency's concerns, wrote Fon, were solely about Chan, not the entire Chinese Canadian community. That did not go down well with some of the newspaper's readers. The *Post*'s editor, Helen Wang, said later she was called into the office of her immediate boss, Joe Zhang. He told her he had received complaints from the Chinese consulate in Toronto and from the *Post*'s proprietor, Wei Chengyi, a supermarket chain owner who was also president of the Confederation of Toronto Chinese Canadian Organizations (CTCCO). Wang said she was instructed to run more articles supporting Michael Chan and to attend and report on a news conference held by the CTCCO to support Chan and to demand that *The Globe and Mail* apologize. She said her working relationship with Zhang continued to deteriorate as she tried to adhere to journalistic standards of balanced coverage. On July 17, Wang was fired. After that, the newspaper added a weekly column by Michael Chan. (The *Chinese Canadian Post* has its roots in the CCP. According to the National Ethnic Press and Media Council of Canada, it used to be called *The Red Army Post* and was mostly printed in Beijing, but around 2013 it was taken over by Wei Chengyi.)

In May 2016, there was a serious example of failure by a Canadian government minister to stand up for freedom of the press and freedom of speech. Chinese foreign minister Wang Yi visited Canada that month, ending with a joint press conference in Ottawa with his Canadian counterpart, Stéphane Dion. Amanda Connolly, a reporter for the online newspaper *iPolitics* (for which I write a weekly international affairs column), asked Dion why Canada was pursuing closer ties with China in the light of Beijing's human rights record. She cited the abduction of Hong Kong booksellers, the detention of Canadian Kevin Garratt, and China's building of military bases on artificial islands in the South China Sea. Dion gave a non-answer, but Wang waded in and launched a rant at Connolly: "I have to say that your question is full of prejudice against China and arrogance where I have heard that come from and this is totally unacceptable." He listed Beijing's economic achievements and said Chinese people were the best judges of human rights conditions in China, not foreigners. "So, I would like to suggest to you please don't ask questions in such an irresponsible manner."

What leapt out at many who watched or read about this episode was that Dion remained absolutely silent, when he should have come to the defence of Connolly and Canadian free speech values. It was not just mainstream Canadian journalists who picked up on Wang's intimidation tactics and Dion's silence. Xin Feng, a Toronto-based writer for the popular Chinese-language news website 51.ca, wrote an article criticizing the Chinese foreign minister for his arrogance and rudeness. Xin quickly became a target for hate comments. Someone posted underneath the article, "Be careful that your whole family doesn't get killed, be careful when you walk outside!" That could be dismissed as just the usual ravings of online trolls, except for the record of attacks on journalists. Another comment under Xin's article said, "Butcher this pig. He's an animal, not a human."

Gao Bingchen, a freelance journalist who for more than a decade wrote regularly for the *Global Chinese Press*, based in the Vancouver suburb of Burnaby, had his column cancelled after he criticized Wang on social media. Gao said he was told by his editor at the paper, "Some people don't want to see your name in the newspaper." Gao, however, made a virtue of notoriety. In his blog posts he hit out at what he called "problematic" leaders of the Chinese Canadian community, alleging corrupt practices. That drew civil suits against Gao, claiming defamation, but also drew support from many in the community and donations to his legal defence fund.

Global Chinese Press again made its own news in July 2017, when the deputy editor, Lei Jin, attempted to run an obituary of Liu Xiaobo, the imprisoned Chinese writer and human rights activist who had won the 2010 Nobel Peace Prize and who died in prison of liver cancer. Senior editors withdrew the obituary Jin had slated to publish and fired him a week later. Si Xiaohong, the owner and president of *Global Chinese Press*, said in an email to *The Globe and Mail* that Jin's firing had nothing to do with the Liu obituary. "Out of consideration of our paper's staff deployment, [the company] made the decision to lay off Mr. Jin," she said.

Back in the mid-1990s, a senior Hong Kong official used to tell an amusing story against herself. She had held a highly responsible financial post in the colonial government, but in a shuffle had been demoted to a senior post in the administration's information department. "Soon after, I went to Beijing where I was greeted with broad smiles and congratulations on my promotion to this senior position in the propaganda department."

That little vignette not only illustrates the importance the CCP places on control over information, it also shows something of the divide in political cultures between Beijing and Hong Kong. And that draws back into focus the CCP's use of Xinhua not only as a source of news reports for both the public and party members but also as an espionage operation.

At around the same time in the early 2000s that the CCP was moving to gain control of Chinese-language media catering to the diaspora in Canada and elsewhere, it also embarked on a major expansion of Xinhua's foreign operations. This included introducing a twenty-four-hour English-language broadcast news station and disseminating highly profitable financial information. Xinhua doubled its overseas offices to about two hundred, employing about six thousand journalists abroad. To achieve this, Xinhua took the unusual step of employing non-Chinese for some positions in the foreign bureaus. Among these was Canadian Mark Bourrie, who had just returned to freelance reporting after two years teaching journalism at Carleton University in Ottawa. Writing about his experience in September 2012 in Ottawa *Magazine*, Bourrie said a chance meeting with Xinhua bureau chief Yang Shilong in 2009 at a Christmas party on Parliament Hill produced an immediate offer of freelance work. Yang told Bourrie that Xinhua was keen to join the burgeoning legions of mainstream media that had found international audiences over the web. The news agency wanted to hire a raft of Canadian reporters to provide political and financial news and analysis for Xinhua's rapidly expanding audiences in China and elsewhere. Bourrie was keen to accept the offer, but he was not naive. Xinhua was well known as a front for Chinese intelligence agencies, and Bourrie didn't want to have his reputation tainted by working for the news service. Before agreeing to work for Xinhua, he talked to a friend of his in the Canadian military. Bourrie's military contact said the secrets of the Canadian Armed Forces were not vulnerable to Chinese spies. The real vulnerability was spies operating in companies and universities involved with the high-tech industry. The friend recommended that Bourrie put his mind at rest by calling the Canadian Security Intelligence Service and asking for advice. This Bourrie did, but he was unable to talk directly to anyone at the service. Instead, he was directed to leave a phone message. He never heard back.

Bourrie's experience is instructive on a number of levels, but two aspects stand out. One is that the ccp's intelligence gathering agencies are just as willing to recruit or otherwise use non-ethnic Chinese as they are Chinese. Another lesson from Bourrie's experience is that there are chaotic aspects to ccp intelligence gathering. That is to be expected when so many amateurs are drafted into the espionage network and so many sources of information are recruited by coercion of one form or another. The ccp's operatives sometimes appear to substitute activity for accomplishment and volume for quality. How much really useful intelligence ends up on the desks of the ccp leaders in Beijing?

Bourrie started work for Xinhua as a freelancer, being paid for each story he filed, but in summer 2010 he negotiated a better deal and was paid a monthly retainer. This coincided with the arrival of Zhang Dacheng as Xinhua's new Ottawa bureau chief. Bourrie wrote that Zhang told him he had been an army officer — many men of his age and education would have done a stint in the People's Liberation Army — and that he had worked for Xinhua in Iraq and East Africa. Zhang's wife, Shi Li, reported on financial affairs for the agency. It rapidly became clear to Bourrie that Zhang was woefully ignorant about democracy in general and the Canadian parliamentary system in particular. "In the two years that I worked for him, he seemed mainly to shuttle from his house in Alta Vista to the Chinese Embassy and to Chinese cultural events around town in his SUV," Bourrie wrote in 2012.

Bourrie doesn't say so directly in his account of his Xinhua interlude, but it is apparent that in hiring the local journalist, Zhang assumed he had acquired access to the corridors of power on Parliament Hill. Bourrie said he would sometimes get excited emails from Zhang demanding that he immediately get interviews about political events with people such as the Speaker of the House of Commons or the Governor General. Zhang assumed from the titles that these were important figures in Canada's day-to-day politics and didn't understand the subtleties of a constitutional monarchy with a parliamentary political system. According to Bourrie, Zhang also wore the blinkers of a child of a one-party state. He dismissed the opposition parties as troublemakers and therefore of no interest.

Bourrie wrote hundreds of run-of-the-mill political and economic stories for the Xinhua wire service. When stories about opponents of the Beijing regime surfaced, Bourrie began to worry about whether Zhang was using him to gather intelligence rather than news. In June 2010, the G20 summit was held in Toronto, and Chinese President Hu Jintao visited Ottawa en route to that meeting. It was an important moment in Sino-Canadian relations. The Conservative government of Prime Minister Stephen Harper had reluctantly been drawn out of its initial suspicion of doing business with the Beijing regime by a concerted lobbying campaign by Canadian business people and academics. Canada had just been named by Beijing as an approved destination for Chinese tourists, and there were prospects of a revival of investment in both directions. But when Hu arrived in Ottawa on June 23, a small group of protesters from Falun Gong lined part of his route into the city. As described previously, the protest was overshadowed by busloads of Chinese university students brought in by the embassy to enthusiastically welcome President Hu. Bourrie was presented with a taste of things to come when Zhang said he needed to know who the Falun Gong protesters were and where they were staying. Bourrie quotes himself as replying, "Canadian reporters don't do that," adding, "the subject was quickly dropped."

This incident, however, had awakened Bourrie to the difference between the regular news reports he filed that would go out on the Xinhua network and material he was asked to provide that would never appear in news reports but would go to CCP officials and intelligence services. Bourrie wrote that in the fall of 2010, Zhang asked him to provide a report on how Canada "governs the religious organizations," how it "restrains evil religions and worship," and how it "restrains racial and tribal discrimination and hostility." After explaining to Zhang that freedom of religion in Canada is guaranteed under the Charter of Rights and Freedoms, Bourrie researched and wrote a story. However, Bourrie later wrote, he got a brusque email from Zhang saying the story Bourrie had filed was not what he wanted. Zhang set out a list of questions he wanted answered, such as which government department was in charge of managing evil cults, how many evil cults there were in Canada at that time, did the government limit or attack the cults, would evil cult practitioners be charged and tried, and how did Canada differentiate between religions and evil cults?

Bourrie's sensitivity about the line between acting as a journalist and acting as a fact gatherer for China's intelligence agencies came to a head when the exiled Tibetan spiritual leader, the Dalai Lama, visited Ottawa in April 2012 to attend the Sixth World Parliamentarians' Convention on Tibet. The Dalai Lama had fled to India in 1959 after China invaded and took over his country in 1951; his continuing international popularity remains a major irritant for the ccp. Prime Minister Harper's decision to meet the Dalai Lama in his office in Ottawa was seen by Beijing as a studied insult. The meeting was undoubtedly intended to be a warning by the Tory government to both its Chinese counterpart and Beijing's supporters in Canada that it was not to be taken for granted. Bourrie reports that he received instructions from Zhang to cover the Dalai Lama's press conference and to use his sources to find out what had been said between Harper and the religious leader during their meeting. "I asked if this material would be used in any kind of news story," wrote Bourrie. "Zhang said no — Xinhua does not report on Tibetan separatists." Bourrie said that he then reminded Zhang that the news conference with the Dalai Lama was open only to accredited members of the Parliamentary Press Gallery, but Xinhua was using that privilege not for journalism but to gather information on critics of the Chinese government. "We were allowed to be there as journalists," Bourrie wrote in an email to Zhang. "We were not working as journalists. We were, by your description, gathering intelligence for China." Bourrie said that later the same day he sent an email to Zhang resigning from Xinhua.

TEN
CONTROLLING THE THOUGHT

They're funding Confucius Institutes in most of the campuses across Canada. They're sort of managed by people who are operating out of the [Chinese] embassy or consulates. Nobody knows that the Chinese authorities are involved. They have organized demonstrations against the Canadian government in respect to some of our policies concerning China.

— DIRECTOR OF CSIS RICHARD FADDEN, MARCH 2010

THE CHINESE COMMUNIST Party has always seen schools, colleges, and universities at home and abroad as critical battlefields in its quest for survival and aggrandizement. The party sees both foreign and domestic academia as portals through which it can acquire important economic and military technologies. Equally beneficial is the use of friendly ties with overseas students and educational institutions to generate foreign political support — or, at worst, acquiescence — now and in the future, when today's students have become tomorrow's movers and shakers. From the start, an essential part of this quest has been the attempt to ensure that educational institutions impart versions of history and socio-political analysis that are in line with the CCP.

In the early years of the CCP regime, skilled foreign supporters were encouraged to come to China to share their knowledge. As well, arrangements were made for foreign students, especially overseas Chinese, to come to Chinese universities to learn Mandarin and the culture of the mother country. Those programs were impeded by the Cultural Revolution in the late 1960s and early 1970s, as was the ability of Chinese nationals to attend foreign colleges and universities. That changed with the end of the Cultural Revolution and the death of Mao Zedong in 1976, followed by the diplomatic and economic opening up of China launched by Deng Xiaoping. Since then, the CCP has focused on Chinese students studying abroad and overseas Chinese students in the diaspora studying at colleges and universities in their own countries.

Agencies were put in place to monitor and control Chinese nationals attending academic institutions in Canada, Australia, New Zealand, the United States, and the United Kingdom. Principal among these agencies are the Chinese Student and Scholar Associations (CSSA). They operate in most universities and colleges around the world where Chinese students travel to study and earn foreign qualifications. They undoubtedly provide an important support service for Chinese students who are far from home and in unfamiliar cultures, but these government-sponsored agencies also have a more sinister purpose, monitoring and controlling the activities of Chinese students studying abroad. Chen Yonglin, a Chinese diplomat in Sydney, Australia, who defected in 2005, provided insight into the extent of operations pursued under cover of the CSSA. In many interviews after his defection, Chen said the CSSA are overseen by the education officers in the nearest Chinese diplomatic missions. As well as monitoring Chinese students, a primary objective of the CSSA is to lobby Western governments at all levels in support of CCP policies on issues including blocking official contact with the exiled Tibetan leader, the Dalai Lama.

Chen said the associations' ties to Chinese diplomats are well known among students, who are accustomed to being under constant surveil-lance at home. They are often drawn into involvement with the CSSA through the prospect of getting favourable reference letters from the Chinese diplomatic missions. There is also the opportunity to fund extracurricular activities and scholarships and get invited to special events. But keeping in the good graces of the missions depends on supporting CCP positions and not getting involved in things of which Chinese diplomats disapprove.

Zhang Lingdi, a computer science student at the University of Ottawa, said in an interview with *The Epoch Times* in July 2007 that she had recently received a sharp warning in an email from an officer of that university's

CSSA. "According to reports from some other students and the investigation done by the association's cadre," read the message, "you are still a Falun Gong practitioner. Watch out."

The same *Epoch Times* story reported a similar incident in April 2006 at the University of Calgary. Members of the university's CSSA received email messages from someone referring to himself as Li Qin and claiming to be a special agent for the Chinese Public Security Bureau, urging association members not to attend a weekly movie show organized by the Friends of Falun Gong club: "Please do not attend this activity. Otherwise your name and photo will be submitted to the Central government."

According to Chen Yonglin, the CSSA have other functions for the Chinese diplomatic missions. "Often, it is not convenient for the Chinese mission to do certain things," Chen said in one interview. "So to use student organizations, with a neutral name, is more effective. Such groups are in fact controlled by the Chinese mission and are an extension of the Chinese communist regime overseas."

In 2004, the University of Toronto CSSA wrote to the City of Toronto, urging the council not to pass a motion recognizing a Falun Gong Day in the city. In 2005, when the Falun Gong-linked New Tang Dynasty TV applied for a license to broadcast in Canada, one of the letters of objection sent to the Canadian Radio-Television and Telecommunications Commission came from the CSSA at the University of Ottawa. In both cases, the wording of the messages sent by the CSSA was identical to letters of objection sent by Chinese diplomats.

Canadian security authorities have occasionally moved against CSSA espionage activities. A good example is the story of Yong Jie Qu, who came to Canada from China in 1991 as a master's student at Concordia University in Montreal. Qu became active in the university's CSSA, and in August 1994, he applied for permanent residence in Canada at the Canadian consulate in Buffalo, New York (at the time, all such applications had to be made from outside Canada). In February 1995, Qu was interviewed by a visa officer, and as a result of that discussion his application was referred to the Canadian Security Intelligence Service. Two CSIS agents interviewed

Qu a year later, in February 1996, and he was seen again in September 1998 by a visa officer who told him his application for permanent residence had been rejected. The refusal letter given to Qu read in part:

At your interview, I expressed to you my serious concerns that there was reasonable grounds to believe that you had engaged in acts of espionage and subversion against democratic governments, institutions or processes as they are understood in Canada. I pointed out that by your own admission during the interview, you had engaged in a consistent pattern of reporting to the Embassy of the People's Republic of China in Ottawa; provided intelligence on the activities of individuals in a Canadian student organization known as the Chinese Students and Scholars Association (CSSA); and attempted to subvert this organization to meet the goals and objectives of a foreign government. At that time, I asked you to disabuse me of my concerns, and advised you that failure to disabuse me of my concern would lead to the refusal of your application.

You responded by denying that you were an agent of a foreign government, but readily admitted to numerous contacts with Chinese diplomats over a protracted period when you were instrumental in "re-organizing" the CSSA. You also admitted that you provided information to Chinese diplomats regarding individual members of the CSSA and admitted further that you were in open disagreement with pro-democracy students of this organization, that you had identified and reported on these individuals to the Embassy, and that you had sought to change the direction of the CSSA using funds provided by the Embassy in support of certain activities, to make it "sensitive to the Chinese Government and Chinese officials." You argued that any congruence between the objectives and policies of the Chinese government and your activities was purly coincidental, and that you acted strictly out of personal conviction. I noted however, that your admitted activities were so clearly those of an agent that your argument lacked all credibility, and that I was obliged to treat your denial as self-serving.

The letter went on to note that Qu had received a rare waiver from the Chinese embassy, meaning that he did not need to attend the classes at Concordia that the Chinese authorities were paying for. The obvious implication, the visa officer's letter noted, was that Qu was a paid full-time spy for the Chinese authorities.

"There are reasonable grounds for me to believe that you are a person who has engaged in hostile and subversive activities on behalf of a foreign government, directed towards gathering information used for intelligence purposes, that relate to the Charter Rights of individuals in Canada," concluded the letter, ending with the judgment that Qu came within "the inadmissible class of persons" under the Immigration Act.

In the early 2000s, as the CCP's confidence in China's re-emergence as a super-power grew, it developed a general strategy of using the attractions of Chinese language and culture in a soft power campaign aimed at foreigners, particularly foreign colleges and universities. Western educational institutions were besotted by all things Chinese at the time. Not only were China, its language, and its culture the chic scholastic disciplines of the moment, it was also becoming clear there was a lot of money in them. Chinese students were already being milked of large international student fees, and boundaries were being pushed on what proportion of foreign students a university could legitimately admit. Specialist institutes within universities were jumping on this profitable band-wagon. Asian studies institutes, often dominated by a Chinese component, began to thrive. Business and management faculties saw that the corporate world was eager for help addressing the Chinese market, of which it had fabulously exaggerated expectations, and it was willing to fund training establishments.

The CCP saw that the door in Western academic institutions was wide open for partnerships with China. What Beijing came up with is ironic, considering that China had only recently emerged from the Cultural Revolution, whose battle cry had been the destruction of the "Four Olds" — customs, culture, habits, and ideas. Central to this feast of iconoclasm was casting aside the feudal templates devised by the scholar Confucius, which had provided China with cultural, political, and administrative cohesion for more than two thousand years. But the CCP realized that when dealing with the Western world, invoking Confucius as the patron saint of modern China would be far more attractive than, say, trying to clean up the ideological corpse of Mao Zedong to make him a presentable champion.

The CCP decided to create a worldwide network of Confucius Institutes in universities, colleges, and schools. The institutes would have Chinese teachers to provide instruction in Chinese language and culture and would be subsidized by enough money from Beijing to make them an attractive proposition for the host institutions. The first trial run of a Confucius Institute was in June 2004 in Tashkent, Uzbekistan. The trial worked so well that just five months later, in November 2004, the first full-fledged Confucius Institute opened in Seoul. By the beginning of 2018, the program's governing body, the Office of Chinese Language Council International, known as Hanban, said there were 511 institutes abroad. There were twelve Confucius Institutes in Canadian colleges and universities and thirty-five Confucius Classrooms in Canadian high schools.

At the start and on the surface, the Confucius Institutes appeared unobjectionable. Chinese officials made much of them being like the cultural outreach organizations operated by several European countries, such as France's Alliance Française, Germany's Goethe-Institut, or the British Council. At the government's end, Hanban's position on the formal structure chart put it under Beijing's Ministry of Education. Thus, the agreements Hanban makes with foreign higher education establishments and district education authorities to provide funding and teaching staff for the institutes and classrooms look like legitimate educational exchange programs. It takes little examination, however, to reveal that the Confucius Institute program is a major CCP international propaganda and espionage operation masquerading as a cultural exchange program. In the October 22, 2009, edition of *The Economist*, Li Changchun, the fifth-highest ranking member of the Politburo Standing Committee, was quoted saying the institutes were "an important part of China's overseas propaganda set-up." It has later emerged that they are much more than that. In most cases they are espionage outstations for Chinese embassies and consulates through which they control Chinese students, gather information on perceived enemies, and intimidate dissidents. At the time of writing, the chair of the Confucius Institute governing council is Vice-Premier Liu Yandong. She is not only a member of the CCP Politburo, she is also a former head of the United Front Work Department. Other senior members of the council are senior CCP officials from the ministries of finance, education, and foreign affairs, as well as from the State Council Information Office, the National Development and Reform Commission, and the State Press and Publications Commission.

The first Confucius Institute in Canada was established in February 2006 at the British Columbia Institute of Technology (BCIT). The opening was a lavish affair. On the Canadian side, among the two hundred guests were federal, provincial, and municipal officials, including the deputy premier of British Columbia at the time, Shirley Bond. The Chinese delegation was even more impressive, led by senior CCP member and minister of education Chen Zhili. Questions soon surfaced about exactly what the BCIT Confucius Institute was up to. Early in 2008, *The Vancouver Sun* education reporter Janet Steffenhagen received copies of receipts for money sent to BCIT from Beijing for the institute, totalling about $400,000. Steffenhagen went to the institute in downtown Vancouver and found "little sign of activity," as she wrote in a story published on April 2, 2008. "Three recent visits by *The Sun* to BCIT's eighth floor found an unstaffed reception desk carrying the Confucius Institute name. On one visit, the entire eighth floor was vacant; on another, classes were in session but all were sponsored by other organizations." In an interview with Steffenhagen, Jim Reichert, the BCIT vice-president, said the college was still gearing up to determine what types of courses would best serve British Columbians hoping to enter the Chinese market. "We're not aiming for big numbers," Reichert is quoted as saying. "The real purpose of the Confucius Institute is to build bridges between the host country, the host institution and China."

Steffenhagen pinpointed some of her questions about the BCIT Confucius Institute in a blog associated with the newspaper that she wrote at the time. "Receipts for about $400,000 were leaked to me, but the total spending could well be more," she posted on April 4, 2008. "I've been told that during that time [since the opening in February 2006], the institute has enrolled fewer than 100 students in part-time programs. BCIT says the number is closer to 250 students, but that includes students who took one-day programs such as Mandarin In One Day. Why would China want to spend so much money on so little action? And how has that money been spent? I don't have the answers because the agreement that BCIT signed with Beijing is secret, as are all financial reports about the Confucius Institute."

There are indeed strong secrecy requirements in the agreements between Hanban and the host institutions, along with stipulations that give Hanban the upper hand in deciding what are and what are not politically acceptable topics for discussion at the institutes. The basic secrecy clause in the agreements is draconian. It reads: "The two parties to the agreement will regard this agreement as a secret document, and without written approval from the other party, no party shall ever publicize, reveal, or make public, or allow other persons to publicize, reveal, or make public materials or information obtained or learned concerning the other party, except if publicizing, revealing or making it public is necessary for one party to the agreement to carry out its duties under the agreement."

Perhaps most bizarre is Article 5 of the standard agreement, which requires activities at the Confucius Institutes to follow the customs, laws, and regulations of China as well as those of the host country. In Canada and all of the Western countries in which Confucius Institutes have been established, this is impossible. There is no equivalence between the rule of law and the social foundation of the Charter of Rights and Freedoms in Canada and what happens in China, where there is no acceptance by the CCP of the rule of law and where the country's constitution is a malleable document that can be acknowledged or not depending on political expediency. Disenchantment with Confucius Institutes at some Canadian universities and schools began because of clashes arising from this clause. A growing number of Canadian academics and administrators began to be concerned that the presence of the institutes in their colleges and universities would debase their reputations for scholastic rigor and excellence.

If the Canadian Security Intelligence Service had not already been interested in the nature of the Confucius Institutes, setting one up at the British Columbia Institute of Technology, one of Canada's major science and technology colleges, certainly caught the agency's attention. Just a year later, in February 2007, CSIS prepared a report that portrayed the institutes as agencies of soft power propaganda ahead of the Beijing Summer Olympics in 2008. An edited version of the report was obtained under the Access to Information Act by the Canadian Press news agency and published in May 2007. The report says the institutes appear to be primarily to promote Chinese language and culture. "In other words, China wants the world to have positive feelings toward China and things Chinese," the report said. "For China to achieve these goals, people must admire China to some degree. While academics debate the relative importance of hard power — tanks, missiles, guns and the like — versus soft power, the People's Republic of China government views the soft power concept as useful."

There must have been sterner assessments of the institutes' objectives in the redacted portions of the report, because even as it was being prepared, CSIS agents were visiting schools and colleges that were making agreements with Hanban. Dawson College in Montreal opened a Confucius Institute in October 2007. Meng Rong, the head of the institute, told a CBC reporter later that CSIS agents came to see her on the day of the opening. It was the first of three interviews in which agents questioned her about the objectives of the institute. "We told them very clearly, [the school] has nothing to do with politics or spying," Rong told the CBC. She said the agents showed her a list of names, but apart from the Canadian ambassador to Beijing, Robert Wright, she didn't recognize any of them. After the CSIS agents came to her home, Rong said she told them she would file a human rights complaint if they didn't leave her alone.

As the Beijing Olympics approached in 2008, the CCP deployed huge resources to try to ensure that China's coming out as a global power was not diminished or besmirched. The event was, of course, a ready-made platform for opponents of the Beijing regime to make their cases. Riots in Tibet against Beijing's oppression and what is seen as cultural genocide began in the capital, Lhasa, in March. They spread quickly to Tibetan populations in Gansu, Qinghai, and Sichuan provinces. Reports in Western media of the riots and the crack-down by authorities became a daily feature of coverage of the run-up to the games.

There was a backlash against Western media by the CCP and its supporters. At the Confucius Institute at the University of Waterloo in southwestern Ontario, Yan Li, an instructor who was also a former Xinhua reporter, launched her own campaign to confront media sympathetic to "Tibetan separatists." She later recounted on a website serving Chinese literature scholars in North America the efforts to get her students to "work together to fight with Canadian media." She devoted class time to explaining to her students Beijing's view of the history of Tibet and the current situation. The scholars' website reported, "Under her influence, some Canadian students bravely debated with anti-China elements on the Internet, some wrote to television stations and newspapers to point out that their reporting was not according to the facts." Yan was quoted as saying that none of this push-back against Canadian and Western views of China's occupation of Tibet would have been possible without the CCP's efforts to establish the Confucius Institutes. "What deeply touched me was that though the state still has many areas still needing urgent improvement, they invest such a huge amount of money abroad to establish Confucius Institutes one by one," Yan said. "From a strategic perspective, perhaps this is a necessary part of the long-term plan, to gain the world's understanding and friendship as China is rising again."

Yan's actions weren't illegal or even blameworthy in Canadian terms. But there are many occasions when the angry reactions of Chinese students to views they hear in Western colleges and universities about past or present events in China goes well beyond what might be considered acceptable. Academic institutions in Australia and the United States, as well as Canada, have experienced unreasonable outbursts from Chinese students against views expressed, sometimes by other Chinese students, sometimes from non-Chinese.

A controversy at the Confucius Institute at McMaster University in Hamilton in southern Ontario was rather different from the experience at the University of Waterloo in 2008. In 2011, Sonia Zhao was assigned by Hanban to move to Canada to teach at the McMaster institute. She said later she was happy to make the move and take up the job. But a year later, she resigned and then complained to the Human Rights Tribunal of Ontario that McMaster University was "giving legitimization to discrimination" because her employment contract forced her to hide her adherence to Falun Gong. A copy of her employment contract, signed in China, was shown to *The Globe and Mail*. It warned teachers "are not allowed to join illegal organizations such as Falun Gong." In an interview with the newspaper, Zhao said in her pre-posting training in Beijing she was told that in discussions with students she should either avoid sensitive topics such as Tibet, Taiwan, and Falun Gong or "say something the Chinese Communist Party would prefer."

The case raised troubling questions for the university administration, especially about the hiring decisions in China, over which they had no influence because of the agreement with Hanban. "We were uncomfortable," McMaster's assistant vice-president of public and government relations, Andrea Farquhar, told *The Globe and Mail* in February 2013, "and felt it didn't reflect the way the university would do hiring." As a result, McMaster decided not to renew the agreement to continue its five-year relationship with the Confucius Institute when the contract with Hanban expired on July 31, 2013.

In the following weeks and months, a campaign against the Confucius Institutes gathered steam. In December 2013, the Canadian Association of University Teachers (CAUT), which represents about seventy thousand professional academics in Canada, passed a resolution calling on all universities and colleges playing host to Confucius Institutes to close the facilities and sever their ties with Hanban. CAUT executive director James Turk said in the statement, "Confucius Institutes are essentially political arms of the Chinese government. They restrict the free discussion of topics Chinese authorities deem controversial and should have no place on our campuses." CAUT's American counterpart, the American Association of University Professors (AAUP), publicly supported the Canadian organization's position. "Allowing any third-party control of academic matters is inconsistent with principles of academic freedom, shared governance, and the institutional autonomy of colleges and universities," said the AAUP statement issued in June 2014. The statement said the AAUP agreed with CAUT's recommendation that Canadian colleges and universities cut their ties with Hanban unless the host institutions are guaranteed control over all academic matters, recruitment of teachers, determination of curriculum, and choice of course texts. Also, Hanban must give all teachers at Confucius Institutes the same academic freedoms as in the host country, and the texts of all agreements between Hanban and the host colleges and universities must be publicly available.

The positions taken by CAUT and AAUP had remarkably little obvious effect. Of the six Canadian universities that sent replies to the CAUT exhortation, only the Université de Sherbrooke said it would be severing ties with Hanban, which it did on December 31, 2013. The university closed its Confucius Institute after months of failed negotiations, saying that the Hanban arrangement no longer met the university's international plans. The University of Manitoba decided not to invite in a Confucius Institute because of concerns about political censorship, which it deftly described in its official responses as "logistical issues." Other major universities such as the University of Toronto and the University of British Columbia didn't contemplate making agreements with Hanban because they already had faculties generating revenue from teaching Chinese language and culture. They didn't need the subsidy or the hassle. Smaller universities with Confucius Institutes judged that the benefits of maintaining their arrangements with Hanban outweighed the threats to their communal order or reputations for academic integrity. At this time, the institutions with Confucius Institute agreements were the University of Regina, University of Waterloo, Brock University, University of Saskatchewan, Dawson College, St. Mary's University, Carleton University, Seneca College, the British Columbia Institute of Technology, the Toronto District School Board, the Edmonton Public School Board, the New Brunswick Department of Education, and the Coquitlam School Board.

In two of those cases — the Coquitlam School Board and the Toronto District School Board — the Confucius Institutes became matters of bitter controversy. The decision by the Toronto District School Board to open Confucius Classrooms in May 2014 set off a loud and angry debate among parents, many of them Chinese Canadians. The matter got murky when the board chair, Chris Bolton, who had been the driving force behind the campaign to do a deal with Hanban, resigned in June. His departure, apparently to take up the direction of a Canadian school in Vietnam, came after *The Globe and Mail* revealed TDSB staff investigated donations for a Toronto elementary school that Bolton had redirected to his own charity before he was elected school board trustee. Bolton's departure left the pro-Confucius Institute faction without a dominant champion. Trustees were deluged with emails and other messages demanding that the board withdraw from the agreement because of the institutes' ties to the Chinese Communist Party and political censorship in their curriculum. Defence of the institutes was just as vehement. The Confederation of Chinese Canadian Organizations in Toronto, which has strong ties to the CCP, told trustees, "Don't make this a political issue. It is about culture and language." In the end, the trustees decided it was about politics. At the end of October 2014, the Toronto District School Board voted to sever ties with Hanban, even though it meant repaying $225,000 it had been advanced by the Beijing government to set up the Confucius Classrooms.

In the case of the Coquitlam School Board, questions about the probity of the trustees arose when it was found that many had taken handouts as part of the Confucius Institute deal. Hanban's arrangement with the board started in April 2008, when Confucius Classrooms were set up in the district; however, in 2012, Hanban agreed to upgrade the program from

Confucius Classroom to Confucius Institute. "We chased the designation because we thought it was important," school superintendent Tom Grant told *The Vancouver Sun* in a story published on February 27, 2012. This higher status would benefit the district's international education program, Grant told the newspaper. It also attracted a good deal of money from Beijing. As an institute, the district would receive $1 million worth of books and about $30,000 to help with community language courses. The district also became eligible for up to $150,000 from Hanban for programs and activities that could include field trips to China for sports teams or school choirs. And it transpired that money didn't only cover trips for students. In December 2017, a local newspaper, the *Tri-City News*, reported, "For the past few years, some trustees, district officials and teachers have been taking 10-day trips during March break paid for by Hanban, an arm of the Chinese government that funds the Confucius Institutes." The newspaper reported Coquitlam School Board chair Kerri Palmer Isaak as saying the trips, "which cost the Chinese government about $8,000 a person, [were] a boon to the school district." School superintendent Patricia Gartland was quoted as telling the newspaper the trips "provide a vital cultural exchange in a globalized world. It's important for students and educators to exchange ideas, and that bilateral exchange will change the world for the better. And I think the Confucius Institute plays an important role in that." This logic did not impress the former chair of the Vancouver School Board, Patti Bacchus. She told the *Tri-City News* the free trips should raise a number of red flags about ethical behaviour, including public servants taking handouts from foreign governments. Bacchus said there should be a lot more scrutiny of Hanban to ensure it is not subjecting Canadians to Chinese government propaganda during these all-expense-paid junkets. "Clearly, there is a conflict of interest," Bacchus said, adding that she didn't buy the excuse that the cultural exchange aspects of the trips justified taking a handout.

Money — the lust for getting it and the fear of losing it — has as much influence over the relationships between Canadian academic institutions and China as it does in the business and political sectors. In 2017, there were several examples of academic publishers engaging in self-censorship or bowing to Beijing's demands to cut or rephrase text on issues on which the CCP holds immovable views, such as Tibet, Xinjiang, Taiwan, and Falun Gong. Kevin Carrico, of Australia's Macquarie University, is quoted in an *Inside Higher Education* article as saying the willingness among Western academic publishers to contemplate self-censorship flows from the assertiveness of the CCP regime and the erosion in the West of support for core liberal-democratic values. "People have come to [the] realization," Carrico said, "that there's no longer any kind of great firewall between academic practice in China and academic practice outside of China. There is this kind of increasing pressure on academics working outside of China, and ironically, I think this increasing pressure is leading people to realize just how problematic the current system is in China."

The number of people in Western academia who have recognized that problem remains limited. Many universities in Canada and elsewhere have made themselves prisoners of the large amounts of money that they are now receiving from international students, especially those from China. With that reliance on revenue from China goes an unwillingness to do or say anything that might annoy the CCP and cause Beijing to turn off the tap. At the same time, the ever-increasing proportion of foreign students being accepted by Canadian universities is beginning to create social frictions within Canada. It becomes more and more difficult for Canadian students to get places at this country's best universities when these publicly funded institutions of higher learning are admitting 30 percent foreign students. And in far too many cases, the qualifications of those foreign students are questionable. A whole industry has grown up in China providing fraudulent paper qualifications for students wanting places in Canadian and other foreign universities and colleges. There are also well-founded judgments that for many of the Chinese foreign students and their families, the prime purpose for getting a foothold in Canada is not education. Education is only a useful by-product, while the principal purposes are moving private wealth out of China and paving the way for Canadian citizenship and passports.

For many Chinese, the first step on that ladder is getting their child into one of the Canadian high schools that have sprung up in China since 1995. In that year, Sherman Jen, an immigrant from mainland China who made a fortune in Hong Kong's textile industry, opened the first of his Maple Leaf International schools in the northeastern Chinese port city of Dalian. The mayor of Dalian at the time was Bo Xilai, whose father, Bo Yibo, was closely associated with the Canada-China Business Council. A 2008 report, *Canadian Offshore Schools in China*, prepared by Hans Schuetze, of the Department of Educational Studies at UBC, for the Asia-Pacific Foundation of Canada, says Jen "convinced the provincial Minister of Education of British Columbia that the export to China of B.C. schools, which use the B.C. curriculum and employ B.C.-certified teachers, would also profit the province since education would be a great door opener to the Chinese market for other B.C. products." The project has been a remarkable business success. A March 2017 edition of *Forbes* reported that Jen's education empire had fifty-six schools in all major cities across China, with twenty-five thousand students enrolled. Ontario was not far behind on the trail blazed by B.C. By 2016, the Ontario Ministry of Education had authorized twenty-one private schools in China to grant credits toward an Ontario Secondary School Diploma. In January 2018, Global Affairs Canada listed eighty-two primary and secondary schools across China that have arrangements with various provinces across Canada to follow their curricula and give credits toward diplomas.

The 2008 Asia-Pacific Foundation of Canada report points out that from the start there was a myriad of cultural, institutional, legal, and administrative problems with the rush of entrepreneurial education into China. A fundamental difficulty, says the report, is the very different objectives of education in China and Canada. Schuetze notes that the province's Ministry of Education mandate is to educate young people for a "democratic and pluralist society." In contrast, the objectives of the CCP are to prepare students for "patriotism, collectivism and socialism." Equally problematic is provincial control of education in Canada, a relic of the difficulties of confederation. "Canadian offshore schools are sponsored, certified and controlled in different ways," says the report. "The resulting differences in standards and procedures, positive in terms of variety and choice, become a problem, for example when some schools acquire the reputation of being low quality. This reputation affects potentially all Canadian offshore schools."

Not least of the regulatory problems has been the variety of policies followed by different provinces toward inspecting and accrediting the schools. B.C. requires that schools it accredits must be inspected every year by Ministry of Education officials and must have an external evaluation every two years. In contrast, once the Ontario Ministry of Education has granted certification, that's it. "They are no longer inspected and evaluated by the Ontario government," said the Schuetze report.

Another conflict is that Chinese students are confronted with trying to get both their Chinese and Canadian high school diplomas. "A completion of the two parallel programs is very demanding. Not many succeed," notes Schuetze. Most students decide to concentrate on their Canadian diplomas. "As a consequence, most graduates go on to Canadian [and other Western] universities and some of the Canadian universities have started considering these offshore schools as feeder schools for their undergraduate programs."

Such is the hunger among Chinese families to get children into foreign universities that administrators of Canadian schools in China are constantly faced with temptations to cut corners and maximize fees. School fees are about $15,000 a year, totalling $45,000 for the three years required to complete a Canadian secondary school program. Over the years, there have been numerous allegations against specific schools in the Canadian school network, many of them launched by expatriate Canadian teachers. The charges have generally been that schools in China are not following the required provincial curriculum, are employing unqualified senior teachers, or are using unethical methods to ensure students obtain diplomas (including teachers accepting money to inflate grades or students being allowed, in return for a fee, to take the same exam repeatedly until they achieve a passing mark).

The Canadian International Academy in Shanghai came under scrutiny by its accreditation partner, the Ontario Ministry of Education, in 2016 after numerous allegations of wrongdoing made by members of the staff. In a May 2016 report on the situation published in the *Ottawa Citizen*, a letter of complaint by fired teacher David May is quoted. "In general," said the letter, "there is a disregard for student interest and they are primarily treated as sources of money, not as people to mentor and help develop. The students, on multiple occasions, have come to teachers expressing that they know that this school is effectively a credit mill. Many parents [of] students who recently graduated complained that they have been cheated and blamed [the school] for not doing enough to support them."

As the Schuetze report said, there is a natural tendency for the reputation of all Canadian schools in China to be tainted by the misdeeds of a few. But the report is equally clear that the conflicts in the two systems make it challenging for a Chinese student to emerge from the obstacle course with a diploma of certifiable value.

At the time of writing in mid-2018, there are more than 350,000 foreign students at Canadian schools, colleges, and universities, over 100,000 more than there were only seven years earlier. A fifth of those students — more than 70,000 — are from China, according to Immigration Canada figures. For many Canadian academic institutions, attracting foreign students has gone well beyond its beginnings as a humanitarian outreach to developing countries and has become big business. For several, it has exceeded even that and has become essential to the health of the bursar's coffers. This has been compounded, according to several studies, by provinces cutting their funding to post-secondary institutions. Early in 2017, the Federation of Post-Secondary Educators of B.C. issued a report saying that per capita funding for the province's domestic students had dropped by 20 percent during the previous sixteen years. Provincial officials dispute that number, but several academic studies set out evidence of declining government grants. Some analysts contend that universities and colleges have had to chase high-paying foreign students in order to make up the shortfall and that provincial departments of education have taken advantage of the situation and cut funding knowing full well the schools would look to foreign students.

A good example of this financial dependence is UBC. In the 2017–2018 academic year, the university expected to bring in $277 million in tuition fees from foreign students — $50 million more that the $227 million from domestic students.

In its annual review of Canadian colleges and universities, published in November 2017, *Maclean's* revealed that just behind UBC's 31 percent foreign students in the first undergraduate year is McGill, with 30.7 percent. Third on the list is Bishop's, with 29.6 percent, and fourth is the University of Toronto at 25.7 percent. The proportion of foreign graduate students is highest at Windsor with 57.2 percent. Newfoundland's Memorial University comes next, followed by Concordia, Regina, Brock, and Waterloo, with the University of Alberta at seventh place with 40 percent foreign graduate students.

Universities Canada (formerly the Association of Universities and Colleges of Canada) publishes the tuition fees charged to domestic and foreign students. These show that for the most popular institutions, fees for foreigners can be five times what Canadian students are charged. For less high-profile universities and colleges, two to three times the domestic tuition fee is more normal. The University of Alberta charges Canadian students about $5,300, while tuition for foreigners is nearly $20,400. The picture is similar at UBC, where foreign students pay up to $30,400 for tuition, compared with around $6,700 for Canadians. At U of T, the fees for Canadian students range from $6,400 to $11,500, depending on the faculty or program, but for foreigners the range is from $31,000 to $42,560. These numbers put U of T and its colleges firmly at the top of the list of most expensive Canadian academic institutions for foreigners.

For many foreign families, particularly Chinese, these fees are acceptable because education is only part of their purpose for sending their children to be students in Canada. The inflated tuition fees can be considered a modern version of the head tax entry fee into Canada that Chinese were charged by the authorities in the nineteenth and early twentieth centuries.

One major reason for having a student in Canada is to facilitate transferring private wealth out of China, where there are severe restrictions on exporting capital. Another is that higher education in Canada is one of the most dependable routes to permanent residence status and then citizenship. About three out of ten foreign students go on to become citizens, which gives them the opportunity to sponsor their parents through Ottawa's family reunification program.

The extent to which foreign money, principally from China, played a part in the extraordinary inflation in property prices in Vancouver and Toronto in the 2010s remains a matter of debate and conjecture. There is evidence, however, from figures gathered by the Canada Mortgage and Housing Corporation, that property bought in the name of Chinese students was part of that phenomenon. A study of home sales in six months in 2015 by urban planner Andy Yam, the head of Simon Fraser University's City Program, found that 70 percent of homes in Vancouver's upscale West Side district were bought by mainland Chinese. Of those buyers, 36 percent gave their occupations as either housewife or student. The average price of the homes bought by students was $3.2 million, and most were paid for outright with cash transfers. The most eye-catching was a mansion in the Point Grey area of the West Side bought by Chinese student Tian Yu Zhou for $31 million.

ELEVEN
BIG MOUNTAIN: GOLD MOUNTAIN

The rapid rise of Da Shan, the Norman Bethune for the 1990s, received the active support of both the Chinese propaganda system and the Canadian government and Canadian businesses, an arrangement of benefit to all parties.

— ANNE-MARIE BRADY, *MAKING THE FOREIGN SERVE CHINA*

We are not going to change our principles or soften our position for the completion of a free trade deal, and we reject the use of political conditions as bargaining chips in a negotiation for an economic agreement.

— CHINESE CONSUL GENERAL IN VANCOUVER TONG XIAOLING

THE CHINESE COMMUNIST Party's changing attitude toward Canadians and Canadian business is neatly encapsulated in the person of Mark Rowswell, a Canadian from Ottawa who became a fluent Mandarin speaker and achieved instant celebrity when he hosted an international singing competition on Chinese television in November 1988. Rowswell's on-air personality, Dashan, meaning "big mountain," was created soon afterwards. He became a fixture on Chinese television and the country's most famous foreigner. Rowswell's forte was the century-old Chinese slapstick comedy routine called *Xiangsheng*, usually translated as "crosstalk." *Xiangsheng* performances are rapid-fire chats between two performers, rich with puns and fast-paced repartee; they have been described as a Chinese version of Abbott and Costello's early vaudeville acts. Rowswell's instant stardom came as much from wonder among the Chinese audience that a foreigner, and a hulking great Canadian at that, could master an art form springing from the country's rough-and-ready street culture. He became a fixture on Chinese television through the 1990s and early 2000s. Rowswell appeared in many educational programs, notably a series teaching Chinese as a foreign language, which was produced by CCTV International. He also made a foray into drama, appearing as American reporter Edgar Snow in a stage play based on *Red Star Over China*.

Canadian diplomats and business people swiftly latched on to the blossoming of Dashan as a commercial brand. Yet there was something a bit unseemly about the fervour with which Canadians scrambled to jump on the bandwagon. It displayed an underlying lack of confidence about dealing with China. It was as though they needed the comfort of a mascot to cling to that reassured them that they really did have a two-way relationship with their Chinese counterparts. In this role, Rowswell was frequently hired as a host or presenter at Canadian-organized commercial gatherings and trade fairs. Indeed, when Prime Minister Jean Chrétien led the first Team Canada mission to China in 1994, Dashan was much in evidence. He was hired to be team attaché by the Canadian Olympic Committee for the Summer Olympics in Beijing in 2008, and he was commissioner general for Canada at the World Expo in Shanghai in 2010. In 2012, Prime Minister Stephen Harper named Rowswell Canada's good-will ambassador to China. In 2014, Rowswell was appointed to a three-year term on the governing council of the University of Toronto. This appointment was renewed for another three years in 2017, and he was also assigned to the university's Asia International Leadership Council. In June 2018, Rowswell was given an honorary doctorate by the University of Alberta.

Few people saw the irony here. Within a generation, the image of Canada presented to hundreds of millions of Chinese had changed out of all recognition. It veered from Norman Bethune, the flawed hero of the CCP's revolutionary war whose dedication to injured fighters and whose death on the battlefield led to his beatification by Mao Zedong, to a TV comedian, albeit a skilled and clever one.

The Dashan phenomenon is part of a broad realignment of Canada's orbit in the solar system of countries of importance to China. More than that, the period from the Tiananmen Square massacre until the present is the time when Canada's quest to fulfill the dreams of the missionaries and social engineers to change China has died. But that message has yet to get through to Canada's political and social evangelical classes, as China's position in respect to a free trade agreement suggests. Ottawa's attempts to include labour, environmental, and other social standards as part of a free trade agreement were rebuffed brusquely by Beijing, as the quotation from Consul General Tong at the head of this chapter shows.

What is more troubling for the future, however, is that Canada in general, and the political classes in particular, do not seem to realize that while Canada has no hope of changing China, the Chinese Communist Party is changing Canada. Those changes are most evident in the business world, where CCP practices of corruption, contempt for the rule of law and the sanctity of contracts, hierarchical arrogance, and disdain for social disparity have deeply infected the Canadian corporate world.

Canada's importance in the eyes of the CCP shrank quickly in the 1980s and 1990s as other countries found themselves orbiting closer to China's sun. This change is evident in the trade figures. Canada was China's fourth largest trade partner at the time of mutual diplomatic recognition in 1970. By 2016, Canada ranked twenty-first, and it is continuing to sink. Canada had served its purpose, opening the door to global society in the 1970s and ending the CCP's international purgatory after the Tiananmen Square massacre with its Team Canada trade mission in 1994. A brusque assessment of the relationship was given by Professor Bernie Michael Frolic, of the political science department at York University, in his September 2011 Asia Colloquium paper, *Canada and China at 40*: "More and more it appeared we were becoming 'a hewer of wood and a drawer of water' for China's burgeoning economy.... After Tiananmen we realized that our presumed influence over China's leaders had been exaggerated. At the time of the millennium it was apparent that China had become a world power, and Canada was no longer one of China's favourite partners."

Canada has continued to be useful to the CCP and its extended family among the red aristocracy, though not as a partner — more as an ATM and safe deposit box for money laundering.

As has already been described, the Canadian Security Intelligence Agency's 1997 Sidewinder report expressed concerns that the CCP was working to gain influence over Canadian politics by investing in Canadian companies. The report tied this campaign by the CCP to the start of the entrepreneur immigration programs in the 1980s and estimated that over two hundred Canadian companies "have passed into Chinese influence or ownership." China's importance as an affordable manufacturing centre grew in the 1980s and 1990s, as Beijing enticed principally Western-owned businesses to relocate their factories to China, where the CCP could provide them with inexpensive facilities and workforces. Most of the people working in the new manufacturing centres had left their rural homes, in defiance of the *hukou* household registration system that requires all Chinese to work where they are officially identified as living. Thus, most people in the factory workforces could be arbitrarily deported back to their villages at any time if they complained about wages or working conditions or pushed back in any way against the regimentation of China's new "open" economy. This state-managed capitalist system garnered vast profits for the state-owned companies associated with the CCP. While some of the money was used to invest in various infrastructure projects within China — energy projects like the Three Gorges Dam, a huge network of roads, airports, railways, and ports, and an extraordinary eruption of city building — much of the money was spent on foreign investment. There were two major targets: one was to secure access to natural resources to feed China's manufacturing industries, whose continued growth since the death of political reform in Tiananmen Square had become the CCP's sole legitimate claim to power; the other was to buy foreign companies whose assets included cutting-edge technologies that China wanted for either economic or military purposes.

The CCP's drive to control access to natural resources is revealing. It says quite clearly that even though Beijing professes to embrace market economics (with Chinese characteristics), in reality it does not. With its roots still firmly anchored in authoritarian Marxism, the CCP doesn't trust the global marketplace. Nor does the party trust private Chinese companies over which it does not exert direct control. The CCP is equally suspicious of foreign companies operating in China. In 2017, the CCP began beefing up its control of both state-owned and private companies. It didn't stop there. The party started expanding its cells operating in foreign companies doing business in China, with the aim of overseeing and influencing the companies' decisions. This was contained in a report circulated by Oxford Analytica, the highly regarded British-based global political and economic risk assessment company, to clients on January 23, 2018.

The report said the CCP is reaffirming that "enterprise is not an independent sector." Until recently, private business had been largely regulated by the state, not the party. But this arm's-length control was not close enough for the increasingly authoritarian regime being crafted by Xi Jinping, who wanted commerce to be controlled by the CCP. In October 2017, a directive ordering party cells to be set up in both domestic and foreign private companies in China was issued by the 205-member Central Committee of the Communist Party of China. The Central Committee is the vehicle through which the orders of the two more senior bodies, the twenty-five-member Politburo and the pinnacle of power, Xi's seven-member Politburo Standing Committee, are relayed.

The Oxford Analytica report said the order reaffirmed the party's role as the vanguard organization of all aspects of Chinese life, including the requirement for "closer guidance of entrepreneurs and demands that entrepreneurs be 'patriotic.'" The report said that as a result of the edict, "Hundreds of stock market–listed state-owned enterprises amended their articles of association in 2017, vowing to consult Party committees on major decisions." At the same time, the Oxford Analytica paper revealed, there were a growing number of party cells being embedded in foreign companies, giving the CCP greater capacity to know about and influence business decisions by those corporations. The new directive said that if there are three or more CCP members within any organization, they should form a party cell. The obligation of those cells, according to Article 46 of the party charter, is "to see to it that the Party's line, principles and policies are implemented."

Since the founding of the People's Republic of China in 1949, the CCP has controlled all major institutions and the appointment to all important positions in the Chinese economic and administrative hierarchy, whether those people were party members or not. That control became more relaxed after Beijing's apparent adoption of market economics in the mid-1980s spurred the growth of private enterprises. As the economy grew by leaps and bounds in the 1990s and early 2000s, the party appeared happy to leave direct control of non-strategic state institutions to the State Council, the public face of the government of China. At the same time, the CCP took little interest in private enterprises because they were too small to be significant or to challenge the economic supremacy of the party-controlled state-owned enterprises. And private entrepreneurs were still tainted by the old communist stigma that they were bourgeois leeches on the working classes. That changed in 2001, when, as part of the drive to join the World Trade Organization, the CCP allowed entrepreneurs to become party members. In any case, because of pervasive corruption in China, many of the new entrepreneurs were already relatives or cronies of CCP officials.

At that time, continued the Oxford Analytica report, only 3 percent of private companies in China had party cells. In the years since, the role of private companies in the Chinese economy has risen, but so have the presence of and control by CCP groups in those companies. The report indicated that of the 3.6 million private enterprises established since 2015, slightly more than half had CCP cells embedded. Within those companies, party members tended to occupy the most powerful positions. The report cited the example of the Internet firm Tencent, where only 23 percent of the staff were CCP members but they occupied 60 percent of the key positions. By 2002, there were party cells in 17 percent of the foreign companies in China. "Today, 70 percent of foreign-funded firms in China [some 750,000 enterprises] have set up Party groups."

The CCP's anxiety about losing control is understandable. The survival of the regime is now based on being able to deliver an ever-improving lifestyle and meeting the growing expectations of its 1.3 billion people. That cannot be done from China's domestic resources, which fall well short of what is needed to fulfill the CCP's promises. There just isn't enough arable land. Only about 11 percent of China's land mass is suitable for farming, representing about 10 percent of the global total of land suitable for agriculture. But China has 20 percent of the world's population. As a result of unregulated industrialization, a great deal of that farming land is polluted by heavy metals. Much of China's agricultural produce is poisonous to one degree or another, and many Chinese people are wary of eating what is for sale in their own markets and stores.

One major cause of land contamination is water pollution. This too arises from unregulated industrialization. Water pollution has reached the level where the water from rivers in most major cities is unsuitable for both agricultural and industrial purposes. In 2006, the State Environmental Protection Administration produced a report saying 60 percent of the water in Chinese rivers and lakes nationwide is not suitable for drinking. In the same year, an article by the Chinese embassy in the United Kingdom stated that about three hundred million people across the country have no access to clean water. Almost 90 percent of groundwater in cities is affected by pollution, as well as 70 percent of China's rivers and lakes. Aquifers have been grossly over-exploited to provide water for exploding urban development, to the extent that parts of several cities, including Shanghai, are sinking into the caverns left by extracted groundwater. China is blessed with one of the world's largest and most varied stocks of mineral resources; however, the country has been so energetic and successful in its mining efforts in recent years that the relationship between production and reserves is now in the danger zone. As a 2014 report by Ernst & Young, *Mergers, acquisitions and capital raising in mining and metals*, set out: "In order to overcome shortages of essential mineral commodities, as well as to secure long-term sustainable supplies for its ambitious economic development strategy, the government of China entitled a number of local state-owned and private companies to actively pursue mining deals throughout the world."

Canada has been only one target. Beijing's state-controlled investment houses and companies have also been on buying sprees in Southeast Asia, Central Asia, Australia, Africa, and Latin America. And China was not the only Asian country eager to invest in Canada. The Asia-Pacific Foundation of Canada's *Investment Monitor Report* for 2017, published in January 2018, says that Japan and Australia were also major investors in Canada in the early 2000s, and together represented 70 percent of the money coming in from Asia-Pacific nations. Japan led the league of Asian investors in Canada in the first third of the period examined by the report, from 2003 to 2016. But in 2008, when China's "Go Global" foreign investment campaign got underway, it quickly overtook Japan and remained the dominant Asian buyer in the Canadian market. The report says that from 2003 to 2007, Chinese state-owned and private companies made twenty-five deals in Canada worth $677 million. Between 2008 and 2012, the number of acquisitions jumped to eighty-two and the value to $21.4 billion. There was another jump, though not so large, between 2013 and 2016, when there were eighty-seven acquisitions, but their value was more than double those of the previous period at $48.9 billion.

According to the report, the main target of Chinese investment throughout the period from 2003 to 2016 was Canadian energy companies and resources. Almost $60 billion of the total investment was in energy companies, with Canadian mining and chemical operations coming in a distant second at just over $9 billion. This single-minded focus by Chinese investors triggered national security concerns in 2013. The Conservative government of Stephen Harper, which had from the start made clear its skepticism about the benefits of over-enthusiastic commercial relations with China, was not as eager as the preceding Liberal governments to receive business investments. In July 2012, Calgary-based Canadian oil and gas company Nexen Inc. announced that it was being taken over by the China National Offshore Oil Corporation (CNOOC) for $15.1 billion, China's largest foreign corporate acquisition at the time. Getting a foot-hold in the

North American oil industry seems to have been something of a hubris-driven quest for CNOOC. In 2005, it had withdrawn an $18.5-billion bid for American oil company Unocal when it became clear American politicians and regulators — traditionally more wary of Chinese investment than their Canadian counterparts — were going to force an interminable approval process. The Nexen deal gained approval from Canadian regulators in December 2012 and from the United States Committee on Foreign Investment, whose agreement was needed because of Nexen's assets in the Gulf of Mexico, early in 2013. But there were many misgivings among members of the governing Conservative Party about the deal. The concern was that it gave CNOOC, an arm of the Chinese Communist Party, ownership of Nexen's assets in the North Sea, the Gulf of Mexico, West Africa, and the Middle East, as well as billions of barrels of oil reserves in the Alberta oil sands.

The Harper government eventually approved the deal, but it announced it would not allow state-controlled companies from any country to take any further majority stakes in the oil sands. The Conservatives then went further and began taking a very cynical view of the takeover of Canadian technology companies by Chinese enterprises, especially when the buyers had links to the CCP.

In July 2015, the Harper Cabinet ordered Hong Kong–based O-Net Communications to abandon its bid to take over a Montreal company specializing in developing secure communications systems. ITF Technologies' website said it offered "a range of robust, high-power components" that are military grade for the defence market. The company had done work for Canada's national cryptology agency, the Communications Security Establishment. This is a key part of the Five Eyes intelligence alliance between Canada, the United States, the United Kingdom, Australia, and New Zealand, set up at the end of the Second World War. The Harper government never publicly explained why it blocked the takeover, but on January 23, 2017, *The Globe and Mail* published what it said was a national security assessment of the deal prepared for Cabinet by the Department of National Defence and the Canadian Security Intelligence Service.

The newspaper quoted the assessment: "If the technology is transferred, China would be able to domestically produce advanced-military laser technology to Western standards sooner than would otherwise be the case, which diminishes Canadian and allied military advantages." The concern of the writers of the security assessment was heightened by O-Net's corporate promotional material, which said the company was 25-percent owned by a subsidiary of the state-owned China Electronics Corporation. Peter Kent, the Conservative Party's foreign affairs critic at the time, who had been chair of the parliamentary Standing Committee on National Defence when the ITF Technologies decision was made, was quoted by *The Globe and Mail* as commenting, "Even a minority control by the Chinese government has to be considered as Beijing-controlled and any Canadian companies they might buy would be under their control."

O-Net launched a legal challenge to the purchase ban, and in a court filing in late 2015 it claimed, "ITF ... does not own any technologies that could be transferred to O-Net Communications that are not readily available in the marketplace." Further court action became unnecessary after the Liberal Party returned to office in November 2015. A year later, in late 2016, the government of Prime Minister Justin Trudeau agreed to review the ban. On March 27, 2017, O-Net issued a statement saying that as a result of the review, Cabinet had agreed to allow the company's purchase of ITF Technologies. There were some provisos; however, these have not been made public. It appears that some conditions on the sale were issued under sections of the Investment Canada Act. These could limit O-Net's scope of operations, security standards, and employee hiring practices, or impose reporting obligations in Canada. Some speculative reports said that the Trudeau government believed ITF Technologies faced dissolution without the O-Net investment. By allowing the purchase, the government thought it was keeping the company and its expertise in sensitive fibre laser technology in Canada.

Observers inevitably saw this decision in the context of the Trudeau government's professed desire for a free trade agreement with Beijing. And the ITF Technologies decision came a few days after the Chinese ambassador to Canada, Lu Shaye, had made a typically blunt comment about aspects of the trade talks: "China will regard as trade protectionism any attempt by Canada to invoke national security to block state-owned firms from buying Canadian companies or doing business with the federal government."

Optimists at the time said the ITF decision did not set a precedent, but that began to look questionable a few months later. In June 2017, the Trudeau government approved the sale of the British Columbia–based satellite communications company Norsat International Inc. to Hytera Communications of Shenzhen in southern China. The Norsat sale immediately rang alarm bells at the United States Congressional U.S.–China Economic and Security Review Commission. And no wonder: Norsat's customers included the U.S. Department of Defence, the U.S. Marine Corps, the U.S. Army, aircraft manufacturer Boeing, the North Atlantic Treaty Organization, Ireland's Department of Defence, the Taiwanese army, and several major media organizations, including CBS News and Reuters. The head of the congressional commission, Michael Wessel, was quoted in Canadian media: "Canada's approval of the sale of Norsat to a Chinese entity raises significant national-security concerns for the United States as the company is a supplier to our military. Canada may be willing to jeopardize its own security interests to gain favour with China, but it shouldn't put the security of a close ally at risk in the process."

There was good reason to be suspicious of Hytera Communications. Even though it appeared to be a private company, 42 percent of it was owned by billionaire Chen Qingzhou, who had a long-standing relationship with China's Ministry of Public Security, the department responsible for China's police forces and thus the frontline agency of the authoritarian state. Hytera had won many contracts to supply mobile and digital radio systems to various Chinese police forces and other agencies of the Ministry of Public Security.

The Trudeau government approved the takeover after conducting only a routine security analysis and not a full-fledged national security review to assess the potential impact of transferring the Norsat technologies outside

Canada. This was odd, especially because earlier in 2017, the British government had conducted a full security review after Hytera made a bid for the Cambridge-based mobile digital radio equipment manufacturer Sepura. As a result, the British government imposed strict limitations on the purchase.

There were other reasons to be suspicious of Hytera. In March 2017, Motorola Solutions, the Chicago-based communications company, launched a lawsuit against Hytera alleging theft of intellectual property and trade secrets. The suit said Hytera had hatched a "deliberate scheme to steal and copy our technology." Hytera did this, said the suit, by luring away three of Motorola's employees in 2008. Up to that point, Hytera had produced only analogue radios, but after the three Motorola engineers — Samuel Chai, Y.T. Kok, and G.S. Kok — joined Hytera, the company developed digital radios "at a very quick pace. Motorola has been building its radios and its reputation for almost a century, and Hytera tried to hijack both in just a few months — and continues to do so today," claimed the lawsuit.

By early 2018, the Liberal government appeared to have perceived that among the general Canadian population, there was a significant group of people deeply suspicious of and uncomfortable with the takeover of Canadian companies by Chinese corporations controlled by the CCP. But the Trudeau government was unable to produce a consistent policy with a clear public message. In March 2018, Minister of Public Safety Ralph Goodale told Parliament the government would not block Chinese company Huawei Technologies from selling smart phones and telecommunications equipment to Canadians. Goodale insisted his government had taken steps to protect Canadians from any attempts by Huawei to use the equipment for espionage. The minister was challenged in Parliament by the Conservative opposition after several American intelligence agencies told the American Senate Intelligence Committee that Huawei smart phones could be used to spy on Americans. The heads of the Federal Bureau of Investigation, the Central Intelligence Agency, the National Security Agency, and the Defense Intelligence Agency all said smart phones, especially those built around the next generation of 5G technology, could be preprogrammed to spy on the user. These warnings were echoed by Canadian experts, including two former heads of CSIS, Ward Elcock and Richard Fadden, and the former head of the Communications Security Establishment, John Adams.

Huawei has been operating in Canada since 2008, and although there have been no reports of problems, several cybersecurity experts caution that the Canadian government has not been as assertive as other countries, especially the United Kingdom and the United States, in testing Huawei's equipment for espionage potential. Huawei is ostensibly a private company founded in 1984 by Ren Zhengfei, a former engineer with the People's Liberation Army and a man with solid ties to the CCP. He was a member of the National Congress of the CCP, and several Western intelligence agencies view his company as a major arm in the party's campaigns of cyber-attacks and corporate espionage. Commenting on the link between the company and the party, former CSIS head Ward Elcock said, "It's hard for me to believe that a company such as Huawei would not do the bidding of the Chinese government and would not build trap doors into its technology on behalf of the Chinese government." Those trap doors would allow CCP intelligence agencies to have access to sensitive data carried on the telecommunications networks. "I would not want to see Huawei equipment incorporated into a 5G network in Canada," Elcock said.

The Huawei story raised even more serious questions about CCP efforts to pillage Canadian intellectual property when, on May 25, 2018, *The Globe and Mail* published a three-page account of the company's activities in Canada. The report, researched and written by Sean Silcoff, Robert Fife, Steven Chase, and Christine Dobby, focused on Huawei's use of research facilities at Canadian universities with the aim of dominating the world market for the next generation of wireless communications, 5G mobile technology. According to the story, since 2008, Huawei has spent about a quarter of its $600-million 5G research and development budget in Canada, and almost nothing in the United States, "where it is viewed as a security concern." That budget includes spending about $50 million in thirteen leading Canadian universities. The company has worked with nearly one hundred professors (and hundreds of their graduate students) who have been given additional hundreds of millions of dollars in grants from the National Sciences and Engineering Research Council of Canada, said the report. Little or none of this taxpayer-funded work is for the benefit of Canadians. A review by *The Globe and Mail* reporters of patents registered as a result of the research shows that "in 40 cases, the academics — whose work is largely underwritten by the taxpayer — have assigned all intellectual property rights to the company."

Adding to the picture of Canada being bought and outfoxed with its own money were details in the report of government and other grants Huawei received. These included a $22.5-million grant from the Ontario government to help the company expand its operations in the province. The Ontario Research Fund granted $740,000 to support a five-year Carleton University research program that generated seventeen inventions and thirteen patents. Huawei also received a 15-percent tax credit on its research and development costs from the federal government and provincial governments in Ontario, Quebec, and B.C.

Scott Bradley became Huawei's vice-president of corporate affairs in 2011, and he emerges in *The Globe and Mail* story as the almost perfect representation of the Canadian businessman most sought by Chinese companies. "Mr. Bradley, [Huawei's] public face, is a tall, gregarious and connected former telecom executive with Bell Canada who has been twice recognized by *The Hill Times* as one of the top 100 lobbyists in Ottawa," the story reports. "He ran unsuccessfully as a Liberal candidate in the 2011 election, serves on the board of the Canada-China Business Council lobby group and is the brother-in-law of Susan Smith, a co-founder of Canada 2020, an influential think tank with close ties to the Liberal government — and which is partly funded by Huawei."

As a result of *The Globe and Mail* story, political clamour grew for Prime Minister Justin Trudeau to instruct security agencies and top policy makers to determine the security threat and economic cost of transferring Canadian intellectual property to Huawei Technologies.

The Huawei story was not the only indication that public skepticism was pushing a sea change in the Liberal government's attitude toward the activities of corporate tentacles of the CCP regime. Early in 2018, the government showed that it had noticed the public's doubts about the benefits of investment in Canada by associates of the CCP and felt obliged to respond. The change of attitude surfaced in Ottawa's reaction to the proposed acquisition for $1.5 billion of one of Canada's largest and most diverse construction companies, Calgary-based Aecon Group Inc., by the Chinese company CCCC International Holdings Ltd. CCCCI is the overseas investment and financing arm of China Communications Construction Company Ltd., one of the world's largest engineering and construction groups. The Chinese company is nearly 64-percent owned by the government; this could lay Aecon open to control and manipulation by the Chinese Communist Party. A group of Canadian construction companies lobbied the government to reject the deal, arguing it could make the domestic market less competitive. The group pointed out that Aecon held contracts for potentially sensitive assets, such as telecommunications infrastructure, nuclear facilities, and the Site C hydroelectric dam in B.C. The counter-arguments were that Aecon's contracts typically consisted of routine work, like burying fibre optic cables or refurbishing turbine generators at nuclear facilities, and therefore wouldn't give CCCCI intellectual property access. In February, the government ordered a security review of the proposed takeover. In March, the two companies put off completion of their deal until July, pending completion of the security review. But near the end of May, the government stepped in and vetoed the takeover. Explaining his action, Trudeau referred to events in Australia in February, when the government restricted foreign investment in land and infrastructure. "One can easily look at the example from a similar investment in Australia where the Australians suddenly realized they had a significant portion of their energy grid ... owned and controlled by a government that is not their own. There are always going to be concerns about the ability of a country to continue to protect and deliver essential services to its citizens in a way that enhances and maintains their own sovereignty," Trudeau told reporters. "We take seriously the work that our intelligence and security agencies do ... and they made a very clear recommendation that proceeding with this transaction was not in the national security interests of Canada."

As was to be expected, the decision drew a curt response from Chinese officials. Lu Kang, a spokesman for the Chinese foreign ministry, said, "We are opposed to political interference under the pretext of national security. We hope the Canadian side can abandon prejudices and create a level playing field for Chinese enterprises." The Chinese embassy in Ottawa chimed in with a statement: "There is no doubt that the decision made by the Canadian government is by no means a good news for the investment co-operation between China and Canada. This will seriously undermine the confidence of Chinese investors."

In the long run, giving pause for thought among state-owned enterprises and other corporations closely linked to the CCP is undoubtedly a good thing for Canada. But the immediate market response to the veto by the Liberal government was confusion, because it appeared to fly in the face of the previously open-handed approach to the takeovers of Norsat and ITF Technologies. It remains to be seen whether the Aecon story has produced new benchmarks that will determine how the Liberal government judges investments in Canada by companies with ties to the CCP. Whether the Huawei and Aecon stories indicate a decisive shift in the Liberal government's stance toward Chinese investment or merely passing political expediency will have major effects on the Ottawa-Beijing relationship. Most immediate will be the effects on the on-again, off-again negotiation of a bilateral free trade agreement.

Even before the May decision on Aecon, Chinese officials had expressed irritation at the attitude of Canadians — not the Liberal government — toward the takeover of domestic companies by what are essentially arms of the Chinese government. In April 2018, the Chinese ambassador to Ottawa, Lu Shaye, while speaking at a symposium on China's $1-trillion Belt and Road Initiative for building infrastructure across Asia, Africa, and Europe, went ranted about Canadian attitudes. "Some people in Canada regard Chinese state-owned enterprises as monsters. These people attempt to weaken the competitiveness of Chinese enterprises by defamation. These approaches are immoral and will be in vain," Lu said. He insisted that

China could be trusted and would act only in the best interests of Canada. "China is not that formidable and we never think of doing anything harmful to Canada," he said. "We hope Canada could adjust its mindset and do not always see China through tinted glasses, nor create barriers for the two countries' co-operation at the excuse of national security."

Yet stories of overpowering investments by arms of the CCP have made Canadians uncomfortable with the idea of a free trade agreement with China. Public opinion polls show that when Canadians are asked simple, un-nuanced questions about whether or not they favour free trade with China, they are evenly split. An Asia-Pacific Foundation of Canada 2016 poll is standard fare. It found 46 percent of respondents were in favour of free trade with China and 46 percent were opposed. But once pollsters start introducing more detail into the questions, such as the gross imbalance between the sizes of the Chinese and Canadian economies and societies and the domination of state-owned enterprises in the Chinese market-place, Canadian respondents become much more wary. For example, a Nanos Research poll published in December 2017 found that 88 percent of respondents were "uncomfortable" or "somewhat uncomfortable" with opening up the Canadian economy to Chinese state-owned companies. There are good reasons for Canadians to be hesitant, because it is evident that the things Beijing and Ottawa want from a free trade deal are very different and, to a large degree, incompatible. Charles Burton, political science professor at Brock University and former Canadian diplomat at the embassy in Beijing, put the dilemma crisply in an article for the Macdonald-Laurier Institute in July 2017. "China's interest in Canada goes well beyond trade to a commitment to establish a 'strategic partnership' between our nations. This encompasses a broad range of non-economic elements, raising the possibility of Canada becoming more economically reliant on Chinese trade and investment," he wrote. "While the Canadian side focuses on promoting prosperity, Beijing sees free trade as a tool to facilitate its overall geopolitical interests, as part and parcel of China's comprehensive rise to power."

When the Liberals returned to office in late 2015, they came with a desire to seek a free trade agreement that contained their own version of geopolitical interests. The Liberals touted what they called a "progressive trade agenda." This envisaged incorporating into free trade agreements matters such as codes of labour conduct, human rights, provisions for the advancement of women, and environmental protection standards. This idea had some traction when dealing with countries with values similar to Canada, such as the free trade agreement with the European Union and the ongoing discussions with Japan. But Beijing signalled from the start that it would have no truck with this notion, which it equated with gross interference in its internal affairs and a demonstration of contempt for its sovereignty. In April 2017, Beijing's newly arrived ambassador to Ottawa, Lu Shaye, made this abundantly clear in an interview with the *Hill Times*. Lu said he objected strongly to "non-trade factors" being included in free trade discussions: "I think it's an insult to democracy and human rights to take them into negotiations. If so, people will ask how much democracy and human rights cost." Somehow, Trudeau and his government didn't get the message. Early in December 2017, the prime minister and a high-level delegation flew to Beijing for what was clearly orchestrated to be a lavish announcement of the start of formal free trade talks. Trudeau and his team wandered around the Chinese capital for a couple of days with little accomplished and no significant announcements. The Chinese balked, as they'd already said they would. What was astounding was that the visit to Beijing was allowed to go ahead when it had been clear for months that there was no mutually acceptable base for beginning talks.

The Chinese Communist Party's position was neatly expressed in the words of Tong Xiaoling, consul general in Vancouver, quoted at the opening of this chapter: "We are not going to change our principles or soften our position for the completion of a free trade deal, and we reject the use of political conditions as bargaining chips in a negotiation for an economic agreement." Except, of course, those political conditions that bolster Beijing's aims in a free trade agreement with Canada. After Trudeau's Beijing embarrassment, most of the Canadian organizations boosting a free trade agreement continued to argue that a deal remained possible if negotiated with care and clear vision. Skepticism was high, however, in some quarters, especially among former Canadian diplomats with experience of postings in Asia. Charles Burton, whose regular writings in various publications provide necessary cold showers for China enthusiasts, has already been referred to. Randolph Mank, who was Canadian ambassador in Malaysia, Pakistan, and Afghanistan before becoming a vice-president of Black-Berry and a fellow at the Balsillie School of International Affairs, wrote a significant essay, *Reassessing Canadian Trade in Asia*, published in January 2018 by the Canadian Global Affairs Institute. Mank's paper began, "China probably did us a favour when it rejected Prime Minister Justin Trudeau's efforts to launch negotiations on a free trade deal in December." The pause, he wrote, gives Canada a chance to think carefully about what sort of relationship with China is best for Canada in the emerging world order. The first thing to grasp is that a free trade deal between Canada and China is "a mismatch of epic proportions and we should not delude ourselves into thinking that it's only about trade. In addition to glaringly obvious differences in geopolitical ambition, ideology, governance, culture, language and so on, we face in China a population nearly thirty times larger than Canada's, and economy more than seven times larger and a trade imbalance more than three to one in their favour."

Canada's central trade objectives with China, Mank said, should be to increase exports to China and to obtain greater access to the Chinese market. But that is not so easy and is politically constrained by the CCP. "China's economy is centrally planned and led by a phalanx of state-owned enterprises, along with favourably treated private businesses, China has a whopping 150,000 SOEs, owned by both the central and local governments." Free trade is a beneficial goal in principle, he continued, but "when one partner has a gross preponderance of the advantage, and a system tilted to ensure that this will always be so, theory yields to practical considerations."

Mank's conclusion is that Canada does not need a full-blown free trade agreement with China. "This quick assessment suggests that, rather than a classic free trade deal, what we really need is a much more aggressive trade promotion program in China to boost [Canadian] exports. On the trade policy side, if we need anything at all, it would be highly nuanced and focused sectoral strategy aimed at boosting our exports to China." Canada should increase its efforts to make trade deals with countries that are willing to accept socially progressive elements, such as the ten nations in the Comprehensive and Progressive Trans-Pacific Partnership and the ten countries of the Association of Southeast Asian Nations. "In the end, while nice to have, a Canada-China free trade agreement is no more make-or-break for them than it is for us."

TWELVE
NEVER MIND THE QUALITY; FEEL THE WIDTH

I am concerned our province under the last administration [the Liberals] has gained an international reputation as a scofflaw; as a jurisdiction where the rules do not apply to white collar crime, fraud, tax evasion, and money laundering, where even if the rules do apply, enforcement is absent.

— BRITISH COLUMBIA ATTORNEY GENERAL
DAVID EBY, DECEMBER 2017

WHILE THE CCP was encouraging Chinese state-owned companies and private businesses to acquire assets overseas in the early 2000s, individual wealthy Chinese saw that this was also a strategy to protect their own fortunes. A 2012 report by Shanghai based consulting and media group Hurun Report Inc., in a joint study with the People's Bank of China, found that 60 percent of China's millionaires and billionaires were either in the process of emigrating or were determined to do so. Another analysis by Hurun Report found that on average, China's wealthiest people keep 20 percent of their assets abroad. In 2015, a story appeared on the website of the state-controlled *People's Daily* newspaper revealing that another study had found more than 50 percent of wealthy Chinese are seeking to emigrate. The story was up on the site for only a short time before CCP officials realized that figure did not inspire confidence in the stability of the regime. The censors moved in, and the story was deleted.

Why are so many wealthy Chinese determined to get themselves and their money out of the country? These are, after all, the red aristocracy, the people who have benefited most from the economic revolution launched by former paramount leader Deng Xiaoping in the 1980s. These are either members of the ruling CCP elite or are close to them through family or business ties. They are the people who ought to feel most secure in the new China, yet they clearly do not. A clear picture of just how powerful is the imperative to have a family member and assets abroad came in a 2014 study by the Communist Party's Commission for Discipline Inspection, the party's internal police force. It found that 91 percent of the 204 members of the party's Central Committee, its third most important body after the Politburo Standing Committee and the Politburo, had close relatives abroad. More than that, the commission then looked at its own members and found that 88 percent of them had close relatives who had emigrated and acquired foreign citizenship.

China has evolved a magnificent, stable culture that survives changes of regime unchanged but that has never managed to produce a government the citizenry can trust. Hiding family assets at home or abroad has a long history. In a country with eternally uncertain politics, it is essential to have resources hidden away beyond the knowledge and reach of whoever holds power at the moment. Starting in about 2005, wealthy Chinese began getting money out of the country in increasingly large amounts and investing it in property, companies, and other assets. This was a particularly uncertain time under the leadership of lacklustre president and party leader Hu Jintao. There was civil unrest across China on a huge scale, but only a few specific incidents came to the notice of (or were able to be reported on by) Western journalists. The Chinese Academy of Social Sciences (CASS), the main research arm of the State Council, kept and for many years published reports on the number of "mass incidents," defined as outbreaks of social unrest by one thousand or more people that required the fielding of riot squads or the People's Armed Police to be quelled. CASS stopped publishing these annual reports when the number became too embarrassing: about 180,000 a year toward the end of the first decade of the new century. But the numbers were still collected, and reports usually seeped out into the public domain. The number remained at about 180,000, or on average nearly 500 major incidents every day, for many years. What made this unrest containable for the CCP was that the riots and demonstrations were always sparked by local incidents. They never generated a national umbrella movement such as the Tiananmen Square students or Falun Gong that could effectively challenge the CCP.

The causes of these five hundred riots a day all arose from corruption of local party officials from a relatively limited list of categories. A major form of corruption throughout China was the requisitioning by local officials of peasant farmers' land, part of corrupt deals with real estate developers to feed China's building boom. Another was owners and managers of failing businesses shutting down factories overnight, absconding with any remaining assets, and leaving their workers without pay or pensions. In the early 2010s, an important shift occurred when the cause of more than half the demonstrations became protests against local factories or other industries polluting the air, water, and soil to levels that were a threat to the health of people living nearby.

A new perspective on the unrest was published in November 2017 by Christian Gobel of the University of Vienna's Department of East Asian Studies. His analysis accepted that there are around 200,000 protests a year in China, but on examination of 74,452 protests from all over China, Gobel disputed the seriousness of most of them. The typical protest involves only a handful of people, said the paper, and few of them turn violent. Most take place in manufacturing hubs around Chinese New Year and involve unpaid wages at a time when workers plan to go home for the holiday. But the report notes a steep increase in the proportion of protests by homeowners — the emerging middle class. These demonstrations are usually because of conflicts with property developers who have failed to live up to their commitments. The development company may have gone bankrupt, failed to return down payments, or just not completed a building on schedule and with the promised quality.

The arrival in power of Xi Jinping in 2012 changed the equation for security within China. On the one hand, Xi's ramping up of internal security and his appeals to hyper-patriotism with his imperialist doctrine of the "China Dream" seem to have quelled unrest. His regime also took significant steps to overcome the country's appalling pollution problems. On the other hand, Xi's uncompromising drive for personal power masquerading as an anti-corruption campaign — in which hundreds of thousands of out-of-favour party functionaries have been disciplined — has reminded everyone in the top echelons of the red aristocracy that in modern China there is no personal security. A second passport and family assets hidden abroad are essential survival tools in Xi's China.

The destinations for wealthy Chinese were countries whose legal systems protect private property, such as the United States, Australia, New Zealand, countries of the European Union, and some places in Southeast Asia, especially Singapore. Canada was a favourite destination because of the Immigrant Investor Program and the open doors for students, as already described. An additional attraction of Canada was the lack of any serious attempts by officials to keep publicly available records of the beneficial owners of property or companies. Canada was an easy place to launder and secrete money. Vancouver and Toronto were favourite destinations to hide money. *Hurun Report* magazine has said that Vancouver in particular was favoured over other target cities such as Sydney, London, and Singapore. The attraction, said the magazine, was its clean environment, relatively short flying time to China, good schools, and established Mandarin- and Cantonese-speaking populations.

A far more pointed analysis was published in March 2017 by Transparency International (TI), the global coalition against corruption, based in Berlin. The report, *Doors Wide Open: Corruption and Real Estate in Four Key Markets*, examined experiences in the United States, Australia, the United Kingdom, and Canada in dealing with floods of money from "corrupt elites." The TI report took as its launch point the findings of the Financial Action Task Force on Money Laundering, a body established by the G7 countries in 1989. In 2013, the task force found that 30 percent of criminal assets confiscated by authorities between 2011 and 2013 had been invested in real estate. This was usually done using shell companies or trusts.

"The ease with which such anonymous companies or trusts can acquire property and launder money is directly related to the insufficient rules and enforcement practices in attractive markets," said the TI report. Among the four countries examined, Canada was judged to have "severe deficiencies" under four of the ten main loopholes used by money launderers. In the other six areas "there are either significant loopholes that increase risks of money laundering through the real estate sector or severe problems in implementation and enforcement of the law."

The report continued, "Transparency International Canada's analysis of land title records found that nearly half of the one hundred most valuable residential properties in Greater Vancouver are held through structures that hide their beneficial owners. Nearly one-third of the properties are owned through shell companies, while at least eleven percent have a nominee [a surrogate to hide the identity of the real owner] listed on title."

The TI report found Canadian requirements for real estate agents, developers, accountants, and lawyers to report "suspicious or large cash transactions" to be full of loopholes. For instance, the Supreme Court of Canada has ruled that it is unconstitutional for lawyers to report on suspected money laundering because it "interferes with the lawyer's duty to keep client information confidential. Given their [lawyers'] role in real estate closings, the lack of an anti-money laundering obligation is a major loophole," said the report.

Canada scores no better on establishing who are the beneficial owners of property. "In Canada, the law and guidelines do not require non-financial professionals involved in real estate closings to identify beneficial owners when conducting due diligence on customers," said TI. This curtain of anonymity provides the perfect cover for red aristocrats to keep assets well away from the prying eyes of the agents of the CCP's Commission for Discipline Inspection.

The Canadian real estate market is just as useful for money laundering by companies as individuals. "In Canada, there are no registration requirements for foreign companies when purchasing property," states the report. "Moreover, Canadian land title offices do not retain information on the beneficial owners of property. Only information about the title holder — which can be a shell company, a trust, or a nominee — is recorded." These rules could have been written for the benefit of money launderers and others intent on hiding assets.

The TI report found that Canada, along with Australia and the United States, puts too much reliance on financial institutions finding and reporting money laundering in the course of their background checks on real estate transactions. This ignores the reality that in these countries, "a large proportion of real estate purchases use cash and so do not require the involvement of a financial institution. This is particularly the case in purchases of high-end property by foreigners." A 2015 report by the Department of Finance identified cash purchases or large cash down payments as major vehicles for money laundering.

Canadian institutions naively expect that real estate agents, developers, and accountants "submit a suspicious transaction report for every financial transaction that occurs or is attempted, if they have reasonable grounds to suspect that the transaction is related to money laundering," says the TI report. However, in a hot real estate market it is extremely optimistic to expect accountants, real estate agents, and developers to look too closely at transactions from which they stand to make large amounts of money. The TI report quoted the Financial Transactions and Reports Analysis Centre of Canada (FINTRAC) as noting there are "minimal" reports of suspicious transactions in the real estate market. There were 127 reports filed by real estate brokers over a ten-year period and 152 by other professionals involved in real estate, such as bankers and securities dealers. "To put these figures in context," said the TI report, "over $9 trillion in mortgage credits were negotiated and approximately 5 million real estate sales took place in this period, 2003–2013." Real estate agents, lawyers, and banks involved in these sales reported only 279 questionable real estate transactions in that decade.

Even if those involved in real estate transactions were driven by the spirits of probity and honesty, their training and responsibilities with respect to matters of money laundering are spotty and inconsistent. The TI report said that in Canada, real estate licences are a provincial responsibility, and there is no common template across the country. In some provinces, applicants are required to take anti-money laundering training in order to get a licence. In other provinces, they are not. The upshot is that there is no universal awareness among real estate agents and brokers across Canada about money laundering and how to respond to it.

The situation is even more opaque for lawyers involved in real estate transactions. The TI report quotes the 2015 Department of Finance Canada report on money laundering: "These lawyers can knowingly or unknowingly provide legitimacy and/or obscure the source of illegally sourced funds ... lawyers and their firms in Canada are not obliged to establish anti-money laundering programmes or conduct due diligence on their clients when involved in real estate transactions." A 2016 report by the Canadian Press news agency "shows that over 60 percent of 800 real estate companies visited and audited by FINTRAC over four years had significant or very significant deficiencies in their readiness to prevent money laundering."

The TI report applauds FINTRAC as the best model among the countries examined for "supervising financial institutions and designated non-financial businesses and professions such as accountants, notaries, and real-estate agents for money laundering." It notes that FINTRAC has increased by one-third its examinations of real estate deals across Canada and has quadrupled its efforts in B.C. "However, there is still a need to strengthen FINTRAC's sector expertise and increase supervision of the real estate sector."

One of FINTRAC's weaknesses is its limited power to apply sanctions or penalties to people who transgress. "Between 2010 and March 2015," said the TI report, "only seven administrative monetary penalties were applied to real estate agents, totalling $197,310, with two agents being publicly named. The fines for non-compliance have typically been in the thousands of dollars, which is lower than a commission on a single sale."

The TI report doesn't put it this way, but the picture it paints is of a Canadian system that goes out of its way to allow and even encourage the use of its real estate market to launder ill-gotten gains and to hide questionable assets. Others have been more forthright. Canada, and Vancouver in particular, has achieved an international reputation as the destination of choice for not only wealthy Chinese but also Chinese criminal gangs to hide their money. The image is so fixed that when John Langdale, of the Department of Security Studies and Criminology at Australia's Macquarie University, gave a talk on money laundering to some of the country's intelligence officers in November 2017, he referred to the "Vancouver model" of transnational crime.

The result of Canada's open door to questionable foreign money was an explosive increase in the prices being paid for houses at the top end of the Vancouver and Toronto markets. This quickly began dragging up the prices for properties lower down the scale of desirability. By 2017, the median price for a home in Vancouver was $1 million. The effects on Vancouver of this incoming torrent of wealth were profound. Above all, it contributed significantly to the perception that Canada was having its traditional social equity taken away and was becoming a country like many others where wealth disparity between a tiny rich elite and the rest of the population creates dangerous societal divides. Some people who were already homeowners or who became flippers made a lot of money buying and selling properties as a result of the feeding frenzy. Wise people cashed in their Vancouver properties at inflated prices and moved elsewhere in Canada, where their profits could buy a bigger and better house with money left over to pad retirement funds. Others, less farsighted, began drawing credit on the supposed value of their homes, perhaps to invest in renovations or simply to finance their chosen lifestyles. Many abandoned investing in fund-based retirement plans. After all, when the money invested in their homes appeared to be growing at 30 percent or more a year, what was the point in putting money into mutual funds producing a measly 5 or 6 percent? However, this left people highly vulnerable to a downturn in the property market. For young people in particular, the inflated market made near impossible the natural Canadian expectation to be able to own a home. By the mid-2010s, the property market in Vancouver was so distorted that companies were beginning to find it hard to recruit or keep staff. Businesses that could began moving to parts of the province or the country not hit by the influx of Chinese money. Vancouver mayor Gregor Roberston said in media interviews in November 2017 that the flood of money hit the lower mainland of B.C. "like a ton of bricks. The big problem we've had is that provincial and federal governments didn't do their job regulating the influx of global capital and the real estate industry, ensuring that taxes were being paid and speculation and flipping was under control." What he didn't say is that all levels of government made money from the bubble caused by the incoming money and weren't inclined to look too hard at the implications of their revenue bonanza.

David Eby, attorney general in the New Democratic Party government that came to office in 2017, addressed this question in a speech on money laundering in Vancouver in December of that year. Eby said he believed the previous Liberal government, led by Christie Clark, had considered cracking down on white-collar crime, fraud, and money laundering, but decided it was more beneficial to leave things as they were. He said it was hard for him to avoid the conclusion that the Clark government thought that a lax attitude toward money laundering gave the provincial economy a competitive advantage. "It is clear, in my opinion, that the previous administration was aware we had a serious and growing reputational issue."

In other words, Eby suspected there was a conscious decision to turn British Columbia into a modern-day Tortuga, because the spinoff money from criminal activities filled the government's coffers. Whether or not that was true, by the time it was clear that the market had become dangerously distorted, it was too late for government to do anything to restore order. Any rules, regulations, or effective tax systems were likely to leave tens of thousands, and perhaps hundreds of thousands, of Canadians shackled to negative equity in their homes and a lifetime of debt. The government imposed a 15-percent foreign buyers' tax, but this had little effect. For many Chinese wanting to store wealth abroad, the tax was inconsequential, and it was easily avoided. One simple way of evading the tax, as the TI report indicated, was to have the property owned on paper by a numbered company registered in a tax haven like the British Virgin Islands. The property could then be sold simply by selling the numbered company, leaving no record in Canada of the new owner.

Restrictions on exporting money from China were intended to be strict. Chinese citizens were allowed to take only the equivalent of $5,000 on any trip abroad and no more than $50,000 in a year. So the clandestine nature of the capital flight makes it difficult to know exactly how much fled the country each year. In the past, estimates from China's central bank, the People's Bank of China, have been some of the lowest of the illegal outward cash flow. In a report in the mid-2000s, the bank is quoted as believing the equivalent of about US$130 billion has been siphoned out of the country since the mid-1990s. The bank reckoned these were the ill-gotten gains of the between sixteen and eighteen thousand corrupt Communist Party officials, business people, and others known to have disappeared abroad in that period. But by most other estimates, US$130 billion during about twenty years is well short of the reality. Indeed, in most of the first fifteen years of this century, that amount was disappearing from China every six months or so. In 2015, US$250 billion fled China in August alone.

Among the most authoritative estimates in recent years was a *Wall Street Journal* calculation published in 2013 that in the twelve months leading up to the end of September 2012, wealthy Chinese illegally slipped US$225 billion out of the country. This was nearly double the flow of US$121 billion direct foreign investment into the country over the same period. Wealth-Insight, a London-based analytical company, estimated in 2015 that wealthy Chinese have a total of nearly $670 billion stashed offshore. Around the same time, the Boston Consulting Group put the total significantly lower at US$450 billion. Some of the most credible numbers come from a Washington-based group that lobbies to close money-laundering loopholes and other pathways for corruption. Late in 2014, Global Financial Integrity said it calculated the total illegal money coming out of China in 2012 at just under US$250 billion and that the outflow since 2003 had averaged US$125 billion a year for a total of US$1.25 trillion over the decade. In 2015, statistics gathered by the People's Bank of China began to catch up with other estimates of the fleeing cash. In May 2015, the bank published financial flow data for the first quarter of the year. A couple weeks later, a major French bank, BNP Paribas, put out a report analyzing the People's Bank statistics. The French bank concluded that in the first three months of 2015, just over US$80 billion fled China illegally, projecting US$320 billion for the whole of 2015. This was up from the US$244 billion in 2014 that the French bank extrapolated from the Chinese government figures that year. In fact, the estimate of US$320 billion for 2015 fell far short of the reality. The Bloomberg financial news agency reckoned that US$367 billion left China in just the fourth quarter of 2015. The last word goes to the Institute of International Finance, which estimates that just under US$1 trillion fled China in 2015.

The tricks used for getting money out of China are many and varied. Where possible, wealthy Chinese try to establish a foreign link that gives them a seemingly legitimate case to put before the authorities for export-ing money in excess of the $50,000-a-year limit. The most trusted route, of course, is by private credit deals with relatives abroad. Those relatives may be emigrants or children studying at foreign schools, colleges, or univer-sities. Canada, like most Western countries, allows people with student visas to open bank accounts, buy property or other assets, and open lines of credit.

Hong Kong is a global banking centre and is a channel much used by wealthy Chinese to get money to other parts of the world. So is Macau, whose casino industry, the largest in the world by far, is set up to facilitate money laundering and the movement of fortunes out of China to destina-tions worldwide. For a while, casinos in Canada, especially B.C., managed to keep the money launderers at bay. But by the mid-2010s, a criminal circle had evolved that provided Chinese high-roller gamblers with loans of cash generated by the street drug trade in Canada, which they used to buy chips in Canadian casinos. The system not only used B.C. casinos to launder drug money, it enabled wealthy Chinese to get money into Canada to buy property or companies. The high rollers, sometimes called "whales," paid in China for the stakes they received in Vancouver, thus evading Chinese restrictions on exporting currency. It quickly evolved into a huge and highly sophisticated business. In September 2017, Postmedia newspapers published the results of a six-month inquiry by reporter Sam Cooper into drug and casino money laundering that focused on an investigation by the RCMP, code-named E-Pirate. The target of E-Pirate was Paul King Jin and the Richmond office of his company Silver International Investment. Based on interviews with members of various police forces and other law enforcement agencies, along with material gathered from freedom of information applications, Cooper described how catering to wealthy Chinese gamblers meshed with laundering the proceeds of drug trafficking. Silver International's business started with funding Chinese high rollers, many of whom were approached in Macau and persuaded to try their luck at Vancouver's casinos. The stories quoted an audit of the B.C. Lottery Corporation by accounting firm MNP LLP as saying Chinese "whale" gamblers were "provided with a contact in Vancouver, either locally [in China] or prior to arriving in Vancouver." The gambler would then "contact the person via phone for cash delivery," with which they bought chips at the casinos. The gamblers would repay the cash advances "through cash holdings in China." When the gamblers redeemed their remaining chips at the casino — and this was part of the objective of the transaction — they would be left with money available for buying assets in Canada. An RCMP inspector told Postmedia that typically, someone from Silver International would meet the Chinese gambler outside the Vancouver casino — the River Rock Casino Resort in Richmond was a favourite — with $100,000 in cash in a hockey bag. It was no great leap to link the bundles of cash being given to the whales to the need of drug dealers to launder cash gathered in their transactions. According to the RCMP officer quoted by Postmedia, Silver International became a hub for laundering drug money and wiring credits around the world. On any given day, drug dealers would take about CAD$1.5 million in cash to Silver International. The cash would be used for loans to Chinese gamblers, and the drug gangs would get credit. "Silver got so sophisticated that it evolved into an operation that could wire funds to Mexico and Peru," said the Postmedia story, "allowing drug dealers to buy narcotics without carrying cash outside Canada, and cover up the international money transfers with fake trade invoices from China."

When the RCMP raided the offices of Silver International in October

2015, officers found detailed ledgers on the office computers indicating that in one year, Silver International had laundered CAD$220 million in cash in B.C. and sent more than CAD$300 million offshore.

These and other media reports prompted Attorney General David Eby to contract the former deputy commissioner of the RCMP, Peter German, to take a close look at money laundering in B.C., especially through the province's casinos. German's report was published in June 2018, and concluded, "Vancouver is a hub for Chinese-based organized crime." It claimed, "A complex network of criminal alliances has coalesced with underground banks at its centre. Money is laundered from Vancouver into and out of China and to other locations, including Mexico and Colombia."

The report said the province's "dysfunctional" regulatory system for casinos — a responsibility shared between the B.C. Lottery Corporation and the gaming and enforcement branch of the provincial government — was an open invitation to money launderers. This created a situation where provincial politicians didn't want to look too closely at what was going on in the casinos because they were making so much money from their cut of casino gambling. Provincial revenues from casinos became second only to general taxes.

The growing use of credit and debit cards in China has been a great help in the movement of money offshore. Shops and stores in many cities frequented by wealthy Chinese visitors, including Vancouver and Toronto, are often willing, for a fee, to give out large amounts of cash along with fake credit card receipts to be shown to Chinese customs. A surprisingly simple method of getting illicit money out of China is to pack it in a suitcase, bribe the customs officials, and get on a plane. Canada is a preferred destination for suitcase cash because it is hard for the Canada Border Services Agency to find reasons to decide the money may be the proceeds of a crime and should therefore be seized. If the money is declared, it will almost always been allowed in. If the passenger neglects to declare that he or she is carrying more than $10,000 and the cash is found but determined not to be the proceeds of a crime, the fines, especially for a first offence, are minimal. With the fine paid, the passenger is generally allowed to bring the money into Canada, unlike in the United States, where undeclared money is often confiscated.

Vast as the sums of private money leaving China are, by far the largest volume of money coming out of the country travels through business networks. And the most common way of duping the Chinese authorities and getting permission to move money overseas is by false invoicing. For Chinese business people who have established their own subsidiary companies abroad, the process is simple. They can simply inflate the expenses of running the overseas operation and thus move assets into foreign accounts. Similarly, when buying goods and services abroad, their partners may be asked to provide false invoices indicating higher prices. Several analyses, including one by Global Financial Integrity, suggest that false invoicing is the method used for at least 60 percent of the money fleeing China.

Of course, those at the top of the Communist Party food chain have the most reliable and secure routes available for exporting their wealth. In 2017, the International Consortium of Investigative Journalists received copies of millions of confidential electronic files, known as the Paradise Papers, from companies specializing in helping people establish trusts and companies in tax havens. Among the files from Singapore-based Portcullis TrustNet and British Virgin Islands-based Commonwealth Trust Limited were twenty-two thousand involving clients from mainland China and Hong Kong with assets stowed in tax havens. The list included the names of many of the red aristocracy, including the brother-in-law of President Xi, the son of former premier Wen Jiabao, and the first cousin of former president Hu Jintao. In all, the list included close relatives of at least five of the seven members of the Politburo Standing Committee and the heads of most of the major companies in China. According to the British Virgin Island authorities, 40 percent of their offshore business comes from Asia, principally China.

With the earlier leak of the so-called Panama Papers in 2016, the public had learned a lot more about not only tax avoidance and evasion schemes but also the anonymity afforded by numbered accounts in tax havens like the British Virgin Islands and the Cayman Islands.

These documents, along with the report on real estate sales by Transparency International and various federal government studies, underline a critical fact: the money coming out of China into Canada is not clean or benign. The systems used to sneak the money out of China require foreign partners to willingly provide false documents. That means that Canada is importing corruption along with money. Canada is seeing signs of this with corrupt activities in the real estate industry, the turning of blind eyes to patently fake documents such as educational credentials, and purposeful lack of scrutiny of the sources of the money appearing on our shores. The red aristocrats' millions have not created corruption in Canada, of course. Since the moment European settlers set foot on this land, there has been an unhealthy relationship between local authorities and the real estate business in all its forms and sectors. Canada is a country where the links between municipal and provincial governments and the land development industry are often scandalous and corrupt. Canadian municipal councils and local real estate business interests are often indistinguishable because of the number of developers who are members of the councils. As the Transparency International report indicated, the Chinese money has merely slipped through an open door. The threat is that when Canada finally does decide that this tidal wave of money is not an entirely good thing, corruption will be even more deeply embedded than before, and it will take years — or possibly decades — to eradicate.

There is a clear moral, social, and practical responsibility for government and the judicial system to confront the people and practices that have made Canada a haven for international money laundering and corruption. Far less clear, however, is Canada's moral obligation to help the CCP to apprehend and punish people it considers to be criminals. As has been mentioned several times in this book, China has no rule of law as is understood in Western liberal democracies; the judicial system in China works to the advantage of the government only. A criminal in China is someone the CCP says is a criminal, and all too often that means someone who is either politically threatening or who for one reason or another has lost political protection. The huge anti-corruption drive launched by

President Xi Jinping when he came to power at the end of 2012 is a prime example of using the law to accomplish a purge of political rivals and potential opponents. In many ways, Xi's anti-corruption drive accomplished the same kind of internal purge of the CCP as did Mao Zedong's Cultural Revolution in the 1960s and early 1970s.

Canada needs to have a clear-sighted view of how justice operates in China; this is essential for many reasons, but two are most pressing. One is the prospect of a free trade agreement or other enhanced commercial relationship with a regime that does not accept fair arbitration of disputes. Equally pressing is the CCP's demand that Ottawa sign an extradition treaty to provide a legal framework for the return of people the CCP claims are criminals.

In the absence of an extradition treaty, the CCP's secret police have on several occasions come to Canada on tourist visas. They have then hunted down their targets and attempted to intimidate them into returning to China. In most cases, the secret police use the threat of retribution against a fugitive's family if he or she does not comply. The case of Lai Changxing, the master of a vast smuggling operation based in the southern China port city of Xiamen, first brought the problem of clandestine Chinese secret police operations in Canada to public attention. Lai fled to Canada with his wife and children in 1999 when the political winds turned against him. He fought extradition for twelve years, during which time a team of the CCP's secret police came surreptitiously to Canada, bringing with them one of Lai's brothers in an attempt to underline the threat to his family. But Lai was immune to this arm-twisting and fought his case through Canadian courts and refugee tribunals. He was eventually extradited to China in July 2011. The following year, he was sentenced to life imprisonment for smuggling and bribery.

Lai's story is an excellent example of the perils of Canada's making any formal treaties with China when the CCP's legal and judicial systems are used as a means to an end in power plays within the party. Lai's smuggling empire flourished because of his connections and payoffs to military and civilian officials in Fujian province, of which Xiamen is the commercial hub. And Lai's contacts were not just any old provincial officials. His military contacts included Ji Shengde, major general of military intelligence for the People's Liberation Army. There were several credible reports published by Taiwanese magazines of Lai's smuggling operations being protected, sometimes with gunfire, by ships of the PLA Navy. Lai himself was part of the political faction of President Jiang Zemin. The head of the CCP in Fujian was Jia Qinglin, a close associate of President Jiang. Jia was transferred, assuming the position of CCP leader in Beijing in 1996 before going on to be appointed a member of the Politburo the following year. In 2007 he climbed one step higher to the Politburo Standing Committee. While Jia was the ruler of Fujian province, his wife, Lin Youfang, was in charge of the province's trade and commerce department. It takes a huge leap of faith to accept the idea that Jia and Lin were not fully aware of Lai's smuggling operation, if not complicit in it.

The political tide began to turn against Lai in 1998, when the no-nonsense architect of much of China's economic reform, Zhu Rongji, became premier. Zhu had only a marginal attachment to the CCP, whose elders and power brokers were equally skeptical about him. Zhu owed his elevation to the premiership to the high regard in which he was held by foreign governments for his economic skills and his non-ideological pragmatism. The CCP felt he was the best front man to get China accepted as a member of the World Trade Organization, as indeed proved true. But survival in the CCP often depends on unseating your rivals before they destroy you. After taking office, Zhu took the classic route to upending his rivals and launched an anti-corruption campaign. He could not, of course, make a direct attack on Jiang or others in the increasingly corrupt inner circles at the top of the CCP. An obvious surrogate was Lai Changxing, who had taken the wise precaution of acquiring permanent residence in Hong Kong in 1991 and running his empire from what was then still a British colony outside Beijing's grasp. Early in 1998, a special task force in the national customs service completed a lengthy analysis that concluded that Lai's smuggling operation had avoided paying duty on US$10 billion worth of goods. On April 20, the CCP's Central Discipline Inspection Commission sent a team of two hundred professional forensic accountants to go through mountains of papers from Lai's operations and from the provincial government. At the same time, three hundred armed police officers from other provinces were sent to Fujian to help in the raids, secure seized evidence, and detain suspects. As the drive against Lai's empire ran its course, at least fourteen less important figures were given death sentences, hundreds of people were given prison sentences, and roughly a thousand people came under investigation and were detained for varying periods. Lai himself escaped execution in 2012 only because a condition of his extradition from Canada was that he would not face the death penalty.

In the wake of the Lai affair, as Xi Jinping's purge disguised as an anti-corruption drive gathered pace, the CCP began to seek extradition treaties with the favourite havens of the country's fugitive wealthy. Beijing had actually made such an agreement with Australia in 2007, but the treaty was not in force for a decade as the parliament in Canberra refused to ratify it. Matters came to a head in March 2017, when the government of Prime Minister Malcolm Turnbull took ratification off the agenda in the face of a revolt by backbenchers in his own party and the certainty any bill would be defeated in the Senate. Ratification foundered because Australian legislators did not believe that the judicial system under the CCP was based on principles that made extradition acceptable.

Even while China's extradition treaty with Australia was approaching its death, Canada apparently opened the door to the possibility of a similar treaty between Beijing and Ottawa. On September 12, 2016, there was a meeting in Beijing between Prime Minister Justin Trudeau's national security adviser, Daniel Jean, and senior CCP security officials. Jean's purpose was to try to secure the release of Canadian missionary Kevin Garratt, who had been detained for two years on charges of spying and stealing state secrets. The day after Jean's meeting, Garratt was found guilty by a court in Dandong (the city bordering North Korea where he lived) and ordered deported. The price of Garratt's release appears to have been an extradition treaty. Ottawa soon issued a communiqué: "The two sides determined that the short-term objectives for Canada-China co-operation on security and rule of law are to start discussions on an Extradition Treaty and a Transfer of Offenders Treaty as well as other related matters."

A few opinion pieces written in Canadian newspapers by retired diplomats and academics argued there would be benefits from an extradition treaty. Two claims predominated. One was that it would dissuade Chinese secret police from launching clandestine missions in search of fugitives in Canada. The other was that the fear of being deported back to China would deter that country's wealthy from seeking refuge here. But Canadian public opinion was against such an agreement. Even two former heads of csis, Reid Morden and Ward Elcock, said an extradition treaty with China under the ccp was not a good idea. Elcock, director of csis from 1994 to 2004, said Canada could never get from the ccp any worthwhile guarantees that people sent back to China would receive a fair judicial hearing. Morden, director of csis from 1988 to 1992, said he didn't see how Ottawa could agree to an extradition treaty with Beijing until the Canadian government had developed a comprehensive policy on its approach to the ccp's human rights record. Even the most pumped-up cheerleader for enhanced Canada-China relations, Ottawa's ambassador to Beijing, John McCallum, conceded that an extradition treaty was beyond the distance the Canadian public was willing to go. "We are a long, long way from negotiations, let alone agreeing to such an agreement," McCallum told *The Globe and Mail's* Beijing correspondent, Nathan Vanderklippe, early in April 2017. Such a treaty, he said, was "not high on my list of priorities."

What the extradition treaty and free trade issues demonstrate is that there are limits to the leverage that the ccp can apply when dealing with open, representative, and accountable democratic governments. The senior levels of Canada's Liberal Party and their influential supporters in business and other key social sectors are undoubtedly much in favour of closer ties with China. But when public opinion is against them, they have little choice but to drop the subject for the moment in the hope that attitudes will change later.

THIRTEEN
CALLING THE TUNE

First, what is foreign interference? Simply put, it is an attempt by agents of a foreign state to influence the opinion, views, and decisions of Canadians with the aim to obtaining a political, policy, or economic advantage. This is, of course, a broad definition that could involve many facets of behaviour, but it's important to note that for behaviour to be considered as true foreign influence, it must be directed against the interests of Canada and must be deceptive in nature.

— RICHARD FADDEN, DIRECTOR OF CSIS, JULY 5, 2010

RICHARD FADDEN'S STATEMENTS about Chinese Communist Party agents of influence in Canada are supported by what has happened in Australia, New Zealand, the United States, and some European countries. The remarkable similarity of the efforts at subversion of public, academic, and commercial life in those countries should be conclusive evidence that the CCP is intent on being able to influence the internal affairs of any country with which the regime has significant relationships.

The determination to undermine liberal democracy has become more evident in recent years, especially under the leadership of Xi Jinping, as the CCP sees China returning to its historic role as the world's pre-eminent economic and political power. As well as working to undermine democracy and the rule of law in countries like Canada, the CCP also aims to supplant or revamp the international institutions spawned and supported by liberal democracies after the Second World War. The CCP is already creating its own institutions based on its own values, such as the Asian Infrastructure Investment Bank. President and party leader Xi has been very clear in several speeches that China's model of authoritarian capitalism is a much better model for stable government than democracy and is an example that should be followed by countries wanting strong ties to Beijing.

For Canada, the most important lessons from the CCP's subversion in other countries have come from Australia and New Zealand. Our three countries are very similar in their histories, politics, economies, and modern view of the world. And the CCP's efforts at subversion, gaining political influence, curbing academic debate and freedom of speech, and intimidating people in the various Chinese diasporas it considers threats have been drawn from the same playbook. A significant difference is that both Australia and New Zealand have been much more open and vigorous than Canada in exposing and countering the CCP campaign. This has taken much greater political courage in Canberra than it would in Ottawa. China is Australia's largest trade partner and the customer for a third of its exports, most of them raw materials. Australia is also a major destination for Chinese investment, second only to the United States. Between 2005 and 2015, Australia received twice as much Chinese investment as Canada. So there were real risks attached to the stated determination of Australia's Prime Minister Malcolm Turnbull to pursue legislation to curb foreign agents and clandestine meddling in the country's affairs. "We've reached the point where there is almost a consensus forming among the political class: that Australia has to stand up to China," Rory Metcalf, head of the National Security College at Australian National University, said in a media interview in June 2017.

Canada is not yet close to forming a similar consensus. The country's political classes are still a long way from admitting that subversion by the CCP is a problem, though there are some signs that that is changing. The country's various security agencies don't have the same misgivings as its politicians. But as the Fadden affair (discussed briefly in Chapter 9) illustrates, Canada's political leaders are reluctant to accept the advice their security officials are providing them or acknowledge the importance of this information to the survival of the country's social and political values.

Early in 2010, Richard Fadden, the director of CSIS, informed Prime Minister Stephen Harper's national security adviser, Marie-Lucie Morin, that his agents had found evidence of "possible foreign political interference with certain Canadian politicians." Fadden told Morin that his agents were not yet certain whether or not what they had discovered violated Canada's security laws but that he was passing on the information "in order to determine the procedure to be followed once the CSIS investigations were completed." That process was still underway when Fadden gave a speech on March 24, 2010, at the Royal Canadian Military Institute in Toronto, and it was here that his difficulties began. Fadden had had the text of his remarks approved by senior security officials. This was done in full knowledge that Fadden's speech would be recorded by the CBC as part of material being collected for a documentary on the twenty-fifth anniversary of the creation of CSIS. After his speech, Fadden agreed to answer questions from the audience, forgetting, much to his regret, as he said later, that CBC cameras were still running. Fadden maintained doggedly through the months of vilification that followed that he had revealed no secrets. But, as he testified before the standing committee, "I provided a degree of granularity, or detail, to an audience of police, intelligence, and military experts that I would not have provided to the public." The critical remark came in answer to a question from the Royal Canadian Military Institute audience: "There are several municipal politicians in British Columbia and in at least two provinces there are ministers of the Crown who we think are under at least the general influence of a foreign government."

Fadden was a little more forthcoming about people being publicly identified as China's agents of influence when he was interviewed by the anchor of *The National* news program, Peter Mansbridge, on June 22, 2010: "They haven't really hidden their association, but what surprised us is that it's been so extensive over the years and we're now seeing, in a couple of cases, indications that they are in fact shifting their public policies as a reflection of that involvement with that particular country."

Fadden was brought before the House of Commons Standing

Committee on Public Safety and National Security in July. The outraged attitude toward Fadden by committee members is evident in an early question to him by Bloc Québécois MP Maria Mourani after he expressed regret for his comment after the March speech.

"Mr. Fadden," she said, "do you realize that your being sorry does not change the fact that a number of municipal officials from British Columbia and provincial ministers were affected by your comments? Unless you clarify the situation, everyone's reputation will be tainted. Mr. Fadden, who are the current political traitors?"

Fadden replied that the term *traitor* was not an appropriate description of the kind of links with China he had indicated. But a little later Mourani returned to her original tack and asked, "You do not want to specify who those ministers are. I am giving you the chance to do it. Mr. Fadden, who are these ministers who are guilty of treason?"

Fadden reiterated, "There is absolutely no question of treason or a breach of the law. Our primary concern in dealing with this matter is to ensure that Canadian decisions are made by Canadians. We want to protect Canadians. That is what we are trying to do."

It came as no surprise that when the committee published its report and recommendations in March 2011, number three on the list was requiring Fadden to resign. This, in the view of the committee, was "for having stated, in circumstances entirely under his control, that ministers in two provinces as well as municipal elected officials in British Columbia were agents of influence of foreign governments, thereby sowing doubt about the probity and integrity of a number of elected officials and creating a climate of suspicion and paranoia."

The committee offered no evidence that Fadden's remarks had created the unsettled atmosphere it described as a "climate of suspicion and paranoia." And there is no evidence from events and reactions beyond Ottawa at that time to suggest that Fadden's observations had had anything close to this effect. The whole tenor of the committee's questioning of Fadden is of overexcited political correctness. Certainly, the Harper government saw no reason to follow the committee's advice. Fadden moved from csis in 2013 to become deputy minister of national defence, and in 2015 he was appointed national security adviser to the prime minister. He retired in March 2016.

After csis agents had completed their investigation into "possible foreign political interference with certain Canadian politicians" in March 2010, a senior csis official from Ottawa arranged a formal meeting with Ontario Secretary of Cabinet Shelly Jamieson. The topic was the activities of Michael Chan, the minister of tourism and culture in the government of Liberal Premier Dalton McGuinty. *The Globe and Mail* on June 16, 2015, reported the csis agent told Jamieson the service had been alerted to the activities of Chan since soon after his election in 2007 and was concerned he was "under the undue influence of a foreign government."

Chan was born in Guangzhou (the old Canton) in southern China in 1951, when the Chinese Communist Party was completing its victory in the civil war. Chan's father was an official in the ousted Kuomintang regime and was likely to be a target once the communists achieved full control. The family fled to the Portuguese colony of Macau, and then, like tens of thousands of other Kuomintang refugees, moved to the British colony of Hong Kong. From there, in 1969, when Chan was eighteen, the family moved to Canada. Chan first worked in a Chinese restaurant in Toronto before becoming an insurance broker. In 1983, he joined the federal Liberal Party, attracted by Prime Minister Pierre Trudeau's promotion of multiculturalism and the establishment of diplomatic relations with Beijing in 1970.

After the trauma of the Tiananmen Square massacre in 1989, the ccp put significant energy into overcoming sanctions by foreign governments and preparing the ground for future economic ties. To that end, the ccp inspired the creation of many organizations in the Chinese diaspora, especially among the newer waves of Mandarin-speaking emigrants from mainland China. The National Congress of Chinese Canadians, with which Chan became associated, was established in 1991. In 1992, the Chinese Professionals Association of Canada was set up. These groups, together with well-established bodies like the Confederation of Toronto Chinese

Canadian Organizations, are strong advocates of deeper and broader relations between Canada and China. But they are also consistent promoters of the CCP's stance on contentious issues. A Chinese government website said of the CTCCO: "Whenever there is something against Chinese interests, the [confederation] will organize parades to protest or use media to protect the image of China."

That duty to Beijing was heavily in evidence in May 2016. The eighty Chinese Canadian groups making up the CTCCO held a press conference to support Beijing's stance on the ownership of the South China Sea. This came just ahead of a judgment to be handed down by the International Court of Arbitration in the Hague on a petition from the government of the Philippines. For several years, Chinese ships had been operating within the Philippines' exclusive economic zone around Scarborough Shoals, which Beijing claimed as part of a historic suzerainty over almost all the South China Sea. Beijing refused to give evidence to the court, a clear indication that it had no intention of accepting the ruling. It also stuck to its position that its territorial disputes with other littoral states — Vietnam, Malaysia, and Brunei — over ownership of the Paracel Islands and the Spratly Islands should be resolved bilaterally rather than through multilateral agreements. This arrangement would clearly give Beijing much greater heft in negotiations.

The news conference by the CTCCO was a pre-emptive strike against the likely verdict of the International Court of Arbitration. The CTCCO announced that its members "unanimously supported China's proposal and called for more overseas Chinese to encourage the stance of their original home country in order to sustain the peace and stability of the region." The verdict of the court, published on July 12, 2016, was indeed that Beijing's claim was "without legal foundation."

It must be noted that Canada's Chinese diaspora is far from monolithic. It is a patchwork of political views and tendencies that usually reflect what part of China the immigrants came from and from which events in China's recent turbulent history they were fleeing. The growth of pro-CCP organizations has been of concern to many Chinese Canadians whose families or they themselves had emigrated to escape the machinations and control of the communist regime. Most have happily abandoned worries about Chinese politics and focus on their lives as Canadians. But some remain active in Chinese politics, such as pro-democracy advocates from Hong Kong, supporters of genuine autonomy for Tibet and Xinjiang, workers for religious tolerance in China, and defenders of Taiwan's independence. To them, the establishment of these pro-Beijing groups looks like the CCP reaching into their new home in Canada to continue controlling their lives.

In interviews with *The Globe and Mail*, Michael Chan said he was only marginally involved with one of the pro-Beijing groups, the National Congress of Chinese Canadians, and only for a short time. In 1995, Chan moved to Markham, Ontario, where he became president of the federal Liberal Party association for the riding of Markham-Unionville, a seat then held by Liberal MP John McCallum (of whom there will be more to say later). Chan made his own leap into politics at the beginning of 2007, when he won the Markham-Unionville seat in a by-election for the Ontario provincial legislature. He was immediately appointed minister of revenue, and the following October he was made minister of citizenship and immigration.

In 2008, Chan was interviewed by the Xinhua news agency, and, perhaps understandably, he played up his Chinese heritage. He was quoted as saying, "Strictly speaking, I'm Canadian, but I have been always paying attention to the root of my culture. I am much concerned with Chinese affairs." He told the reporter he had visited China about seventy times in the previous decade or so. After his election to the legislature, Chan rapidly established himself as an essential facilitator linking Ontario and Chinese business people, the Ontario and Chinese governments, and pro-Beijing elements in the Chinese Canadian community with the Liberal parties of both Ontario and Canada. Some of Chan's authority arose from his reputation as an effective fundraiser for the Liberal parties among the Chinese Canadian communities. But he was also a divisive figure among Chinese Canadians opposed to the CCP's incursions into Canadian life. Some saw him as mentoring pro-CCP candidates to run for the Liberal Party in provincial and national elections. In June 2015, *The Globe and Mail* quoted Cheuk Kwan, the chair of the Toronto Association for Democracy in China, as saying Chan "has a lot of influence and used it to build up a network of pro-China candidates. My worry is that he's promoting a lot of candidates who don't have the qualifications — except 'I'm Chinese, vote for me.'"

It was against the backdrop of this history that, in March 2010, CSIS agents went to see Shelly Jamieson. "The agency believed Mr. Chan had an unusually close rapport with Taoying Zhu, who was China's consul general in Toronto until 2012," *The Globe and Mail* reported in 2015. "At one point, CSIS alleged, Mr. Chan and Ms. Zhu were having daily conversations. Such frequency can happen from time to time — when countries are negotiating details of a trip or event, for example. But details are not usually settled by officials as high-ranking as a minister and a consul general. They are most often handled by bureaucrats."

The exact nature of CSIS's concerns has never been made public. Chan himself, in an interview with *The Globe and Mail*, said there appeared to be two issues: that he owned property in China and that he had asked Zhu directly to arrange a visa for him. If she had granted him the request and bypassed the formal application process, it could have created an obligation on his part that would have to be reciprocated at some point. Chan told the newspaper both claims were false. His only property was his home in his constituency of Markham, and his frequent conversations with the consul general related to a cultural event in which his department was involved.

After her meeting with the CSIS official, Jamieson informed the Premier's Office about the allegations. McGuinty's chief of staff, Chris Morley, discussed the CSIS information with Chan, and put the whole matter before the Office of the Integrity Commissioner. After the vetting, Chan was held to be in compliance with the Integrity Act, and the Premier's Office dismissed the CSIS concerns. Under the government of McGuinty's successor, Kathleen Wynne, Chan went on to be the minister of citizenship, immigration and international trade, and then, in 2016, the minister of international trade. In April 2018, Chan announced he would not be a candidate in the provincial election due later that year and was retiring from politics because of health concerns.

There was never any implication that Chan's behaviour was traitorous, although he has been an advocate of positions favoured by the Chinese Communist Party. Two issues in particular stand out. In June 2016, in a Chinese-language blog he maintained on the popular website 51.ca, Chan took a stance on human rights issues in China very similar to that of the CCP regime. Chan defended visiting Chinese Foreign Minister Wang Yi, who was much criticized after he castigated a Canadian reporter, Amanda Connolly of *iPolitics*, for asking about human rights during a press conference in Ottawa. In his blog, Chan said that human rights and people's welfare are intertwined. Improving people's livelihood is the more important strand of the two, he said. Therefore, China's economic development is the best route toward advances in human rights. This is the view propounded by the CCP; it argues that economic stability, and the social harmony believed to evolve naturally from it, is more important than human rights at this stage in China's modern history. But it does not begin to convincingly explain why it is necessary to persecute, detain, torture, and kill people from various segments of society who advocate peaceful and measured political and social reform. In 2013, Chan echoed Beijing's stance when he lobbied for the Toronto District School Board to negotiate and conclude an agreement for Confucius Institutes to be installed in district schools. As has been described in Chapter 10, in October 2014 the school board cancelled its agreement with Hanban, parent organization of the Confucius Institutes, over the issue of whether the institutes were political.

There remain questions about whether the process used to vet Chan's activities was adequate for the situation. Ontario's Members' Integrity Act deals only with foreign property ownership and conflicts of interest. It does not offer a comprehensive template for how Ontario ministers or members of the legislature should deal with foreign governments and what are the legitimate boundaries of those relationships. That poses the question whether Canadian provincial and municipal governments are currently capable of recognizing and dealing with foreign interference and influence. The anecdotal evidence is that they are not. Certainly, much of the energy expended by the CCP on achieving political influence in Canada appears to be targeted at these more vulnerable lower levels of government.

In September 2014, former CSIS analyst and co-author of the Sidewinder report Michel Juneau-Katsuya told Sam Cooper, then reporting for *The Province*, that CSIS "found evidence that the Chinese Consulate in Toronto was directly interfering in elections, by sending Chinese students into the homes of Chinese-language-only households and telling residents which candidates the Consulate wanted voters to choose."

Cooper quoted Juneau-Katsuya as saying, "There are lots of members of council in Toronto, for example, who were on CSIS's watch list. Some have been able to move up to the provincial and federal level, and remain a great source of concern."

ONE OF THE most direct allegations of CCP interference in Canadian elections came in October 2018. A couple of weeks before voting day on October 20 both the Mounties and the Vancouver City Police issued statements saying they were investigating claims that an organization linked to the CCP's United Front was attempting to buy votes. The allegation was that the Canada Wenzhou Friendship Society had used the Chinese social media platform WeChat to offer voters a $20 "travel allowance" if they would vote for people on a list of ethnic Chinese candidates. Wenzhou City is in Zhejiang province on China's southeast coast and the friendship society is one of those organizations designed by the United Front to ensure people who have immigrated to Canada continue to have strong links with their home town.

Another contentious issue is the main reception at the annual meeting of the Union of British Columbia Municipalities (UBCM). In 2012, the Chinese consul general in Vancouver, Liu Fei, held an invitation-only reception for delegates. The consulate has since become a regular sponsor (sometimes co-sponsor along with the B.C. provincial government) of the main informal social gathering of the annual meeting. Members of the UBCM include 190 regional districts and municipalities and 8 First Nations. In theory, there is nothing wrong with Chinese diplomats in Canada being able to meet and form business relationships with municipal officials and elected leaders. But it must be remembered that it is the CCP these business people and municipal officials are dealing with, and these associations have to look at that in the context of everything else the party is doing in Canada.

No other foreign government has hosted receptions for the UBCM members, and the scale of the Chinese consulate's hospitality has raised many eyebrows among both the union's members and outside observers. The aim of the CCP's diplomats is clearly to turn social relationships with B.C. municipal officials and politicians into ones where the Canadians feel a sense of obligation. One way this is achieved is by offering visits to China paid for by Beijing, mirroring the hospitality offered school board and university officials in the campaign to promote Confucius Institutes. The justification for these trips is usually that they provide understanding and perhaps business links between Canadian municipalities and their Chinese counterparts. An illustration of this phenomenon was posted on the website of the Chinese consulate in Vancouver on December 1, 2015. The centrepiece was a picture of Consul General Liu surrounded by twenty-one people, the executive members of the UBCM with whom she had just had a meeting. "The two sides reviewed the achievements in bilateral co-operation and the visits to China by some UBCM members in the last few years and agreed to continue the exchanges and mutually beneficial co-operation," read the caption.

It is not just municipal and provincial politicians who are lured on free trips to China, usually by offshoots of the United Front Work Department, Xi Jinping's "magic weapon." Records kept by the Senate and the House of Commons show that between 2006 and December 2017, members of both houses took thirty-six trips to China sponsored by either the Chinese government or provincial business groups. *The Globe and Mail*, in December 2017, reported that most of the trips were funded by the Chinese People's Institute of Foreign Affairs, which answers to the United Front. The biggest beneficiary of the CCP's hospitality in that period was John McCallum, who was an opposition Liberal MP during much of the decade. McCallum took trips to China valued at $73,300. What makes McCallum's junkets striking is that when the Liberals returned to power in 2015, he became minister of immigration, refugees and citizenship. In January 2017, McCallum stepped down from Cabinet, resigned his seat in Parliament for Markham-Unionville — the same area represented by Michael Chan in the provincial legislature — and was appointed Canada's ambassador to Beijing. McCallum arrived in the Chinese capital unfazed by Canada's allies' increasing caution about getting too close to the CCP regime and pursued a diplomatic course that included obtaining a free trade agreement and other ties with Beijing. According to the *Toronto Star* on March 27, 2017:

> *McCallum arrived in the Chinese capital 11 days ago, and presented his diplomatic credentials directly to President Xi Jinping within 24 hours of arrival.*
>
> *He said their meeting lasted just five minutes, long enough to tell China's top Communist government leader that he was there to deliver on Trudeau's promise of a renewed relationship.*
>
> *"I said on behalf of our prime minister that Canada wanted to expand and deepen its ties with China beyond what has been agreed to previously by the leaders, that we wanted to do more.*
>
> *"My slogan is more, more, more. We want to do more trade, more investment, more tourists, more co-operation in many areas, particularly in environment and climate change where both countries have an interest," said McCallum."*

McCallum's bubbling enthusiasm overflowed on occasion. During Quebec Premier Philippe Couillard's visit to China in January 2018, McCallum said that on some key issues Canada now has more in common with the CCP regime in Beijing than it does with the United States under the administration of Donald Trump. He cited issues like the environment, global warming, and globalization: "I believe that because of this political situation with Donald Trump, the Chinese are now more interested than before to do things with us." The divergence between the United States and China is a boon for Canada, he continued. "In a sense, it's a good thing for me as an ambassador and for Canada with China because, because of these big differences, it gives us opportunities in China. There is no doubt that Canada wants to do more with China, which is what the prime minister told me when he asked me to come here." Prime Minister Justin Trudeau, who was at the annual World Economic Forum in Davos at the time, was asked about McCallum's comments and said only that his government's approach to foreign affairs was to look for common ground with all countries, including China. Opposition politicians, however, were swift to question what McCallum's relish for deepening ties with an authoritarian and brutal one-party state did for Canada's image among its allies.

The courting of Canadian politicians and officials by agents of the CCP has created an unhealthy climate in which any decisions by Canadian bodies that appear to favour Beijing are regarded with suspicion. One such situation arose in 2006. Vancouver's city council attempted to force the removal of a semi-permanent hut and billboards erected in 2001 by followers of Falun Gong on Granville Street, against the wall of the Chinese consulate. The billboards decorating the consulate's wall illustrated what Falun Gong claimed were methods of torture used by CCP security agents against the group's followers in China. In the hut, followers would sit in Buddhist poses of contemplation day and night. The presentation made a mockery of the entrance to the consulate and the residence of the consul general, as was undoubtedly intended.

In 2006, Mayor Sam Sullivan determined the structure contravened local bylaws, and city staff ordered the hut and billboards removed. Local Falun Gong practitioners appealed the order, and the matter went through the courts. The arguments revolved around Falun Gong's insistence that they had the right to freedom of expression in a public place — the sidewalk —

and the city's contention that the group's encampment interfered with the free passage of pedestrians. In 2009, the British Columbia Supreme Court upheld the city council's decision, and the hut was dismantled. But in October 2010, the Court of Appeal reversed the decision on the grounds that the bylaw was unconstitutional. The city was given six months to rewrite the bylaw. By this time, the political complexion of the city council had changed, and Gregor Robertson was mayor.

From the first, there had been public speculation that Sullivan had moved against the protestors at the behest of the Chinese consulate. In 2011, it was found that Mayor Robertson and city officials had consulted officials at the consulate on the proposed new bylaw on the grounds that they were stake-holders. This prompted outrage in the media, with many commenting that the Chinese government was not a stakeholder in any city bylaws, especially not those concerning freedom of speech, a concept alien to the CCP regime in China. An appeal-proof bylaw was eventually approved, one limiting the kind of structures that could be built to support protests and the length of time a demonstration could be mounted.

There is a strong thread of ambiguity and unresolved questions that runs through many of the Canadian stories that have surfaced, stories that may or may not have their roots in the efforts of agents of the CCP. Some of this persistent fog seems to be generated by Canadian cultural reticence. Some undoubtedly comes from personal concerns that looking too hard at these questions would be considered racist. Even among those who find it legitimate to question the activities of the CCP in Canada, the fear of being labelled racist can be silencing. The result is a general lack of rigour in addressing a problem that is beginning to undermine Canada's values and social structure. The ways in which Australia and New Zealand have addressed the same CCP campaigns of subversion with public dissection and debate are worth examining.

In September 2017, Anne-Marie Brady, a political science professor at New Zealand's University of Canterbury (whose book on the CCP overseas subversion networks, *Making the Foreign Serve China*, has been referred to earlier) produced a lengthy report on the current situation in her home country. She set out evidence that since the accession to power of Xi Jinping in 2012, the CCP's soft power campaign had intensified to influence New Zealand's politics, economy, and society in many ways — including through donations to the campaigns of political parties. The paper high-lighted how a cluster of former senior politicians — including prime ministers and mayors — as well as family members of current government ministers had been appointed to boards of state-owned Chinese banks, companies, and think tanks. Brady also named two elected politicians of Chinese origin who she believed were influenced by the Chinese embassy and community organizations used by Chinese diplomats as front groups to promote the CCP's agenda.

The two politicians Brady named were Jian Yang, a member of Parlia-ment for the centre-right National Party, and Raymond Huo, MP of the left-wing Labour Party. Huo rejected Brady's characterization, saying his appearances at events organized by Chinese community groups associated with the United Front Work Department was just part of his duties as a member of Parliament. Yang's position became more difficult just before the September 23, 2017, national election in which he was re-elected. A joint investigation by the *Financial Times* and an online media outlet, *Newsroom*, published evidence that before immigrating to New Zealand from China, Yang had been a CCP member and had taught English at two Chinese spy schools. Crucially, he had not revealed this part of his previous career when applying for New Zealand citizenship. Instead, he had listed what he called "partnership civilian universities" as his employers. When confronted, Yang admitted teaching English at the spy schools but insisted he himself was not a spy. Even so, the media stories said that after the New Zealand Security Intelligence Service began to investigate Yang's background early in 2017, he was removed from the Parliamentary Select Committee on Foreign Affairs, Defence and Trade, on which he had served since 2014.

Although New Zealand has a small economy and a small military, it is a member of the Five Eyes alliance set up after the Second World War among the United States, the United Kingdom, Canada, Australia, and

New Zealand. Information from both signals intelligence — electronic bugging of various kinds — and human intelligence — spies — is shared. Thus, infiltrating one of the five can open windows to the others.

While Canada has spent years trying to interpret incomplete phrases from a few of its senior security intelligence officials, counterparts in Australia have had little hesitation in speaking publicly about their concerns. In May 2017, the government's most senior Department of Defence official, Dennis Richardson, said in a speech that China was conducting extensive espionage against Australia. "It is no secret that China is very active in intelligence activities directed against us. It is more than cyber," Richardson said. "The Chinese government keeps an eye inside Australian Chinese communities and effectively controls some Chinese-language media in Australia." Richardson spoke specifically about a contentious question from 2015, when Australia leased a commercial and military port in the northern city of Darwin to a Chinese company said to have ties to the People's Liberation Army. The move drew strong rebukes from the United States, which was in the process of setting up a major base for its Marine Corps nearby. As a result, Australia has since blocked several bids on infrastructure projects from Chinese companies. An indication of how seriously the government considered the issue came early in 2017 when Canberra created an infrastructure authority to check whether foreign-led bids for assets such as ports and power grids could pose national security threats. At the same time, Canberra appointed David Irvine, the former head of the Australian Secret Intelligence Service (ASIS) — the equivalent of CSIS — as chairman of the foreign investment advisory committee, which advises the government on offshore transactions.

The following month, June 2017, the head of ASIS told Parliament that the efforts by the CCP to exert its influence in Australia had reached the point where they posed a direct threat to the country's liberties and sovereignty. Speaking to Australia's parliament, Duncan Lewis said espionage and foreign interference in Australia were occurring on "an unprecedented scale. This has the potential to cause serious harm to the nation's sovereignty, the integrity of our political system, our national security capabilities, our economy and other interests."

Lewis's statement came at the same time as a major series of articles and programs on the CCP's subversion and infiltration, assembled by the Fairfax Media newspaper group and the investigative current affairs program *4 Corners* of the Australian Broadcasting Corporation. The six-month investigation found the CCP and its agents made efforts to control dissenting voices among Chinese Australian citizens by threatening their families in China. Chinese student organizations were being used both to spy on the students themselves and to organize protests when the CCP saw its positions attacked on such issues as the South China Sea, the role of the Dalai Lama, democracy in Hong Kong, the independence of Taiwan, or the nature of Falun Gong. The journalists found Chinese diplomats were managing Confucius Institutes in Australian colleges and universities. These are all the same activities that the CCP is pursuing in Canada. They also found a potential problem with former politicians and government officials taking up highly lucrative posts with Chinese companies or institutions after their retirements. This raised questions about whether the prospect of these posts had affected their pre-retirement judgments. This question has not been addressed in Canada, but it undoubtedly should be.

One issue that surfaced in Australia in 2017 was the question of donations by foreigners to political parties. This is allowed in Australia — unlike in Canada and most other Western democracies — though as I write in mid-2018, changes and restrictions are being considered by the government in Canberra.

Since returning to office in 2015, Canada's Liberal Party has courted wealthy Chinese Canadians in the Vancouver and Toronto areas. There are well-documented accounts of private fundraising events with Justin Trudeau as the star attraction. The main organizer on the West Coast was former Liberal minister for Asia-Pacific Raymond Chan, who was the Liberals' main fundraiser in British Columbia in the 2015 election. In the Toronto area, it was business consultant and leading party organizer Richard Zhou. Guests were charged $1,500 per ticket, and on several occasions Chinese Canadian business people brought along contacts from China, including people representing Chinese state-owned corporations or with links to the CCP.

When reports about the fundraisers began to circulate in late 2016, then Conservative Party leader Rona Ambrose charged in the House of Commons, "Rubbing elbows with millionaires at these cash-for-access events does not pass the smell test."

Prime Minister Trudeau replied, "Canadians faced a period of ten years of lower-than-needed growth under the previous government. That is why we have committed, engaging positively with the world to draw in investment. We know that drawing in global investment is a great way to grow the economy and create jobs."

The flaw in Trudeau's retort was shown in statements produced by Liberal Party officials when questioned by reporters about the line between government and party business. Liberal Party spokesman Braeden Caley responded to one such question by saying, "As we have been clear, fundraising events are partisan functions where there is not discussion of official government business. Any individual who wishes to initiate a discussion on such matters is immediately redirected to instead make an appointment with the relevant office."

People coming from a political culture where the ruling party and the engines of commerce are indistinguishable, and where survival and prosperity usually depend on cultivating networks of mutual obligation, cannot be expected to appreciate this nicety. A case in point was one fundraising event with Trudeau held on May 19, 2016, at the Toronto home of the chairman of the Chinese Business Chamber of Commerce, Benson Wong. Among the approximately thirty paying guests were Chinese businessman Zhang Bin and his business partner, Niu Gensheng. A few weeks after the event, they donated $1 million to the Pierre Elliott Trudeau Foundation and the University of Montreal's Faculty of Law. Apparently, of the $1 million, $200,000 went to the foundation and $50,000 to pay for a statue of Pierre Trudeau as a token of appreciation for his having opened diplomatic relations with China in 1970.

There were more blurred lines at another fundraiser featuring Justin Trudeau, this one hosted by real estate developer Miaofei Pan at his home in West Vancouver in November 2016. This event attracted about eighty guests at $1,500 a person. Pan came to Canada in 2006 but is still involved with organizations aligned with the CCP in both Canada and China. He is former president of the Canadian Alliance of Chinese Associations, an umbrella group for about two hundred Chinese Canadian groups across the country. The alliance has close ties to Chinese diplomatic missions and cleaves vigorously to the CCP's line on all current issues, including the CCP's position on the South China Sea and Beijing's claim to Japan's Senkaku Islands in the East China Sea. In 2012, Pan was quoted in a newspaper in Macau, talking about the stance of the alliance. The organization, he said, "declared its stand in newspapers." He insisted, "overseas Chinese were responsible for defending China's territorial integrity."

In addition to people with links and loyalties to both the Liberal Party and the CCP, Trudeau's fundraising events inevitably attracted people with questionable business records. (Although the latter is true of fundraising drives for all parties and from all segments of Canadian society.) But in 2015 and 2016, the Hong Kong-based newspaper *South China Morning Post* ran a series of articles about Vancouver developer Michael Ching, who was not only a contributor to the Liberal Party but also closely involved with Trudeau's campaign to win the party leadership in 2013. Unfortunately, Ching (born Cheng Muyang, and also known as Mo Yeung Ching) was wanted in China for corruption. That in itself ought not to be a conclusive concern. People in China, especially prominent social figures like Ching, whose father was the governor of Hebei province until he was expelled from the CCP in 2003 for corruption, only get charged with crimes when they have fallen out of political favour. But the Ching story added fodder to Conservative opposition in the House of Commons about the probity of the Liberals' fundraising among Chinese Canadians and Trudeau's involvement in the events. In the end, the Liberals put the matter before Ethics Commissioner Mary Dawson. She decided, in a judgment issued in February 2017, that Trudeau had not contravened the Conflict of

Interest Act. "After carefully reviewing the information and documents provided by Mr. Trudeau in response to my request, I have found no reason to believe that Mr. Trudeau contravened sections 7 or 16 of the act in relations to the fundraisers," she wrote.

Yet it is evident that the Liberals — and other political parties at all levels of government — have not being diligent in looking clearly at the connections to the ccp of people they have solicited for donations. Canadian political leaders, government officials, business people, academics, and media proprietors should all be looking at their dealings with the ccp, and its surrogates, much more clearly than they have in the past. They need to understand that the ccp's China is not going to be a benign superpower. No superpower is. It is already intent on imposing its values on the international order, and those values are very different from those of Canada and other liberal democracies.

The challenge of dealing with China for middle powers like Canada will be more intense because of what is likely to be an ongoing political and social crisis in the United States. The phenomenon occurring there is a symptom of deeply embedded national discord that will erode the United States' dominant role on the world stage. Washington, and American society in general, will no longer be the arbiter of liberal democracy that it has been since the end of the Second World War. This is not a disaster scenario for Canada and other Western democracies; however, there are many things Canada can and should do to strengthen its defences against ccp incursions.

Examination of the campaign by the ccp to plant agents of control and influence in Canada also shows significant failures. The ccp has frequently fallen short of its objectives for several reasons. The institutions of established open democracies such as Canada's are not as easy to pervert as some might think. While the ccp is adept at cultivating the venality of individuals, it usually misunderstands and misjudges the strengths of free and open societies. And the ccp regime is no longer built on a viable social contract with the Chinese people. Authoritarian states are able to present a strong and seemingly impregnable facade to the world, sometimes for a surprisingly long time, but these regimes are intrinsically brittle. A tap on the glass in the wrong place at the wrong time can leave nothing but a scattering of shards in the street.

EPILOGUE
TIME TO ABANDON THE MISSIONARY SPIRIT

The choice before us isn't whether or not to engage China. The government and people of China will almost certainly continue to engage us — and on their own terms. The real choice is in determining how we manage our side of the relationship.

— DAVID MULRONEY, *MOVING FORWARD: ISSUES IN CANADA-CHINA RELATIONS*

THE CHINESE COMMUNIST Party is now only one of the threats to Canadian democracy. The rise of what is being called populism in the United States and Europe may well turn out to be as great a danger to Canadian civic values as the CCP. Populism could be more toxic because it is coming from within the fortress of North Atlantic culture and is a symptom of a sickness within liberal democracies that has left many people feeling divorced from their governing institutions. The rise of support for populist nationalist parties over much of Europe, the success of the Brexit referendum in the United Kingdom in the summer of 2016, and the election of Donald Trump to the American presidency five months later all raise the question of whether the survival of democracy is threatened. That is overly pessimistic, though there is certainly evidence that among voters in the democracies of the North Atlantic, there is significant disenchantment with the established social and political order. Many frustrations have bred this discord, and the relative importance of the key elements varies from country to country. A common thread is the sense that quality of life is not improving and is unlikely to do so. In the decades after the Second World War, the expectation took hold that the standard of living would continue to improve and that children could look forward to more rewarding lives than their parents. That is no longer the case in Europe and North America. Globalization of manufacturing and the automation of production have created social and economic uncertainty for large segments of the populations in industrialized democracies.

A feeling of powerlessness has become pervasive among Western democracies, and in many cases there are good reasons for people to think that their civic systems are not functioning as intended. In some countries, there appears to be a disconnect between the values of the political establishment on such matters as immigration and the views of people lower down the social hierarchy who, rightly or wrongly, feel threatened by newcomers. For people who feel frustrated and powerless, there is a natural attraction to the easy answers proffered by people like Boris Johnson in the United Kingdom, Donald Trump in the United States, Marine Le Pen in France, Geert Wilders in Holland, and Viktor Orban in Hungary. Canada is not exhibiting the same wide-spread antipathy toward the governing classes and the tenets of liberalism they expound as is evident in the United States and in European countries. But that could change, and change quickly, if, for example, there were a long-running economic recession on the North American continent. The election in mid-2018 of the populist Doug Ford in Ontario with a simplistic recipe for addressing the province's problems is closely aligned with events in the United States and Europe.

There is clearly a need to refashion Western democracy and forge a new compact between governments and citizenry. But this comes at an inconvenient time of growing external pressures, especially from the CCP regime in China. As China and other non-European emerging countries become more influential on the world stage, the civic values that have dominated international relations since the Second World War will become less influential. Canada and the other Western democracies are going to have to decide how much they are prepared to compromise in the interest of sustaining economic, political, and diplomatic relationships with countries whose domestic social structures and views of the world are profoundly different from our own.

In Canada, these decisions are already upon us. Interference by the CCP in and attempts at the perversion of public life in Canada, coupled with the intimidation and harassment of individual Canadians, demand a response. All too often in the past, Canadian politicians, officials, security agents, business people, academics, and, on occasion, the media have shied away from levelling justified criticism at the CCP and its operatives for their behaviour in Canada against Canadians. This is no longer good enough. There should not be any debate that covert actions by the CCP in Canada are unacceptable and ought to be publicly condemned. It is the responsibility of any government to protect its citizens against intimidation by foreign agents.

There was a sign in May 2018 that Ottawa had finally decided to send a clear message of disapproval of the CCP's infiltration and influence peddling through the United Front. The World Guangdong Community Federation, an association of people from the southern Chinese province of Guangdong, which borders Hong Kong and is made up mainly of Cantonese people, planned its ninth conference in Vancouver. The event was organized by the Overseas Chinese Affairs Office branch in Guangdong province, and about two thousand Cantonese people from China and around the world were expected to attend. But Ottawa refused to give visitors' visas to about two hundred would-be delegates, including officials from the Overseas Chinese Affairs Office and from other branches of the provincial administration. Canadian officials gave no response to reporters' questions for an explanation of the visa ban. But, as has been previously described, local branches of the Overseas Chinese Affairs Office are overseen by the United Front. The refusal to grant visas to United Front agents should send a clear message to the CCP that Canada is no longer a happy hunting ground for intimidation and influence peddling.

More action is needed. The boundaries between acceptable and unacceptable behaviour need to be staked out clearly in a number of areas of Canadian life. Canadian political parties, academic institutions of various sorts, and the media have been far too willing to accept benefits, financial and otherwise, that make them beholden to the CCP. Perhaps most questionable are Canadian politicians and officials who in retirement from public life accept lucrative consultant work or advisory positions with the CCP and its agencies. Such arrangements always raise questions of whether the Canadian was preparing the ground for a comfortable retirement while still in office and was acting as an agent for the CCP. This is not a question that applies only to dealings with China and the CCP, of course. There is a wide and well-trodden path from positions in government to lucrative roles with foreign agencies and corporations.

Canada's security and intelligence agencies, both civilian and military, take the threat of CCP economic and technical espionage a good deal more seriously than do our federal and provincial politicians. Whether the intelligence agencies feel constrained because of the evident lack of political backing is hard to judge. But it is notable that there have been practically no cases of CCP-generated industrial or technical espionage brought to court in Canada over the past three decades. In the United States, meanwhile, there is a steady stream of prosecutions of CCP operatives for stealing technologies that are also available in Canada. It defies belief that the same level of industrial espionage is not going on in Canada as in the United States.

It is very unusual in Canadian history for there to be any question about the loyalties of immigrants who seek public office. One strength of the parliamentary system is that people who are selected as candidates have usually been political activists for some time and have therefore gone through a process of communal vetting. But there are still weaknesses in the system. Political parties have not been able to escape the dangerous mindset of viewing immigrant groups as homogenous voting blocs whose support can be won en masse if the party can capture the right community leader. This is not only insulting to new Canadians, it tends to create a ready-made position for an agent of influence to be supplied by the CCP or other foreign interests.

On the international stage, Canada should not allow its behaviour or its statements on issues to be affected by how the CCP might react. Canada should not keep silent about human rights abuses within China and should decry the CCP's campaigns of imperial expansion in the South China Sea, Tibet, and Xinjiang. Canada should be firm in its support for the maintenance and expansion of democracy and the rule of law in Hong Kong, which, with about three hundred thousand Canadians resident at any given time, is one of the largest Canadian communities anywhere. Canada should affirm its support for democracy in Taiwan and the independence of the island nation. Taiwan should be high on the list of Asian democracies with which Canada seeks enhanced economic and political relationships. There should be repercussions for Canadian companies, such as airlines, that bow to the CCP's insistence that public material should indicate Taiwan is part of China. Ottawa should affirm and expand its political, trade, and military alliances with Asian and Pacific Rim democracies such as Japan, South Korea, Mongolia, Australia, India, Sri Lanka, Bangladesh, and New Zealand, as well as with emerging democracies among the countries of Southeast Asia, notably Indonesia.

Soon after the Liberals returned to office in 2015, a compilation of essays was produced by academics and others with records of advocating for greater Canada-China cooperation. *Moving Forward: Issues in Canada-China Relations* took as its premise, "China and Asia will figure prominently in the Liberal government's foreign policy. The inclinations, instincts and world-view of the leadership are significantly different from those of their Conservative predecessors as seen in the style and tone of Justin Trudeau's first two meetings with President Xi Jinping on the margins of recent multilateral forums." Reports from Ottawa said the booklet became essential reading among diplomats in the newly renamed Global Affairs Canada. In an introductory chapter, Wendy Dobson, professor and co-director of the Institute for International Business at the University of Toronto's Rotman School of Management, and Paul Evans, professor at the Institute of Asian Research and Liu Institute for Global Issues at the University of British Columbia, wrote that "deeper and broader engagement of China is in Canada's national interest." The new government cannot simply turn back the clock to the way things were before the Conservatives came to office. "Rather than restoration we need a reinvention based not merely on past foundations but on a new narrative that is more ambitious and more strategic."

Before that can be accomplished, the Canadian government needs to prepare the ground with a citizenry that is highly skeptical about relations with China. "At the moment, public anxiety is palpable. Canadian surveys in the past two years reveal that while more than two-thirds of Canadians believe China will be more powerful than the United States, only about a third see China as highly important to their economy and support a free trade deal. Only 14% support the prospect of a Chinese state-owned enterprise owning a controlling stake in a major Canadian company," wrote Dobson and Evans. "A majority believe that the human rights situation in China is deteriorating, that it does not respect freedoms of its people, and that its growing military power is a threat. More than half believe that China's influence is threatening the Canadian way of life. The words most frequently chosen to describe China are *authoritarian*, *growing*, *corrupt*, *threatening*, *strong* and *disliked*."

The Canadian public attitude reported by Evans and Dobson shows a more grounded view of China under the CCP and the dangers it represents than do the actions of the establishment classes that have benefited from their relationship with the Beijing regime for nearly fifty years. Ottawa would do well to listen more closely to public disquiet than to fantasies drawn out in vivid colour by the CCP's agents of influence or the romantic notion that the example of Canadian civic values will change China.

ACKNOWLEDGEMENTS

This book has been twenty-five years in the making. It began imprinting itself on my mind when I was appointed to the Southam News Asia Bureau, based in Hong Kong, in 1993. Memories of the Tiananmen Square massacre were still fresh. I was the first reporter for the Southam newspapers, Canada's largest group of metropolitan dailies at the time, to be allowed into China since the massacre. My predecessor, Ben Tierney, had been banned because of his reporting on both the massacre and the Chinese Communist Party's imperialism in Tibet.

How I got a visa and spent lengthy periods over several years travelling around China and reporting from places a long way beyond Beijing's reach is another story. But I learned very swiftly about the enormous complexities of attitudes and histories among people who come from different facets of Chinese culture. That lesson was reinforced when I returned to Canada in 1998 after two decades abroad as a foreign correspondent. My family and I landed in Vancouver, which, like Toronto and other cities in Canada, had become home to people from every tendency of Chinese political thought and historical experience. As I sat down to begin planning this book, that panorama convinced me that I had to write exclusively from the public record. The evidence for the story that I wanted to tell about the efforts of the Chinese Communist Party and its agents of influence to interfere in Canadian public life was sitting there in plain sight on the public record. And I wanted it evident to all readers that I was approaching this story, not as a supporter or advocate for any faction of the Canadian Chinese experience, but simply as a Canadian.

That I have been able to stick to that discipline is due to two gifts. First, there is a strong body of history and analysis of the Canada-China relations in a solid reservoir of books, which are named in the bibliography at the back of this book. Second, and most important, elements of the story of the CCP's campaign of subversion in Canada have been reported consistently by Canadian media over the years. What I have done is assemble the work of many of my colleagues in the Canadian media and present in complete form the story that they have told in daily instalments and episodes. Without my colleagues, I could not have written this book. They, far more than Canada's politicians, business people, and academics, have seen and understood that the CCP is not and never will be a benign actor on the world stage. They have also shown in their reports that it is Canadians of Chinese heritage who are major victims of the CCP, which continues to view them as its subjects despite years and sometimes generations of separation.

On the public record, for anyone who cared to look, is a raft of stories about agents of the CCP spying on and attempting to intimidate Canadian citizens in Canada. In 2017, the Canadian Coalition on Human Rights in China assembled a report on many examples of this gross intrusion by the CCP. The report was presented to the federal government and various Canadian security agencies in April that year. I am grateful to the coalition for making a copy of the report available to me.

From the start of the process to research and write this book, I received encouragement from an old friend and colleague from Hong Kong days, when we marched in allied legions of the media armies of Conrad Black, Chinese scholar Graham Hutchings. Both Graham and another friend and colleague, Clive Mostyn, a newspaper and magazine editor of incomparable experience and judgment, reviewed the first draft and gave essential advice about the structure and compass of the book. I am grateful also to David Mulroney, the former Canadian ambassador to Beijing, for reviewing the manuscript on matters of fact. I first met David when he was Canada's de facto ambassador to Taiwan and I was doing research for my book *Forbidden Nation: A History of Taiwan*.

Doug Gibson, who edited my first book, *The Power and the Tories*, for Macmillan of Canada back in 1973, played a crucial role in the inevitable drama of actually getting a book published. He introduced me to Marc Côté of Cormorant Books. In our early discussions, Marc warned that he is very demanding of authors and it could be a stormy relationship. He is indeed properly demanding, but he is not the martinet he warned me about. His questions and suggestions for cuts, changes, and additions were all well founded. Marc has been a pleasure to work with, and his knowledge and understanding of the Canadian political and social landscape have been invaluable. Finally, I am indebted to Andrea Waters, whose meticulous editing of the manuscript also contained thoughtful suggestions for clarifications in the text.

It is customary in these acknowledgements to absolve all those thanked for their help from any responsibility for the final product. I happily follow the custom.

This is the third book I have written while sharing light housekeeping duties, the rearing of children, and daily joys and sorrows with the love of my life, Petrina. There is more to come.

VICTORIA, BRITISH COLUMBIA, OCTOBER 2018

BIBLIOGRAPHY

NOTES

Austin, Alvyn. *Saving China*. Toronto: University of Toronto Press, 1986.

Andrew, Arthur. *The Rise and Fall of a Middle Power: Canadian Diplomacy from King to Mulroney*. Toronto: Lorimer, 1993.

Brady, Anne-Marie. *Making the Foreign Serve China*. Toronto: Rowman & Littlefield, 2003.

Campbell, Charles M. *Betrayal and Deceit*. West Vancouver, BC: Jasmine Books, 2000.

Cao, Huhaua Cao, and Vivienne Poy. *The China Challenge*. Ottawa: University of Ottawa Press, 2011.

Chan, Anthony B. *Li Ka-shing: Hong Kong's Elusive Billionaire*. Hong Kong: Oxford University Press, 1996.

Chinese Ministry of Foreign Affairs. *The Diplomacy of Modern China*. Beijing: 1990.

Cottrell, Robert. *The End of Hong Kong: The Secret Diplomacy of Imperial Retreat*. London: John Murray (Publishers) Ltd., 1993.

Drake, Earl. *A Stubble-Jumper in Striped Pants*. Toronto: University of Toronto Press, 1999.

Eftimiades, Nicholas. *Chinese Intelligence Operations*. Annapolis, Maryland: Naval Institute Press, 1994.

Endicott, Stephen. *James G Endicott: Rebel Out of China*. Toronto: University of Toronto Press, 1980.

Evans, Brian. *Pursuing China*. Edmonton: University of Alberta Press, 2012.

Evans, Paul, and Michael Frolic. *Reluctant Adversaries: Canada and the People's Republic of China 1949–1970*. Toronto: University of Toronto Press, 1991.

Hsu, Immanuel. *The Rise of Modern China*. Oxford University Press, 1970.

Huang, Chichung. *The Analects of Confucius*. Oxford University Press, 1997.

Hutchings, Graham. *Modern China: A Companion To A Rising Power*. London: Penguin, 2000.

Kurlantzick, Joshua. *Charm Offensive*. Yale University Press, 2007.

Lin, Paul. *In the Eye of the China Storm*. Montreal: McGill-Queen's University Press, 2011.

Ma, Adrian. *How the Chinese Created Canada*. Edmonton: Dragon Hill Publishing Ltd., 2010.

Morgan, W.P. *Triad Societies in Hong Kong*. Hong Kong: Government Press, 1989.

Mounk, Yascha. *The People vs. Democracy: Why Our Democracy Is In Danger & How To Save It*. Harvard University Press, 2018.

Mulroney, David. *Middle Power, Middle Kingdom*. Toronto: Allen Lane, 2015.

Nathan, Andrew, and Perry Link. *The Tiananmen Papers*. New York: Public Affairs, 2001.

Nathan, Andrew, and Andrew Scobell. *China's Search for Security*. New York: Columbia University Press, 2012.

Osnos, Evan. *Age of Ambition: Chasing Fortune, Truth, and Faith in the New China*. New York: Farrar, Straus and Giroux, 2014.

de Pierrebourg, Fabrice, and Michel Juneau-Katsuya. *Nest of Spies*. Toronto: HarperCollins, 2009.

Ronning, Chester. *A Memoir of China in Revolution*. New York: Pantheon Books, 1974.

Sawatsky, John. *For Services Rendered*. Toronto: Penguin Books, 1982.

Stewart, Roderick. *Bethune*. Toronto: New Press, 1973.

Trudeau, Pierre. *Memoirs*. Toronto: McClelland & Stewart, 1993.

Trudeau, Pierre, and Jacques Hébert. *Two Innocents in Red China*. Vancouver: Douglas & McIntyre, 1961.

Wong, Jan. *Red China Blues*. Toronto; New York: Doubleday/Anchor Books, 1997.

INDEX

We acknowledge the sacred land on which Cormorant Books operates. It has been a site of human activity for 15,000 years. This land is the territory of the Huron-Wendat and Petun First Nations, the Seneca, and most recently, the Mississaugas of the Credit River. The territory was the subject of the Dish With One Spoon Wampum Belt Covenant, an agreement between the Iroquois Confederacy and Confederacy of the Ojibway and allied nations to peaceably share and steward the resources around the Great Lakes. Today, the meeting place of Toronto is still home to many Indigenous people from across Turtle Island. We are grateful to have the opportunity to work in the community, on this territory.

We are also mindful of broken covenants and the need to strive to make right with all our relations.